ON
AIR
DEFENSE

ON
AIR
DEFENSE

James D. Crabtree

The Military Profession
Bruce Gudmundsson, Series Editor

Westport, Connecticut
London

Copyright Acknowledgments

All photographs appear courtesy of the U.S. Army Air Defense Artillery Museum.

Library of Congress Cataloging-in-Publication Data

Crabtree, James D.
    On air defense / James D. Crabtree.
      p. cm. — (The military profession, ISSN 1074–2964)
    Includes bibliographical references and index.
    ISBN 0–275–94792–0 (alk. paper). — ISBN 0–275–94939–7 (pbk.)
    1. Air defenses—History. I. Title. II. Series.
UG730.C73   1994
358.4'009—dc20   94–8639

British Library Cataloguing in Publication Data is available.

Copyright © 1994 by James D. Crabtree

Library of Congress Catalog Card Number: 94–8639
ISBN: 0–275–94792–0
     0–275–94939–7 (pbk.)
ISSN: 1074–2964

First published in 1994

Praeger Publishers, 88 Post Road West, Westport, CT 06881
An imprint of Greenwood Publishing Group, Inc.

Printed in the United States of America

The paper used in this book complies with the
Permanent Paper Standard issued by the National
Information Standards Organization (Z39.48–1984).

10 9 8 7 6 5 4 3 2 1

Contents

Photographs follow page 114.

Illustrations

Acknowledgments

I'd like to take this opportunity to thank those people without whom this book might never have proceeded past a vague idea: Mrs. Patricia Rhodes, the Research Historian at Fort Bliss, who took time from her busy schedule to examine critically the initial concept of *On Air Defense* and to give her honest advice for its improvement. The staff of *Air Defense Artillery* magazine, especially Mr. Hubert Koker, Mr. Blair Case, and Mrs. Lisa Henry. Without their enthusiasm and encouragement I might never have developed the confidence to tackle a project as large as a book. The staff of the U.S. Army Air Defense Artillery Museum, who helped provide illustrations and photographs for *On Air Defense*. And LTC Barrie Smith, who served as a mentor in both my military career and my writing. LTC Smith taught me that writing was more than just producing reports and stating plain facts; writing can be the telling of stories and the expression of ideas. I learned more from LTC Smith than from any college professor.

ON
AIR
DEFENSE

1

Early Air Defense

Even before the Wright Brothers flew at Kitty Hawk in 1903, there was a concept of air defense. It was born of experience, as the threat from the air existed even before the airplane. It would take a world war to make military leaders fully aware of the need for air defense, but the origins of antiaircraft artillery came far sooner, when military aviation was more of an annoyance than a true threat.

Man first left the earth by artificial means in 1783 in France. The balloon had been invented, and daredevil "aeronauts" took to the air in flights of experimentation. But, as novel as these early aircraft were, little use could be found for them. Balloons could not be navigated; a balloonist was totally at the mercy of the winds. Balloons could not carry large payloads. Free balloons were useless, and the only thing tethered balloons could really be used for was observation.

France invented the balloon, and naturally it was France that first used the device in combat. The French Revolution had caused conflict and turmoil in Europe; France faced enemies on every border who were determined to crush the popular republic. Despite the obvious problems in using the balloon in warfare (i.e., its relative delicacy, its vulnerability to the elements, the need to generate hydrogen gas), the situation for France was desperate enough to commit the primitive aircraft as scouts. A chemist named Jean Marie-Joseph Coutelle was commissioned a captain and placed in charge of the *Companie d'Aerostiers*. He was then sent to the front to conduct observation missions in his hydrogen balloon.

Facing skepticism by Army officers to whom he was attached and suspicion by the local Committee of Safety, Coutelle soon proved the military worth of the tethered balloon. At Maubeuge, Belgium, he sent excellent reports on Austrian and Dutch positions by means of sandbags filled with messages and by sliding reports on rings attached to a mooring rope.

At this point, active air defense was attempted for the very first time. Aside from the information being delivered to the French, Dutch and Austrian officers were concerned about the effect the balloon was having on their troops. It was the first balloon they had ever seen, and the soldiers thought it was a supernatural object. In response, two Austrian 17-pound howitzers were superelevated by placing their trail-pieces in a ditch, thus making them the very first antiaircraft guns, even if they were only temporarily so.

The Austrians came close to hitting the balloon at least once, barely missing the airbag and grazing the gondola Coutelle was in. But without exploding shells (the gunners were using solid shot), such a large target was difficult to hit at such an extreme angle.

Three more *aerostat* companies were established by the French, as well as a special school for balloonists; but despite initial interest, ballooning technology soon fell by the wayside. Military leaders were still unprepared to adjust to the potential that balloons held for scouting and observation. A few inventors came up with schemes to bombard the enemy with manned and unmanned balloons; but when Austria actually tried experimenting with "pilotless" balloon bombs against Venice in 1849, the results were unsatisfactory. The Venetians were largely oblivious of the bombs that fell from the unmanned balloons when their fuses burned through; most of them dropped harmlessly into the water, and some might have even fallen on the besieging Austrians.

Not until the American Civil War was the balloon tried again in earnest by the military. Ballooning was still considered the realm of the showman and state fairs in America; the only way balloonists could help the army was for the civilian aeronauts to attach themselves on an unofficial basis to Union officers. Nevertheless, a tentative ascent in June 1861 by one of the showmen, Thaddeus Lowe, convinced President Lincoln of the usefulness of the balloon.

Using a telegraph, he wired to the officials below that he could see the encampments surrounding Washington quite well from his perch. In fact, from his altitude of 500 feet (152m) he could see for 25 miles (40km). It seemed that the hydrogen balloon, coupled with the telegraph, had come of age as a weapon of war.

LaMountain, another civilian aeronaut working for the U.S. Army, made an ascent from Fort Monroe in July 1861 that not only provoked rebel fury but also resulted in the creation of the first passive air defense measure: the dousing of campfires at night to prevent the balloonist from estimating the strength of Confederate forces.

Other ascents made by Lowe in Northern Virginia also prompted passive measures. Confederates began camouflaging their troop positions to prevent aerial observation. They also began to build dummy positions, which were armed with "Quaker guns" made of painted logs. The measures took time, but they were deemed effective and necessary by the rebels.

In August 1861 an American aeronaut came under antiaircraft fire for the first time. A rebel officer by the name of Captain E. P. Alexander directed fire from his guns, which according to his report caused a Union balloonist to descend "as rapidly as gravity would permit him." This is entirely possible, as Alexander had exploding shells available to him and would have employed them were he able to get proper elevation.

Artillery had become more advanced since Napoleon's time, although the guns themselves appeared to be little different. Exploding shells were much more reliable, thanks to improved fuses that largely took the guesswork out of how many seconds would pass before they exploded. Also, rifled barrels increased accuracy and range. All this contributed to new attempts to use field pieces against balloons.

The reason so few balloons were actually hit was the mathematical problem involved. When a gun is fired, its round flies in an arc. When used as a field piece, a fairly simple set of formulae determines where the round will land for a flat or nearly flat trajectory. The range of the best rifled guns of the time was only about 2700m. Even though a theory of indirect fire was known, it was rarely needed or wanted.

Elevating the gun barrel above normal trajectories completely changed the arc and made standard formulae useless. In theory, new formulae could have been computed. However, for them to work, the simple sights then in use would have to have been replaced. Although elevation and range to the target would have had to be measured in order to fire an intercepting arc to the balloon, simple optical instruments could have been built with 1860s technology for this purpose. Yet another formula would have been needed to estimate for how many seconds to set the fuse so that it would explode in the vicinity of the target.

This procedure might sound complex, but considering that the tethered balloons moved neither in azimuth nor in elevation it was a fairly straightforward two-dimensional mathematical problem, one that required no new in algebra or trigonometry and very little in the way of new technology (see Figure 1.1). But as no military research and development apparatus was in place at that time, a scientific approach was never tried.

Balloons were never deemed a great enough threat by either side to warrant specialized technology or units to combat them. Usually, whatever gun section or battery was available would be dragooned into fulfilling the air defense role. These guns would get the range by sheer trial and error.

Balloonists continued to fly despite the dangers involved. Apparently, rebel

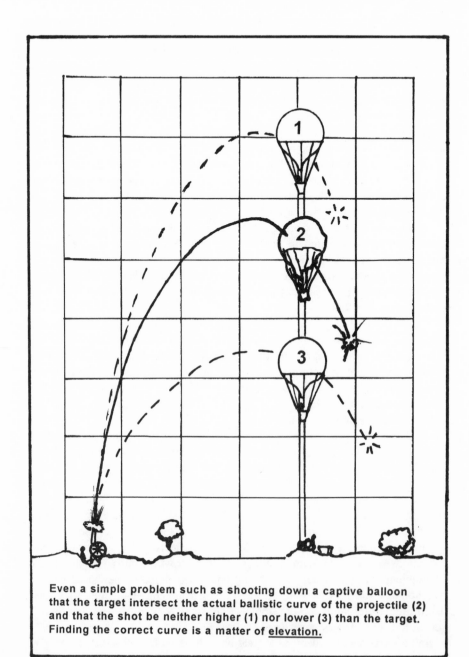

Even a simple problem such as shooting down a captive balloon
that the target intersect the actual ballistic curve of the projectile (2)
and that the shot be neither higher (1) nor lower (3) than the target.
Finding the correct curve is a matter of <u>elevation.</u>

Figure 1.1
Air Defense as a Two-Dimensional Problem

gunfire did little to discourage pioneer aeronaut Lowe; a month after his first experience with antiaircraft artillery he pioneered the use of balloons to correct indirect fire on rebel positions, a use for balloons that would be common during the Great War 50 years later. In deploying his balloon with an artillery spotter on board, Lowe changed the air threat from an abstract danger of observation to the active danger of providing artillery fire.

The newly formed U.S. Army Balloon Corps was ready for service when General McClellan's Army of the Potomac began the Peninsular Campaign in March 1862. With three balloons, Thaddeus Lowe followed the army up the length of the peninsula in its advance to Richmond. His balloons proved themselves invaluable in scouting enemy positions and may even have been decisive in preventing a Union defeat in the Battle of Fair Oaks.

The Peninsular Campaign also saw one of the few attempts by the Confederates to use military balloons of their own. Hampered by a blockade and lacking the industrial base to produce hydrogen gas and rubberized balloons, forays by aeronauts like Captain Alexander (the same officer who tried to shoot down a Union balloon near Arlington) and Lieutenant John Randolph Bryan were few and far between. Bryan was nearly shot down during his first flight, which was also the first flight ever by a CSA aeronaut. He tried to resign from the ballooning service after his brush with Union artillery fire, but the request was refused.

Despite several successes similar to those gained by the French during their revolution, the balloon was not appreciated by the Union high command. Aeronauts sent to South Carolina and Mississippi met cold receptions by the generals they were assigned to serve. Lowe's Balloon Corps was dismantled in 1863 before it could get an opportunity to participate in the Battle of Gettysburg. Military traditionalism seems to have been more of a threat to the aircraft of those days than any existing weapon.

The next major incident featuring war balloons, the one that would inspire the creation of a dedicated antiaircraft weapon, was the Franco-Prussian War. During the Prussian siege of Paris that began in September 1870, balloons became the only contact Parisians had with the outside world. During the four-month siege, 66 balloons managed to carry 2.5 million letters and 102 passengers out of Paris. It was this slim lifeline that the Prussians became determined to cut.

The Prussians tried the time-honored practice of using elevated guns against the balloons, which were well out of reach of the small arms of the day. The field pieces were further refined than most of those used by the Americans during the Civil War, in that they were breechloaders; placing shell and charge in the rear of the gun facilitated rapid fire, and there was no need to lower the gun's elevation to load the next shot. Yet the problem of engaging targets at high elevations proved as difficult for the Prussians to deal with as it had for the Americans.

In response to the problems of antiaircraft gunnery, the Krupp arms company designed the very first air defense artillery piece. It was called a *ballongeschutz*, or balloon gun. A breechloading 25mm rifle, it was mounted on a flatbed wagon and hinged to a swivel that permitted firing 360° in azimuth and 85° in elevation. For targeting, it had nothing more complicated than a gun sight similar to the one used on Krupp's needlegun. With a range of up to 700m, it managed to shoot down at least one balloon during the siege at Paris, thus claiming the first antiaircraft "kill."

Despite the Prussians' monopoly on air defense weapons, they were never able to cut Paris off from the air. When *ballongeshutzen* began to shred the French balloons during their flights into and out of Paris, the aeronauts began to fly at night, making detection difficult and hitting them virtually impossible. This made the French the first to realize that what is difficult to hit during the day is even more difficult to hit at night.

Even though Paris's thin lifeline was never cut, the city was forced to surrender in January 1871 after a continual bombardment by Prussian field artillery. Thus ended the first thought-out attempt to set up a ground-based air defense. It also resulted in a new innovation: As the balloon guns were firing at moving, untethered targets, the mathematical problem had changed from a two-dimensional to a three-dimensional one (as illustrated in Figure 1.2).

Balloons finally began to win acceptance in the military, having proved their worth in artillery-spotting and scouting during the colonial wars prior to World War I. Austria-Hungary, France, Germany, Great Britain, and Russia all established balloon training centers, and aerostat units saw combat in minor conflicts across the globe in the late 1800s. Technological improvements made the military balloon more reliable and more effective: Bottled gas made primitive hydrogen generators obsolete, telephones replaced telegraphs for communication, and cameras made the balloon a more efficient scouting tool.

The Russians, seeing the growing use of balloons and building them themselves, experimented with using their field guns against a tethered balloon three kilometers away. Little came of these trials except a Russian interest in outlawing the use of aerial bombing, which led to the 1899 Hague Convention.

The Hague Convention, which was attended by all of the major powers of the time, addressed several emerging issues in warfare and sought to set up a legal guideline for conducting wars. One of the agreements was that no signatory could launch projectiles from balloons or "other kinds of aerial vessels."

This noble effort was meant to be a temporary ban only; in 1907 the signatories met again and modified the agreement so that undefended cities or towns were not to be bombed, a carryover of the traditional concept of an open city. Only military facilities and other installations that were necessary to a war effort could be legally attacked. Such civilized niceties would not be observed when they proved impractical.

Powered aerostats, or dirigibles, became practical around 1900 after two decades of experimentation and speculation. Ferdinand Von Zeppelin gave the German Empire the lead in their development and use. For many years prior to

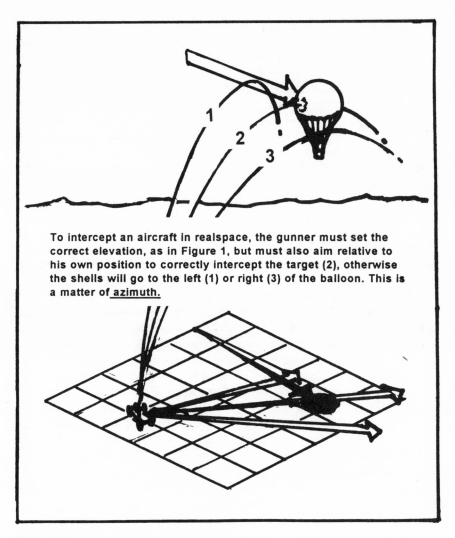

To intercept an aircraft in realspace, the gunner must set the correct elevation, as in Figure 1, but must also aim relative to his own position to correctly intercept the target (2), otherwise the shells will go to the left (1) or right (3) of the balloon. This is a matter of azimuth.

Figure 1.2
Air Defense as a Three-Dimensional Problem

World War I the few people seriously thinking about air defense would consider the dirigible the primary threat because it could carry a considerable bomb load over a great distance and of course could be navigated to a specific target.

The *ballongeschutz* was slowly but surely evolving to meet the threat the Germans themselves were posing. A 50mm model developed by the German Rheinmetall Company was displayed at the 1906 Berlin Auto Exhibition, and two versions were offered for sale: an armored gun that could traverse only 60° and an unarmored model capable of 360° of sweep. These weapons had the advantage of being self-propelled, of going where they were needed under their own power. This would be a key feature for lighter weapons in use with field forces. However, neither of the 50mm guns could elevate over 70°, limiting their usefulness.

Not to be outdone, Krupp developed even more ambitious weapons in time for the 1909 Frankfurt International Exhibition, including 65mm, 75mm, and 105mm designs. The 65mm gun was mounted on a special field carriage, one that allowed for 360° rotation in azimuth and 70° elevation. It was meant to be towed into battle much as field artillery was. The 75mm gun was mounted on a motorized carriage and was equipped with a differential recoil system. The 105mm was designed for naval mounting.

Work was also done by Rheinmetall and Krupp to create appropriate ammunition for antiaircraft guns, ammunition better suited for ripping gas envelopes open, for setting gasbags aflame, and for tracing the flight of rounds. Smoke and flame designs were tried. The problem of fuzing shells was also being faced for the first time. Despite these studies, no effective ammunition type was invented.

Other countries also began working on antiaircraft designs. France began work to adapt its 75mm fieldpiece to an antiaircraft mounting, while working on a tactic of collective ranging. The Vickers firm of England also started work on an antiaircraft weapon, one based on a specially mounted 3-pounder gun. Another English design was an experimental piece made up of the 1-pounder "pom-pom" fast-firing cannon placed on a 6-pounder antitorpedo gun mount. Antiaircraft training was even tried with the weapons available.

In the United States the first work on an antiaircraft automatic weapon was done on the personal initiative of Colonel R. P. Davison, the commandant of the Northwestern Military and Naval Academy. His Cadillac Balloon Destroyer was simply a Colt machine gun mounted on an auto, but was one of the first (if not the first) air defense automatic weapons built.

When such weapons were placed on the international arms market, they met with lackluster sales. Britain, France, and Russia had access to the fledgling air defense artillery pieces but general consensus seemed to be that the need for a dedicated defense against airships would be sporadic at best and did not justify the added expense.

There was little work done in the field of air defense doctrine. The Esher Committee established in England in 1909 made the determination that air defense would consist of two elements: mobile and fixed. Mobile defenses would consist of friendly airships and airplanes, as well as mobile guns that would rush about the countryside in the manner of a fire brigade. Fixed defenses would consist of passive air defense measures (like camouflage) and static guns. The Garrison Artillery was given the task of air defense in England by default. This left the problem of field army air defense open.

Scarcely noticed was the development of the warplane. The early-model airplanes were extremely dangerous to fly until technical refinements made them easier to pilot; their lack of reliability left something to be desired, according to the military. At first the military establishments could find little use for the machines: Scouting and artillery spotting were better done by balloon, and the airship had far greater potential as a bomber. The primary advantage of the aeroplane lay in its superior speed, but few officers understood how to exploit it.

Not long after their deployment to North Africa during the Italo-Turkish War in 1911, Italian planes were used to bomb Turkish positions with grenades. The following year the Italians had the dubious honor of having the first airplane shot down by ground fire as the Turks, lacking dedicated antiaircraft weapons, set up a good deal of rifle fire. The Turkish gunfire limited dirigible operations as well, but the Italians claimed to have succeeded in "dampening the enthusiasm" of the enemy. On the other hand, the Turks had confirmed that, when nothing else is available, small-arms fire would prove able to bring down aircraft.

The Balkan Wars of 1912–13 saw some limited air activity but little use of planned air defense. However, the first successful engagement of an airplane occurred when a civilian aviator flying for Bulgaria was killed by small-arms fire. The native uprising in French Morocco was put down with the help of a French *escadrille* that saw no attempts to bring their planes down other than a few rifle shots. The airplane was becoming more and more commonplace in war.

Airships (and airplanes, to a lesser degree) proved able to navigate at night, which protected them from engagement to a degree. Night operations by airplanes and airships would lead to the further development of searchlights and the invention of sound detectors to penetrate the darkness.

Searchlights were originally designed for naval use. By creating an intense light source, usually electrical, and using mirrors to concentrate it into a beam, searchlights made it possible to find and identify ships that were operating at night or in inclement weather. Carbon arcing was the preferred light source for most designs, although some nonelectrical designs used the burning of acetylene as a source. The beam was directed by moving the entire assembly by mechanical means, or even manually if the searchlight were small enough.

Ships were able to make most use of the searchlight because of their large power plants; electricity produced by means of an AC generator hooked up to the vessel's engines allowed liberal use of the device. The searchlight was next adopted by the U.S. Coast Artillery for shore use against enemy ships. When the airship became a threat to be dealt with by Coast Artillery, locating and identifying the airborne enemy at night was deemed another use for the searchlight.

Several countries went one step further to look at the use of searchlights with their field armies. Mobile carriages were invented for the machines, and field generators capable of providing enough electricity to operate them were adapted for use on the battlefield. A 1914 German design was available that could be broken down into small components transportable by mule or horse. The result was the deployment of searchlights to many potential targets from the very beginning of World War I, and countries that did not possess mobile searchlights when the war began wasted no time in procuring them when their utility was demonstrated.

Searchlights, properly used, can locate aircraft operating at night and to a limited degree identify them. Later models would dwarf the early models used in World War I and would grow in sophistication. Some were designed to be operated with sound locators, and others to give firing data to antiaircraft guns. The searchlight would continue to provide good service to air defenders many years after radar took over its duties.

All the technology needed to combat aircraft effectively was known and potentially available to all the great powers. All that was now needed was a substantial air threat to trigger the creation of a dedicated antiaircraft artillery.

2

World War I Air Defense: The Central Powers

World War I bogged down within a few months into trench warfare. Mobility rapidly became a distant memory. As neither side could do much more than stare at the other, greater reliance was placed on primitive aircraft to scout out and attack the enemy. In turn, air defense would prove not only practical but necessary in the new ways of waging wars, new ways that would just begin to touch on a separation in air defense between the tactical battle of the field armies and the strategic defense of the home cities.

Airplanes were deployed by most of the European powers at the very beginning of the war in 1914. In the ten years since its invention the airplane had increased in reliability and performance to the point where it had become an effective scouting instrument. The airplane's relative high speed, excellent observation ability, and relative immunity from attack had sold the traditionalist armies of Europe on its value. Had the airplane kept to its role as a scout, air defense would certainly not have grown in importance as it did during the war.

But military aviators did not stick to scouting. The stalemate that ground the armies into trench fighting limited the need for aerial observation. Some intrepid pilots began to shoot at their opposite numbers with pistols and rifles, a far cry from the very beginning of the war, when they would wave at or salute their fellow aviators. Then machine guns were mounted on the airplane, and it became a true killing machine: The fighter had been born.

Aircraft of the time were constructed of wood and fabric, relatively simple materials that might be easy to penetrate but still allowed little practical damage. Both sides typically used biplane designs, although there were a few single-wing and triplane designs. Power was provided primarily by air-cooled rotary engines, although some in-line types were available. Performance of early models was up to 150kph, operating as high as 5000m. Mounted machine guns not only could destroy other airplanes but also proved to be effective in attacking soldiers on the ground.

Airplanes also began dropping bombs on troops. At first the bombs were just grenades dropped over the sides of the plane by the pilot. But with the needs of war accelerating the advance of technology, airplanes soon proved able to carry larger bomb loads. Bombs themselves were improved, and specially designed bombsights increased accuracy. Planes and airships began attacking the enemy not just in the front lines but also in the rear echelons and even at the enemy's capital.

As warplanes became a common sight, the need to identify them as either friendly or hostile arose. National markings were adopted by each of the warring powers: a Maltese cross for German and Austrian planes and a roundel system for the Allies. Roundels used the national colors of the country of origin. Even so, fratricide was not uncommon when weather conditions and range made visual identification difficult. What would become known as aircraft recognition was begun, in which ground troops and pilots were trained to tell the difference between enemy and friendly planes by their silhouettes.

Meanwhile, air defense weapons were needed for the troops on the ground and the people at home. German exercises in 1909 using Maxim machine guns and Mauser rifles to engage balloons proved ineffective. The job of shooting down aircraft was officially deemed an artillery problem.

But in 1914 German Army maneuvers had established the impracticality of using field guns for antiaircraft fire. Steps were taken to acquire dedicated antiaircraft guns from the models becoming available from German firms, but the number of pieces available to the German Army at the beginning of the war was minimal, a mere 36 guns, even though Germany had a head start in the design and production of such weapons.

The German High Command had determined that dedicated antiaircraft guns were needed. Next, it determined where the guns would be used. The initial gun requirement would be to protect rear-echelon elements from observation. Movable guns were to be acquired for each army and divisional field headquarters, but not enough were delivered prior to the outbreak of war to fulfill this goal.

The few antiaircraft pieces available were not even with the armies in the field when war broke out. Zeppelin sheds at Metz and Friedrichshafen, as well as two Rhine bridges, were protected by the guns. These four areas were the only locations with any sort of ground-based air defense at the beginning of the war.

As Allied warplanes became more persistent in their attacks against German ground forces, the need for some sort of fixed defense became more acute. Most use was made of improvised weapons, as the already heavy demands on Germany's industrial base precluded a large-scale shift to antiaircraft artillery production.

Captured field artillery pieces were pressed into use after modifications had made them suitable for an air defense role. On the eastern front, the Putilov M1903 field piece was mounted on a pedestal, enabling it to fire at higher angles. In the west, French 75mm guns were rebored to accept German 77mm shells.

The sight of German antiaircraft bursts came to be nicknamed ''Archie'' by Allied pilots. Archie also came to mean Allied antiaircraft artillery. But to describe their new weaponry, the Germans used the term *Flugzug Abwehr Kanonen*, or *Flak* for short. Flak would become an almost universal term for antiaircraft fire.

Germany's industry took up the slack in antiaircraft guns during the last two years of the war. Several calibers of heavy guns were available by war's end: 10cm, 9cm, 7.5cm, 8.8cm, and 10.5cm (marine). The heavier guns could reach up to 6000m. Typically, German antiaircraft was deployed two guns per position. The Germans came to rely on strong concentrations of mobile antiaircraft pieces to protect field units.

The accuracy of heavy antiaircraft guns was poor at the beginning of the war, but antiaircraft fire forced observation aircraft to higher altitudes, lessening their value. Guns also helped coordinate fighter support; as no radio was available for ground-to-air communications, guns would fire a line of bursts to point toward enemy aircraft that had been spotted.

Barrage fire became a common air defense tactic. Because accuracy would always remain a problem, the simple expedient of firing large numbers of exploding shells into the path of an enemy aircraft was adopted. The very sight of exploding shells over a target often had a deterring effect on pilots. The term *barrage* was adopted from the field artillery; with its use in air defense, barrage would come to mean different types of mass air defense measures.

Machine guns were the obvious point-defense weapon against air attacks, but they were heavy and unwieldy to use against air targets. Until special mounts could be designed and built, some machine guns were placed on upright wagon axles, with one wheel stuck firmly in the ground and the other providing a platform several feet off the ground that could be rotated 360° and several degrees in elevation.

Dedicated mounts, which were slow in coming, included a tub mount that allowed a gunner to fire straight up by lying on his back. Among the model guns in use were Spandaus and Maxims.

To counter the growing threat of antiaircraft fire, Allied pilots changed altitude and course frequently during missions. Against barrages, a steep dive was recommended until the lower end of the barrage was reached; then the pilot's course was to be corrected. German antiaircraft fire was described as dense, active, and accurate. Strafing was especially dangerous for Allied pilots because of the threat posed by ground fire.

Allied pilots began experimenting with flak suppression, deliberate attacks made to destroy or damage known antiaircraft positions. This tactic began in order to attack German spotter balloons, which were usually guarded by anti-aircraft guns.

When Allied aircraft developed the means to operate at night, the Germans in turn had to find the means to combat them. The Germans would use search-lights in large numbers at the front, but their antiaircraft and machine-gun fire was usually sparse at night. The Germans did not believe in wasting ammunition on targets they couldn't see.

Despite the glamour and daring of many of its pilots, the German Air Service developed a passive style of warfare, fixing most of their patrols behind their own lines. In this way, the Germans had both their fighter aircraft and their guns available for air defense duties and downed pilots could be recovered. Of course, this procedure also turned the initiative over to the Allies.

The Germans developed a fighter tactic they named *luftsperre*. It was a kind of barrage, based on the use of fighter aircraft to form a barrier across a single sector of the front. It required large numbers of aircraft to mount, leaving other sectors defenseless or weak, and was hardly impenetrable. The Germans flew more patrols behind the *luftsperre* to intercept "leakers."

The passive style of warfare was probably bad for morale. There were in-stances in which pursuit aircraft were grounded during air raids, their pilots taking shelter in dugouts. Of course, this was at the end of the war, when German aircraft routinely found themselves outnumbered as they rarely flew in formations of more than five.

The first challenge to German air defense was the bombing raids on their zeppelin sheds. The sheds were large, and most of their locations were well known to the Allies, making them logical targets. Because the Germans realized how vulnerable the sheds were, they made certain to deploy antiaircraft guns in their defense at the beginning of the war.

The very first bombing raid of the war was mounted against the sheds, when a single French *Aviation Militaire* airplane attacked the zeppelin facility at Metz-Frescaty in August 1914. England soon followed suit, attempting to hit zeppelin sheds in Cologne and Dusseldorf in September. Out of the four Royal Naval Air Service planes in the raid force, only one reached Dusseldorf to drop its three bombs, all of which failed to explode. The Allies began to attack in for-mation, abandoning for the most part raids by individual aircraft.

Most of the Allies' early attacks concentrated on the zeppelin bases; very little force was committed to attacking other military targets in territory held by the Germans. Even though strategic attacks were conducted by the British and French, the Germans initially concentrated on a point defense of the zeppelin sheds and devoted nothing to an overall national air defense system. Indeed, such a system was unheard of at that time and would have required great imag-ination and foresight. Meanwhile, the growing antiaircraft defense of the sheds was taking a toll on the attackers.

The early Allied raids on Germany proper virtually came to a halt after the airfield at Antwerp was captured in October 1914. After the occupation of most of Belgium, British planes were sent to France to operate. But attacks could still be mounted on western Germany from behind the front. One such attack, on Freiburg in December 1914, proved that Allied bombers could reach the important factories in the Alsace-Lorraine region.

Such attacks resulted in piecemeal air defense allocations, whereby the few guns available were deployed to whatever community or factory clamored for them loudest. Deployed in this haphazard manner, guns usually didn't arrive at a potential target until a raid had already taken place. Air defense was only beginning to be understood as a 4-dimensional problem, as shown in Figure 2.1.

At the beginning of the war all home air defense measures were localized, the responsibility of the individual German states. But although the states were given the responsibility, they had very little in the way of material to actually carry out air defense. Guns arrived a few at a time for the defense of individual factories until the summer of 1915, when large numbers of converted enemy guns were made available. Early warning was virtually nonexistent; no formal observation posts were in place, and Germany's decentralized telephone system made rapid communications difficult.

In 1916 the German High Command finally saw the need for a centralized antiaircraft defense. Major von Keller was appointed Inspector of Home Air Defenses, with the task of designing and implementing air protection for Germany. He set up joint committees of military and civilian authorities to deal with the matters of air-raid shelters and other passive measures and to provide input on establishing a possible early warning system.

Soon a double cordon of observation posts was established, behind and parallel to the front lines, that enemy aircraft would have to cross to reach targets. These watchers provided early warning, but there were few posts in the German interior to track aircraft. The watchers who were available were often of poor quality. Even when an observer was fortunate enough to be at the right place at the right time to spot enemy aircraft approaching, he would have to find the nearest telephone to call the nearest military authorities. As a result, the system was prone to false alarms and tardy warnings.

To alert localities prior to an attack, signal bombs, telephones, and factory sirens were used to announce air raids. But because the Germans never approached the problem of aircraft tracking in a scientific way, whole areas were alerted unnecessarily. The warning system was still in the process of being revamped at the end of the war.

Home-front antiaircraft artillery was concentrated at key points. Von Keller knew that to try to protect all of the potential targets would mean diluting his weapons to the point where none of them was being adequately protected.

The Military Air Service was made responsible for both antiaircraft artillery at the front and the Home Air Defenses in 1916. The Inspector of Home Air Defense was placed in actual command of the home units, with centralization

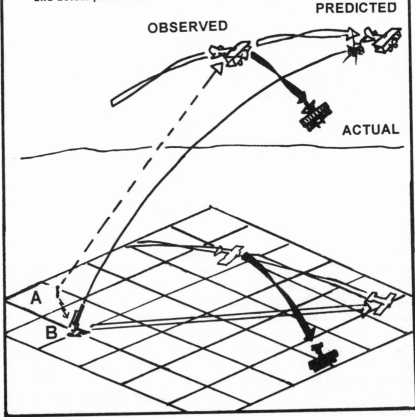

To hit a fast-moving target, an observer (A) notes target speed, range, and direction, calculates the target's probable future position and sends elevation and azimuth values to the gunner(B) to intercept. But fast-moving aircraft can manuver drastically, throwing off calculations: note the difference between predicted and actual positions.

Figure 2.1
Air Defense as a Four-Dimensional Problem

placing the home defenses headquarters at Frankfort. The threatened frontier of Germany was divided into three separate air defense zones, and the Saar district was transferred from Field General Headquarters to Home Defense jurisdiction.

Formal training was instituted to help improve the quality of the air defenses. Observers gained valuable knowledge at an air-raid reporting school in Saarbrucken; and antiaircraft batteries were rotated to the front at Ostend, where enemy air activity was frequent and the gunners would almost certainly engage actual aircraft. Special detachments replaced the units in rotation.

Though the gunners were needed to destroy and discourage enemy aircraft, there was a distinct disadvantage to the use of guns: shrapnel. The debris caused by the destruction of the shells rained down on the very area the guns were meant to defend.

Such collateral damage could be substantial. In Joeuf, an occupied French town, damage from Allied bombs caused 10,000 francs worth of damage, while shrapnel damage from German batteries caused 40,000 francs worth of damage. Another 40,000 francs worth of damage was done by flak at the nearby Wendel smelter works, a legitimate military target and the focus of Allied attacks, as opposed to 30,000 francs of intended damage caused by bombs. The amount of flak damage is all the more remarkable considering that only a single antiaircraft battery was present in the town.

Such collateral damage seemed to be unavoidable in defended areas, causing both property damage and deaths (another reason to get under cover during an air raid). It would also turn out to be a problem for Allied air defenders.

Extensive measures were taken to protect machinery and personnel in war production. For instance, Thionville's Carl Foundry took important steps to protect itself. Dugouts were built for workers, consisting of underground structures of masonry or cement. Concrete roofs were built to protect vital equipment. The cost for these measures came out of the company's own funds, reaching 90,998 marks in 1918.

Up to this point the home defense had no aircraft assigned to it; any interceptions that took place in Germany were the result of chance, of Allied aircraft meeting a German aircraft in transit to or from the front. But because of their experience with antiaircraft guns, the Germans concluded that a mobile element would have to make up for their deficiency in antiaircraft artillery. By the end of 1916 nine flights of interceptors were available to the Inspector of Home Air Defense.

The defense potential for interceptors was limited by diluting the flights into small detachments, each detachment positioned to fly in defense of a particular target. But, by the time aircraft were alerted by the early warning system, they rarely had the guidance or time to find the enemy. This system was later minimized in favor of patrols and sorties that cut across likely enemy routes.

In 1917, improvements on the home air defenses included barrage balloons and searchlights. Barrage balloons represented a passive air defense measure, with hydrogen balloons anchored to the ground by means of steel cable. The balloon cables could shear off a wing, even though the pilot might never see them. To avoid them, the pilot would have to fly around them or above them. If the plane flew around the cables, antiaircraft guns might more easily engage it; and if it flew above the barrage, its bombing accuracy would be decreased.

The balloons could remain airborne for 10 to 14 days once they were charged with gas. The maximum altitude was 3000m for the balloons, but they were usually tethered between 2000m and 3000m. Balloon barrages were deployed in the cities of Cologne, Esch, Hayange, Knutange, the Saar Valley, and Occupied Luxembourg.

The Germans were slow in adopting searchlights for air defense, but they had little choice when the Allies began experimenting with night bombing. Searchlights became available in large numbers in 1917; but the Germans avoided using them en masse prior to a raid, believing that such a "searchlight barrage" would only serve to guide enemy bombers to their target.

Though sound detectors began appearing in 1915 around German cities, they were never available in large numbers. The reason might have been the already enormous strain on Germany's production base, or possibly the fact that Allied night attacks didn't reach an intensity strong enough to justify special countermeasures.

In March 1918 British bombers returned in strength to German skies; by June 1918 they would be part of the Allies' Independent Air Force (IAF). The IAF was organized independent of the Allied armies on the continent and given a free hand to choose strategic targets in the German interior.

The primary impetus was the German bombing raids against Britain. The citizens of that country demanded retaliatory raids to make Germany pay as dearly as England. Retaliation raids were resisted by the military, who saw the German raids as militarily ineffective.

Allied military planners wanted to try strategic bombing against important targets, perhaps forcing the Germans to draw off large numbers of enemy aircraft from the front to defend national airspace, as the British had been forced to do. If the raids were effective enough, they might be used as a bargaining chip to make the Germans stop their attacks against England.

Aircraft technology was developing rapidly. Both sides began to develop large, multiengined bombers. Such aircraft possessed superior speed and range. When Handley Page and de Havilland bombers became available late in the war, they gave the Allies the means to strike hard at distant targets.

Meanwhile, Germany not only defended itself from air attack but also provided limited material assistance to the Central Powers, Austria-Hungary, and the Ottoman Empire. Both countries were large, but they had weaknesses in aircraft and weapon production that Germany did its best to correct.

Austria-Hungary possessed aircraft and guns but, as one assessment put it, was fighting on three fronts but with only enough aircraft to fight effectively on one. The most active location was the Italian Front, where Austrian planes flew raids on Italian territory, while Italy conducted a planned bombing campaign against important strategic targets. Germany provided aircraft and other assistance, but the Austrians never used them to build a credible air defense system.

In the Ottoman Empire the military situation was even worse. The Turkish Army was large in numbers, but weak in leadership and material. While the European powers made advances in military science, the Turks had largely stood still. To compensate, Germany instituted a program of military assistance that gave the Ottoman Empire weapons and officers.

Before long the Turks' entire military establishment was heavily dependent upon German military missions. In the Ottoman Empire military aviation and antiaircraft were virtually nonexistent, and German pilots and German gunners helped provide air defense for the Turkish Army facing the Allies in the Sinai. In 1916 the Turkish invasion of Sinai included five sections of German antiaircraft guns; later, when Germany formed the *Asien Korps*, it included an entire antiaircraft battery.

Air assets in the Middle Eastern theater were meager; most German and Allied resources were committed to Europe proper. Turkey came to rely heavily upon German pilots and craft, while British aircraft formed the bulk of Allied commitment.

British aircraft effectively supported the Allied assault into Palestine, working closely with cavalry units and infantry to effect battlefield interdiction. The Germans and Turks often used machine guns for close-in air defense, but the heavy German antiaircraft guns never seemed to be at the right place at the right time.

At home, Germany's situation worsened rapidly as the effects of the Allied blockade and four years of war took their toll. Military supplies started to dwindle, and casualty replacements were increasingly hard to find.

Antiaircraft batteries in the rear areas began running out of ammunition toward the end of the war, and resentful civilians got the impression that officers were trying to save on ammunition. Meanwhile, the town of Trier employed soldiers recuperating in a military hospital to serve as gunners. Inferior fuel was all that was available for interceptors, and maintenance on the machines also fell in quality.

Yet Home Air Defense still managed to bring down attacking Allied bombers, consisting as they did of 17 Home Defense flights of 14 machines each in the Rhine Valley by the end of the war and possessing 2,576 antiaircraft guns of all types. Allied bombers losses were almost evenly split between guns and aircraft.

German aircraft were becoming faster, more reliable, and more maneuverable. The Fokker D.VII could fly as fast as 189kph and could reach altitudes of 6000m, a marked improvement over slower and clumsier prewar models. But maneuverability was also important as pilots learned to fly in the third dimension. Basic fighter tactics were invented in the skies over France and would largely be just as valid 75 years later as they were during World War I.

Growing German skill and improving technology could not hold off defeat. But even as civilian authority dissolved and military units mutinied, most Home Air Defense units remained cohesive and loyal and, more important, maintained the respect of the German populace. Several of them became *Freikorps* units in the chaos that followed the Armistice.

When the Allied bombing campaign came to an end on the Western Front, the IAF had dropped twice the tonnage on Germany as the German Army and Navy had managed to drop on England. The Allies were planning to widen the scope of the war: Three Handley Page V/1500 "giant" bombers were fueled and loaded with bombs for a long-range mission when the Armistice was declared. The planes were immediately grounded. Their target was Berlin. How well they would have done against Germany's thin but effective air defense system will always remain a subject of historical conjecture.

3

World War I Air Defense: The Allies

The French approached the development and techniques of antiaircraft gunnery in the *Ecole d'Ecoute des Avions*, a part of the *Institute Aerotechnique*. French scientists were placed at the disposal of the military to solve the new problems of ballistics, interception, and timing posed by the aircraft.

Like the Central Powers, the Allies all relied on improvisation at the beginning of the war, especially where machine guns were concerned. The French used various expedients to mount them off the ground, including long stakes, wagon axles, and tree trunks. These primitive machine-gun platforms were eventually supplemented by specially designed antiaircraft mounts.

Several machine-gun designs were available for use in the field, including the St. Etienne and Hotchkiss models. The French developed the excellent "infantry corrector" sight, a simple ring sight that was accurate to 1000m.

France had designed the most successful heavy antiaircraft gun to be used by the Allies, the 75mm auto cannon developed by the French before the war. The original *Soixante-Quinze* was a field gun, and it would continue to see service in that role; but its large caliber and relatively high rate of fire (15 rounds per minute) made it an ideal heavy antiaircraft gun once it was adapted for that role.

Semifixed amounts gave the 75mm the elevation and azimuth necessary to engage aircraft effectively. Mobile versions were mounted on a De Dion Bouton motor chassis, allowing guns to be relocated on relatively short notice. The

75mm's reach of 7000m was high enough to engage any aircraft then in German service.

In the first few years of the war antiaircraft duties were the responsibility of small units, first single-gun sections, then two-gun platoons, and finally four-gun batteries. In 1917 the batteries would be organized into individual *Regiments d'Artillerie Antiaerienne* (RAA): the 63rd, the 64th, and the 65th RAA.

The *Defense Contre Aeronifs* (DCA), or tactical air defense, of the armies was initially given to the 63rd RAA. The DCA expanded in 1918 by dividing the 63rd into four new regiments. These new units were more specialized: the new 63rd RAA was equipped with semifixed 75mm guns, the 66th RAA mobile with 75mm guns, and the 67th with RAA searchlights; and the 166th operated semifixed 105mm guns.

The 65th RAA was designated the duty of *Defense Aerienne de Territoire* (DAT), which amounted to France's strategic defense. The 65th RAA was responsible for all interior defenses except for Paris, which was given its own regiment, the 64th.

The French dedicated a good deal of thought to their fire-control methods, which the British and American dubbed technical shooting. Several different devices were invented for antiaircraft prediction: the goniograph, sitgoniograph, telemeter, broqc predicting apparatus, goniotachymeter, and routin mechanical tachymeter, just to name a few.

These devices were all intended to predict mathematically the future position of an aircraft, using its present position and some form of external data such as aircraft speed or rate of climb. These devices were unsuitable for the four-dimensional problem posed by enemy aircraft, but they did tremendously improve the gun's chances of hitting its target.

The other method of fire control was barrage fire, simply laying down pre-planned fire to detonate in a set volume. This was often used at night, when visual acquisition of targets was impossible without searchlights. Primitive sound detectors were developed but were of limited use for directing gunfire.

Antiaircraft training was conducted at the *Ecole DCA*, located at Arnouville-les-Gonesse. The French pioneered in practical training techniques, including an interesting method for training antiaircraft machine gunners. To give gunners experience in engaging moving targets, the French would use a motorcycle with a target mounted high above the rider. Gunners would shoot at the moving target while the rider was protected by a long wall just high enough to shield him.

In the field DCA gunners were set up in sections, 3km-4km behind the front lines. Each section would identify and clear several potential gun positions in its area of the front, then wait at one of them for the opportunity to engage an enemy aircraft. After an engagement the antiaircraft section would immediately pack up and move to one of the other positions; German aircraft would immediately call in artillery fire on antiaircraft guns once they returned to base or, later, radio it. This "shoot and scoot" tactic preserved the meager antiaircraft guns available, but infantrymen hated to see the guns provoke artillery fire and then leave.

By 1915 enough sections were available to be distributed at a rate of one per 6.5km of front. The first line of guns would later be supplemented by a second one equipped with searchlights and operating further behind the front.

The total strength of the DCA, the DAT, and the Paris defenses at their height amounted to 48,000 personnel and close to 900 heavy guns, plus machine guns, balloons, sound detectors, and searchlights. Heavy reliance was placed on antiaircraft artillery, as opposed to fighter aircraft, for air defense. France's aircraft industry was already working at capacity, trying to fill the needs of both its own army and that of its allies; nothing could be spared for dedicated air defense fighters.

On the other hand, British gunners concerned themselves less with the technical shooting then in use with the French than with visual firing techniques. Guns and munitions being as primitive as they were, this was not an unreasonable attitude.

At the beginning of the war, the British air defense arsenal consisted primarily of 3-inch and "pom-pom" guns, rapid-firing cannons. In the English defenses, 1-pounder, 3-pounder, and 6-pounder pom-poms were used. The 3-inch, 13-pounder gun was one of the best designs available, reaching an altitude of over 5000m. Other British heavy-gun designs that would see service were the 13 pdr Mk IV, 13 pdr 9 cwt, 3-inch 5 cwt, the "Russian 10 pdr," and a 3.5-inch experimental gun design. These would be supplemented by French 75mms after they had proven themselves in combat.

Lewis machine guns were widely used for field air defense. Many weapons were improvised, but the British also designed some excellent mounts; their twin-mounted Lewis gun could concentrate double the volume of fire possible from a single gun.

In tactical deployment, the British were slow in acknowledging the need for heavy guns on the front. The Royal Horse Artillery was finally given the task and equipped with modified 3-inch 13 pdrs, set up for high-angle fire and mounted on trucks for mobility as the 13-pounder 6 cwt.

By 1916 the British equipped each British Expeditionary Force (BEF) division with a two-gun section, augmented by 26 guns in the rear areas. This scheme not only provided each division with a point defense but in theory also presented a line of guns that the Germans had to fly across to get to the French interior. In practice, however, it probably only served to dilute available air defense assets.

Efforts were made to establish an early warning network across the front and to relay warnings to guns. Liaison with Royal Flying Corps (RFC) units also assured that fighters would shortly be airborne to destroy enemy aircraft.

The British field commanders did come to appreciate the antiaircraft artillery before the end of the war. After Allied successes in 1918, BEF commander Haig asked for 150 antiaircraft guns and 150 searchlights in October in order to defend newly acquired territory in France. The Armistice came before he got the equipment he asked for.

But if the French can be credited with pioneering the field of tactical air defense, it is the British who led the way in national, or strategic, air defense. On 19 January 1915, three zeppelins of the German Imperial Navy raided the Norfolk coast of England. It was the first of many raids that would be launched against Great Britain by the German army and navy. Even though some warning had been given that the zeppelins were on their way, no guns were fired and no searchlights came on until the first bombs began to fall on a railway station and near a church.

English newspapers had speculated about the possibility of these huge airships being used to bomb Great Britain, but in the early months of the war the German High Command had decided to use them for the purpose for which they had originally been intended: scouting far behind the lines of the enemy armies in the field and searching for the British fleet. There were few enough airships even for reconnaissance.

The British prepared for more raids as best they could, deploying the meager antiaircraft artillery assets of the Royal Garrison Artillery and initiating passive air defense measures, such as an ordinance for London spelling out blackout procedures. It fell short of blacking out the entire city. But with all these precautions the only zeppelins spotted during the remainder of 1914 were airships scouting the English coast.

During the opening months of the war the Admiralty was given the overall job of home air defense until the Army could take it over. Some Royal Naval Volunteer Reserve members were placed into the Navy's new Antiaircraft Corps, manning guns, searchlights, and observation posts as "special constables," signing up for special air defense duties at night or during the day while maintaining their civilian occupations.

After a pause of several months, the Germans began attacking English targets at night in January 1915. At first the zeppelin crews were restricted against raids on London on the personal order of the Kaiser, but as the frustration of stalemate continued this restriction was lifted. On 31 May the first bombs rained on London; only 12 antiaircraft guns and 12 searchlights were available for defense. As the war dragged on and the Germans desperately looked for some way to get England out of the war, the city of London would become the favorite target of attack.

The first raids on London were successful in that no airships were lost, but a failure in that (as in many raids) no military targets were struck. However, the concern it caused the populace was all out of proportion to the actual civilian casualties, and the obvious defects in the air defenses would have to be corrected. Interestingly, pom-poms were removed from the London defenses after the initial raids made it clear that the fast-firing guns were useless against high-flying zeps but very hazardous to civilians as their shells returned to earth.

The problem of combating the zeppelins was a strategic one that demanded sophisticated measures. First, the air defenses would have to be centralized. This was initially done by a Royal Navy office set up for analyzing intelligence and reports of zeppelin sightings.

Second, the defenders had to have warning of an impending attack so that gun crews, searchlights, and interceptors could be alerted. Radio intercept stations monitored careless transmissions from the zeppelin bases that were reliable indicators of impending operations, and sometimes the code experts of the Admiralty could even identify what target was to be hit and what airships would be carrying out the attack.

Lightships anchored off the coast of England were meant to provide a means of navigating treacherous waters, but the airships would frequently use them as beacons to guide them to their targets. Sometimes the war machines would even use them as rally points to gather an attacking squadron together after its long flight over the North Sea. Radios or telephones aboard the ships would warn the coast once the distinctive sound of an airship's engines were heard overhead. Coastal stations would also listen for the sound of the zeppelins.

Occasionally the target was one of England's smaller cities along the coast. If no warning was sent from a lightship, the huge machines might be able to arrive over the target with just the hum of their engines audible before the bombs began falling. But more often the target was London, and the cities and naval stations along the coast served as another line of detection, the newly installed telephone network serving to relay the warning to the "hub" of England.

Finally, the zeppelins had to be engaged and destroyed. Antiaircraft guns along the coast would serve as the first line of defense against the aerial raiders by providing early engagement, by early in the war only a few naval installations had antiaircraft guns. Later in the war picket ships would add their antiaircraft fire to the defenses. The British quickly realized that the zeppelins used landmarks such as rivers, rail lines, and urban centers to navigate by. Antiaircraft artillery sites were frequently set up at these potential waypoints.

The Eastern Mobile Air Defence Force was armed with vehicle-mounted Vicker machine guns and searchlights and organized to pursue or intercept enemy aircraft by road as they flew over the eastern approaches to London. A Southern Mobile Air Defence Force was also organized, but it was short-lived. These mobile forces seemed to have accomplished very little.

In London itself a modest inner artillery zone was set up for the engagement of aircraft, protecting only the "vital area," which included Buckingham Palace and government buildings. Even such a small artillery zone was a strain for the limited air defense assets available. It was later expanded to protect most of the city as more weapons became available and public outcry demanded better protection.

Interceptor aircraft were based in an arc across the zeppelins' avenues of approach. Such interceptors would prove to be a vital part of any strategic defense, as the planes could identify the enemy, pursue him, and destroy him.

But in 1915 the zeppelin held the advantages of darkness and altitude over the primitive airplanes.

The early-model zeppelins could operate at an altitude above 3350m. The British BE2c, which had proven a failure for use on the front because of its inherent desire to remain on a fixed course, was an excellent zeppelin interceptor for the same reason. Zeppelin hunting required tedious tracking, which the BE2c did well. But it took 45 long minutes to reach the altitude of the raiders, out of a two-hour operational limit. Even after it had climbed to its ceiling, there remained the problem of locating the zeppelins, which proved to be surprisingly difficult to find in the darkness despite their size. Usually the interceptors had to wait until the searchlights found the airships before the planes could attack.

Once the Admiralty sent the word of an impending air raid to the War Office, it would in turn send the order to waiting air crews to take off at the exact time that would place the aircraft at the right altitude and airspace to engage the enemy. These planes were the dregs of the Royal Flying Corps, whatever could be spared from the front lines on the continent. A handful of Royal Naval Air Service planes were placed along the coast to fight the airships before they reached maximum altitude. To supplement these meager forces, training squadrons were required to keep one plane available at all times for interceptor duty, and new combat squadrons being formed for duty at the front were placed under the control of the Home Forces.

Even as the machines became available, pilots were a scarce commodity as well, and pilots with experience flying at night were virtually unknown. Training was done at dusk when possible, but sometimes pilots were committed to the attack with no night training at all. The combination of inexperience, fog, and the poor improvised lighting of the airfields for landing led to crashes that deprived the defenses of precious aircraft and personnel.

By the end of 1915 the limited interceptor resources available for England's protection were formed into the Home Defence Wing. RFC Home Defence Squadrons, equipped with SE5cs, Sopwith Pups, and other single-engine biplanes, would rise to fight the giant airships as their experience and equipment improved. An incendiary bullet for their machine guns was perfected to catch the zeppelins on fire, a task that the fighters had found surprisingly difficult.

Meanwhile a naval gunnery expert, Sir Percy Scott, was placed in charge of the gun defense of London. He immediately reorganized the antiaircraft artillery and the searchlights, but he did not forget the importance of the interceptors. He requested a great increase in aircraft, as well as 104 new guns and 50 more searchlights, in London's defense.

The proposed increase in interceptors came as a surprise after a study of the Paris defenses was tendered that suggested guns and searchlights alone were sufficient to ward off air attack. Of course, the zeppelins hadn't been sent against Paris; the Germans had other means to bombard the French capitol, as their huge railroad guns could easily hit the city.

The weapons Sir Scott wanted were French 75mm mobile antiaircraft guns that were proving so successful on the Western Front. The London Mobile Section was formed and was armed with the "75s" as the first renovation of the gun defenses.

Interservice rivalry and high-level meddling made further improvements difficult; in fact, for a few weeks no RFC interceptors were assigned to the defense of London. But in the end the War Office and its Royal Flying Corps was given responsibility for the inland defenses; the Navy and the RNAS would be responsible for interception and early warning when the zeppelins came over the sea.

New airfields linked by telephone were laid out for the Home Defence Squadrons that were closer to London. These new bases were equipped with guns and searchlights as well, spreading the interception net wider. The soldiers had brilliant colored rockets as well, which were fired only when an airship was sighted. These rockets could be seen for miles and would guide airborne interceptors towards the raiders.

Two rings of twin-gun positions were laid out around London, one at five miles and the other at nine miles from the city. Other gun defenses were planned to protect war plants and population centers. Field Marshal Lord French was named commander-in-chief of all Home Forces, unifying the defense and giving it central direction.

Even though it took some months before the first air raider was brought down over England, the antiaircraft defenses shaping up below and above were making themselves felt in collateral effects. The Germans found that they could not safely operate below 2440m (8,000 ft) and climbed above 3000m when they could. This of course affected bombing accuracy. The total blackout instituted in London made it even more difficult to find legitimate targets.

Against interceptors the zeppelins found themselves maneuvering to avoid the guns and bombs of the fighters, wasting ballast that the airships could not replace. Magnesium flares were occasionally carried by the airships in order to blind antiaircraft gunners, taking precious payload space that would otherwise be used by bombs. Sometimes the zeppelins would drop their bombs prematurely in order to gain precious altitude. On occasion, zeppelins would even turn back without dropping their bombs on the target at all if they met heavy enough resistance.

These maneuvers resulted in what is now known as "virtual attrition," a lessening of the effectiveness of the attacker by the known or probable presence of active defenses. The more countermeasures an enemy must take along, the fewer bombs he can carry. The more maneuvering an enemy does, the less accurate is his bombing. Virtual attrition can be a very valuable contribution of air defense even when no aircraft are actually brought down.

The new antiaircraft measures made themselves felt in real attrition as well. In September 1916 the first airship was brought down over England by an RFC interceptor using experimental ammunition. The incendiary bullets started the airbag burning. As the zeppelin was a Shutte-Lanz type, it was framed with wood instead of aluminum. By the time the flames burned out there was almost nothing left of the once-mighty machine. German morale almost seemed to disintegrate as well.

The guns were scoring victories of their own. The bursts of fire that blossomed around the airships did not cause a dreaded fire aboard the first raiders, but they did cause other damage; and the combined action of the guns and an interceptor ended in the downing of the L15 over the North Sea on 1 April 1916. Other airships suffered damage from the guns as well; while some airship commanders managed to reach London virtually unmolested, others seemed to run into guns at every turn. By sheer volume of fire the guns were bound to hit a target. On 24 September the L33 was brought down solely by antiaircraft artillery fire.

The Germans responded to the September losses by outfitting a new class of zeppelin they had been working on, the so-called superzeppelin. The L30 class airships flew at 4900m to 6100m, making it far more difficult for the interceptors to reach them and harder for the guns to hit them: It took several seconds for a shell to reach that altitude, and by that time even a slow-moving target like an airship could get out of the way.

The British had committed 17,000 personnel to air defense duty by 1916. The air defenses were becoming effective enough for the German Army to stop sending their airships against England, leaving the zeppelins of the Imperial Navy to carry on.

In July 1917 the London Air Defence Area (LADA) was established, gradually centralizing firefighting units, police units, antiaircraft gun batteries, searchlight batteries, and home defense squadrons into one command charged with protecting the city. Gun areas and interceptor patrol lines were established (see Map 3.1). LADA was responsible for air defense over southeast England, as well as over London itself. Coordination was through a plotting board in a central command post; operators moved symbols representing hostile aircraft as reports came in from observation posts.

The raiders began turning back at the first sign of determined defense. Others tried flying even higher than 6100m, well beyond the maximum altitude of the guns and interceptors but at a cost of accuracy and bomb load. The freezing temperatures at that altitude also reduced crew effectiveness.

The "silent raid" of October 1917 was purposely not challenged by the antiaircraft guns or searchlights on the premise that they could do the raiders no harm but might instead give away their position and aid the enemy in finding targets. The raid ended in disaster for the Germans: Of the 11 airships that participated, five were lost to French defenses or became victims of worsening weather conditions as they tried to return home. Only one airship succeeded in doing any damage, and that was just in civilian casualties, not military targets.

Further losses to the airships from the improving defenses discouraged more raids on London, but other targets around England still received the attention of the zeppelins. The German Navy persisted in their zeppelin attacks right up

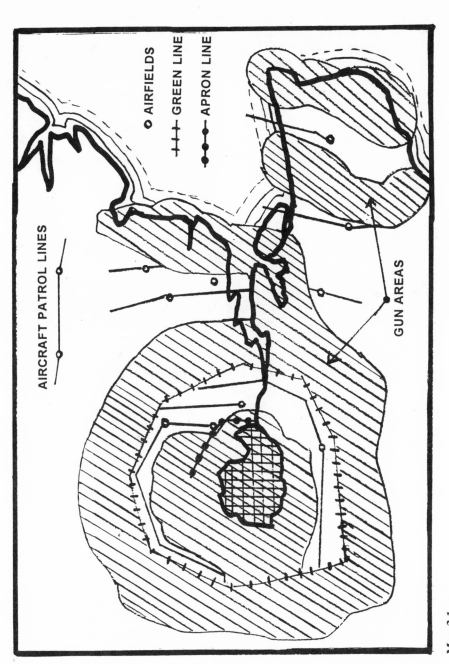

AIRCRAFT PATROL LINES

AIRFIELDS
GREEN LINE
APRON LINE

GUN AREAS

Map 3.1
London Air Defence Area (LADA)

until August 1918, but long before then the Germans had switched tactics and technology; it would be the "giant" bombers that would take the war to London.

German Army planes had been making short excursions to England since 1914, using bases in occupied Belgium. Attacking in ones or twos, these planes occasionally dropped small bombs on coastal towns. London itself was bombed by a lone German biplane on a reconnaissance mission in November 1916. But it would be June 1917 before the Germans began mounting a planned bombing campaign against England, primarily to strike at London.

To mount such attacks the German Army's newly organized *Luftstreitkrafte* (Combatant Air Forces) deployed Gotha G.IV bombers flown by members of *Kampfgeschwader* 3, also known as the England Squadron. *Kagohl* 3 answered directly to the German Army High Command, the *OHL*.

The bombers were large (for the time) twin-engine biplanes. While primitive by today's standards, the aircraft represented a remarkable technological achievement for their time. It had only been a few years since Bleriot successfully flew across the Channel for the first time. A comparable technological feat would have been the USAF beginning regular military flights to the moon in 1975.

The Gothas would be flying from forward bases in Belgium, themselves just barely out of Allied field artillery range. Their route to England brought them close to the Dutch border, and Dutch antiaircraft gunners defended their neutrality with flak. Once past the Netherlands the bombers had to cross hostile territory virtually the whole way. The German planes would be flying at the mercy of the elements, their crews exposed to high altitudes and the vagaries of the weather while manning the plane in open crew stations.

Although London was within range of the planes, it was just barely so. Unforeseen winds, engine trouble, or battle damage could easily ensure that a plane would never return to its base. Part of the dread associated with the bomber attacks was how they seemed to go straight to their targets, regardless of the opposition or difficulty. But the truth was that the first bombers had little choice; they didn't have the time and fuel to test the English defenses gingerly, the way the zeppelins could.

At first the Gothas had an advantage in that the British defenses had been weakened after November 1916, when one of the last large zeppelin raids was mounted, as well as the first bombing of London by an airplane. As subsequent raids against England had caused minimal damage, antiaircraft guns were diverted for use on board merchant vessels and pilots were sent to the front. Guns in London were sent to outlying areas, which seemed to be at greater risk from hit-and-run attacks.

The air defenses continued to be oriented against zeppelin attacks; the threat posed by airplanes was considered by many to be minimal. Lord French ordered his antiaircraft gunners (those not on the coast) not to fire on any seaplanes or airplanes in order to minimize the need for day guns. This incredible directive, which applied to both day and night firing, remained in effect even after several raids, including a particularly damaging bomber raid on Folkestone.

The restriction was lifted on 7 June, and the air defenses were alerted to meet the Gotha threat, as illustrated by the 13 June raid on London. The raiders were met by a few scattered puffs of flak and interceptors, but the entire bombing force returned without a single combat loss.

On 11 July the Prime Minister's Committee on Air Organization and Home Defence Against Air Raids was created to deal with the threat. General Jan Christiaan Smuts of South Africa was the committee member who would virtually mastermind England's improved defensive measures. Smuts was not an airman or artillery officer, but he was a clear thinker who made reasonable conclusions about this new means of warfare.

It was on his recommendation that the War Cabinet established the LADA, giving command of the London defenses to Brigadier Edward B. Ashmore. Ashmore was uniquely qualified for the post: he was both a dedicated Royal Artillery officer and a pilot, having learned to fly just prior to the war. He had command experience in France in both the RFC and the Royal Artillery. The defenses he took command of would be called Ashmore's Shield in some circles.

Lieutenant-Colonel Simon, commander of London's gun defenses, recommended a plan that he had developed during the relative lull in the air battle. His plan would create a barrier of gun sites located, initially, on three sides of London at a distance of about 40 kilometers. Any enemy formation approaching from the north, east, or south would come under fire before it was over the city proper. This would break up the formation, the individual aircraft becoming easier targets for interceptors; British pilots were already learning how dangerous it was to attack bomber formations when they had interlocking fields of fire.

The British established procedural controls to enhance the strengths of the gun and interceptor components of their air defense. The barrier was separated from the city center by a so-called Green Line. Outside the Green Line antiaircraft artillery had priority on targets, while inside the guns would be silenced to give the fighters a chance to destroy the enemy.

Eventually the barrier would form a protective box around London, with a western side added to defend against future German capabilities. The projected gun requirement for the barrier was 190 guns, but there was no immediate change in defense priorities. The eastern gun barrier came into operation first, with 34 guns scrounged from the coast and from the city defenses.

Newer model interceptors and the improving skills of the antiaircraft units took their toll on German bombers. When daylight attacks became too costly, the German bomber pilots turned to night attacks, just as the zeppelin crews had done before them. They did so in order to conserve their strength for a round-the-clock bombing campaign, but by September the bombers were raiding solely under the cover of darkness.

At first the British seemed incapable of finding the bombers at night, either with fighters or with guns. Searchlights were the best means of combating the night raiders, but they sometimes aided the Germans in finding the target area in the darkness.

This rapidly changed: Interceptors flew patrols over London in what effectively became a gun-free zone. The metropolitan center was divided into numbered squares, some of which were given colorful names. Enemy aircraft were tracked by sound and shells were fired in their path to give interceptors (still lacking radio) a bearing.

The antiaircraft artillery formerly sited in London and elsewhere was moved to the defense barrier to give it added depth, and the outer defenses were augmented by additional searchlights. Sound locators came into increasing use, with some manned by blind volunteers. In theory, sight impairment made their hearing more acute.

Experiments were conducted to create an early-warning system based on sound. Various designs were tried, including a huge double-disk design and concrete "sound mirrors" cut right into the channel cliffs. Some of these projects were quite successful, picking up enemy aircraft as far out as 24km, well out of normal hearing range. Greater emphasis was also placed on sound direction of searchlights.

Newer bombers entered German service, including improved Gothas and the R-types—the so-called Giant Bombers. The Germans were finding better range and greater survivability with which to mount their night attacks, which were becoming more indiscriminate. They also started to use incendiaries, in the hope of causing a disproportionate amount of damage.

The British responded by increasing the volume of antiaircraft fire. During one raid over 14,000 rounds were fired, without scoring a single hit. This in turn resulted in a near crisis of supply when antiaircraft ammunition started running low. Crews were exhausting themselves, and many guns were literally worn out. The ground-based air defenses were in danger of burning themselves out.

Once again the problem was met by creating a committee, again with Smuts at its head. Orders were given to increase antiaircraft shell production to 30,000 rounds and to build a reserve of 100,000 rounds. All projected 3-inch gun production was reallocated to London's defense.

British guns and interceptors continued to take a toll on the bombers, causing poor bombing results and even making several planes turn back from their assigned targets. Barrage balloons were brought into service, deployed in "aprons" connected by cables from which trailing cables hung. Eventually, ten such aprons would be placed around the city to snare enemy bombers.

Of the bombs that the Germans did manage to drop on their targets, incendiaries were causing relatively little damage. The Germans began work on a "foolproof" incendiary and started dropping 1 (metric) ton bombs in February 1918. The one-ton bombs were the largest to be used in World War I.

Further modifications of the air defenses occurred before the end of 1917. More squadrons were added. The original barrage balloons, originally set at an altitude of roughly 2700m, were raised to 3300m (10,000 ft) where the Gothas were more likely to be operating. Interceptors, including new Bristol Fighters, or Brisfits, flew patrols staggered at 330m (1000 ft), where they had a good chance of finding the enemy. And finally, searchlights were organized into companies.

But the most important date in the First Battle of Britain was 1 April 1918. On this date the Royal Air Force was created from the RNAS and RFC, making Britain the first country to make its air force an independent service. The use of interceptors during the war amply demonstrated the unique needs and tactics of the new mode of warfare.

Also in April 1918 the British created the North Air Defences, under the command of Brigadier P. Maud. This combined command would protect England north of the LADA, but its main concern was the improved zeppelins then making raids on the Midlands.

On 19 May the Germans launched one final attack on London, causing 49 deaths and over 177,000 pounds worth of damage. While the Germans did finally perfect their incendiary Elektron bomb, no effort was made to burn out the cities of England. With the exception of the August zeppelin raid, the Germans turned their air efforts to the Western Front.

LADA and the Northern Air Defence Area remained strong until the very end of the war, in case the Germans should attempt another sustained bombing campaign. The LADA controlled 304 guns, 415 searchlights, and 11 fighter squadrons; and the northern defenses had a further 176 guns, 291 searchlights, and five fighter squadrons. An effective ground-observer network was in place, and some fighters were equipped with ground-to-air radio for control guidance.

Further improvements were in the works when the Armistice was declared, including two underground hangers for some of the interceptors and the augmentation of existing defenses by 100 guns and 300 searchlights. England had become a veritable air defense fortress.

Over 20,000 personnel were engaged in air defense duties, not counting those people employed by the Anti-Aircraft Experimental Station, known as ''Hill's Bandits,'' after their scientific leader, A. V. Hill. This hand-picked group of mathematicians and electrical engineers did research into the problems of sound location, height and range finding, and antiaircraft artillery ballistics.

Although they arrived relatively late in the war and would not see nearly the same amount of combat service as their French and British allies, the Americans of the AEF's Anti-Aircraft Service would make up for the lost time through professionalism and skill. When America entered the war against Germany in April 1917, there was not a single antiaircraft unit in the U.S. Army, hardly an unusual absence for an armed force of the time. But the need for antiaircraft units was recognized in the planning of the American Expeditionary Force (AEF). In the table of organization that resulted, each corps would possess a machine-gun battalion and a heavy antiaircraft battalion equipped with the

M1917 3 in. gun. This force would be further strengthened by 20 platoons of antiaircraft guns per army.

The field air defense network foreseen by AEF planners, the result of studying the Allied air defenses already in place in France, promised sufficient antiaircraft weapons to deter or prevent enemy air attack. However, there were simply no guns and no personnel to man them in the Army at the time. The M1917 had barely reached prototype stage, and it would take months to begin full-scale production.

The decision was made to make air defense the mission of the Coast Artillery Corps (CAC), a branch of the Army that had experience in engaging moving targets. Another factor was the fact that with the German fleet bottled up by a British blockade, the threat to the American coasts was minimal. The skilled and experienced personnel of the CAC could be better utilized to fill the manpower needs of the expanding AEF, its soldiers forming the core of the new CAC antiaircraft units as well as other U.S. Army artillery batteries.

The AEF plan established a school in the United States for training officers in antiaircraft artillery, with another school for both officers and NCOs in France. A unit training center would also be established in France. French antiaircraft gunnery methods would be the standard, with translated French manuals providing the doctrine base. Officers training in the French antiaircraft school were sent to French units for two weeks of practical instruction and experience. In this way, a mode of warfare previously unknown in the U.S. Army would be rapidly taken up by the Coast Artillery Corps.

The AEF's Army Antiaircraft School at Langres would provide practical experience in antiaircraft gunnery by defending its area with training pieces and student gunners upon attack. Although American antiaircraft doctrine would remain French-based, some CAC officers were sent to the British antiaircraft artillery school at Steenwerk. As British tactical air defense was largely judged to be inferior to the French, few British innovations were adopted.

The American antiaircraft school formally recognized one of the true values of antiaircraft artillery, that of limiting the effectiveness of the enemy's aircraft. Lectures suggested that making the enemy climb to a higher altitude or drop his bombs prematurely or simply preventing the enemy from spying on a particular sector of the front could be considered even more important than destroying the enemy's planes.

Like the Air Service and other Army branches, the CAC would have to be equipped with French weapons. This of course meant the 75mm, but there were difficulties in procuring these weapons. France's industrial base was already stretched to its limits trying to supply the needs of itself and its European allies. AEF needs further strained France's war production.

Few 75mm auto cannons would be available for the AEF in the first few months. In fact, most of the weapons delivered to the Coast Artillerymen were not even on antiaircraft mounts, making them virtually useless for antiaircraft gunnery.

The U.S. Army's ordnance experts designed improvised mounts for the guns, placing them in concrete pits that allowed space for gun traverse and recoil. A gun was fixed in a wooden framework mounted above the pit. There was also available an M1917 gun carriage designed along similar lines, but using steel girders to support the gun. Its main advantage over the improvised mount was its transportability.

This arrangement was less than satisfactory. In the improvised mounts, 75mms were immobile, making them suitable only for defending permanent installations. Mounted guns were also very limited in azimuth and elevation. In this manner, the 75mms were best used in night firing and barrage fire.

The machine gun chosen by the CAC for antiaircraft duties in Europe was the Hotchkiss; the weapon was found to be superior to the St. Etienne. One reason the Hotchkiss was selected was its compatibility with the "infantry corrector" sight.

The Antiaircraft (AA) Service deployed antiaircraft machine guns all across the front, but ultimately it wanted to provide heavy antiaircraft batteries with machine guns. This would have given antiaircraft units at the front a good mix of weapons. However, the French could not deliver enough machine guns to carry this out.

CAC searchlights were manned by Army engineers, who were judged to have the technical skill necessary to operate them. Unlike just about all other war material, the United States was able to supply AEF units with American-made searchlights, taking them from CAC installations in the United States. Even in this area, French equipment dominated American units.

In deploying searchlights the AA Service was deviating from French doctrine, which minimized the use of searchlights in favor of sound detectors. The United States did operate sound detectors to help guide the searchlights, improving upon French night defense methods.

One air defense element the AEF did not employ was the use of barrage balloons. Though American planners did desire them, particularly for airfield defense, none were ever acquired because of personnel and equipment shortages.

Americans were trained in the use of fire-prediction equipment already in use by the French. Although the limitations of the available equipment were recognized by the mathematically inclined CAC officers, they would do little about it; despite efforts to provide effective fire control, the method used by Americans was described by one of them as the "guess-point-shoot-and-pray" system.

Brigadier General James A. Shipton drew up the plans for the AEF's Antiaircraft Service and would become its first chief. The organization he commanded consisted of the Army Antiaircraft School and fixed air defenses in the rear areas. The Chief of the AA Service was also an inspector of the antiaircraft units that were part of AEF armies, providing administration, doctrine, and guidance. In June 1918 Brigadier General Shipton was replaced by Col. Jay P. Hawkins, the Commandant of the AAA School.

Because of the AEF's late arrival in the war, the time spent organizing and training units, and the difficulty in equipping them, relatively few American antiaircraft units saw combat. But the combat record they left behind was impressive.

The most telling fact is the number of rounds it took to bring down an aircraft: the AA Service expended 605 rounds, compared to 4,500 for the French and a staggering 10,000 for the British. Taking advantage of the European's air defense experiences in the first three years of war, the Americans had learned to lay down intense and accurate AA fire.

Back at home, the CAC was busy looking at the need for defending the United States from air attack. Admiral Robert E. Peary, the famous explorer, observing the sudden amount of Central Powers air activity in early 1918 on all fronts, recommended spending a billion dollars in appropriations to defend American cities against air attack.

This was not an unfounded fear. Even as the British were preparing to attack Berlin when the Armistice took effect, the Germans in turn were working on a huge bomber with which to reach New York. Even had the design been completed in time, the cost of attacking America with such bombers would have been prohibitively expensive, not simply in the cost of bomber production but also in losses due to combat and mechanical failures.

4

Developments during the Interwar Period

At the end of World War I the air defense elements of the great powers were largely broken up in the rush to demobilize and return to normalcy. Had the war lasted a year longer and the full implications of strategic bombing become more evident, the antiaircraft artillery arms might have survived intact. Instead, the mad dash of the war's combatants to achieve an air defense capability was quickly forgotten and the air defense artillery units that had been painstakingly built up over several years were rapidly dismantled in a matter of months.

Britain had developed a sophisticated air defense network to protect it against German raids, but against the advice of many of its military leaders most of it was dismantled. By the end of 1919 only one brigade of the Royal Garrison Artillery and one searchlight battalion were available for air defense. The infrastructure of national defense was gone in the rush to resume a peacetime economy.

Demobilization and the reduction of the size of British forces encouraged standardization among the available weapons in order to minimize the number of different types in service. The 3-inch 20 cwt and 13 pdr 9 cwt were retained for active duty and 4-inch guns were held in reserve, but not manned. All other wartime weapons were disposed of, including a promising 3.8-inch antiaircraft gun that did not reach production before the end of the hostilities.

Despite a severe reduction in personnel and equipment, interest in British air defense did not disappear overnight. In 1922 the School of AA Defence was established at Biggin Hill, with 1st AA Brigade RA (Royal Artillery) and the Royal Engineers (RE) Searchlight Wing providing a cadre. Even though the brigade was stationed in England, its main role was to support any expeditionary force deployed to fight for the Empire. Any mission of national air defense was gone at this point.

The Steel-Bartholomew Committee was established in 1923 as part of an overview of British military defense. Its primary finding was that the United Kingdom was inadequately defended from air attack. A recommendation was made for sufficient weapons and organization to defend England from future attack. The resulting zones of defense are shown in Map 4.1.

As there was still a need to defend an expeditionary force from attack, the new antiaircraft forces would come from the British Army's reserve component, the Territorial Army (TA). TA units such as the 4th City of London (Royal Fusiliers), 7th City of London (Post Office Rifles), and 21st London (1st Surrey Rifles) were converted to antiaircraft duties. England would acquire 33 RA antiaircraft batteries and 28 RE searchlight companies, organized to form Air Defence Brigades. RAF fighter wings would also be allocated for air defense duties.

The recommended additions to the antiaircraft forces were not made, at least not to the degree envisioned by the committee. The economy-minded postwar government of Great Britain based its defense spending on the premise that no major war would break out for at least ten years. Some modest expansion of TA antiaircraft forces were carried out, and a few batteries were sent to British possessions overseas for their protection. Hong Kong, India, Gibraltar, Aden, and Singapore were just a few of the corners of the British Empire that received air defense units.

But while budget cuts were limiting England's active defenses, the infrastructure was being planned and emplaced. The Observer Corps was formally established in 1925 and would spend the next decade honing its skills during air defense exercises. With "Forewarned Is Forearmed" as its motto, the corps was kept a virtual secret. As in World War I, Observer Corps reports of enemy aircraft were relayed by means of the civil phone system. As seen in Map 4.2, a new and simpler air defense scheme, the Romer Plan, was adopted.

The corps came under the control of the Air Ministry, just as the RAF did, and was organized along RAF lines. It utilized unpaid volunteers and relied on patriotism to fill its ranks; the small amounts of money spent to maintain it would reap inestimable returns during the coming war.

To control England's airspace, Air Defence Great Britain (ADGB) was established. ADGB consisted of two elements: RAF Bombing Formations and Fighting Area. Fighting Area was made up of ten fighter sectors, Advanced Fighting Squadrons, and General Officer Commanding Ground Troops. GOCGT would control all ground-based elements of air defense, including the Observer Corps. While all this was impressive on paper, the fact was that there were not enough interceptors, guns, or personnel to implement it fully.

Another major organizational development in Britain's interwar period was

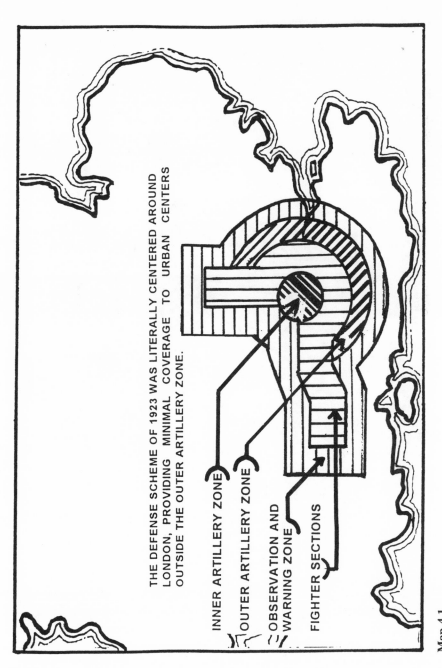

THE DEFENSE SCHEME OF 1923 WAS LITERALLY CENTERED AROUND
LONDON, PROVIDING MINIMAL COVERAGE TO URBAN CENTERS
OUTSIDE THE OUTER ARTILLERY ZONE.

INNER ARTILLERY ZONE

OUTER ARTILLERY ZONE

OBSERVATION AND
WARNING ZONE

FIGHTER SECTIONS

Map 4.1
Steel-Bartholomew Plan, 1923

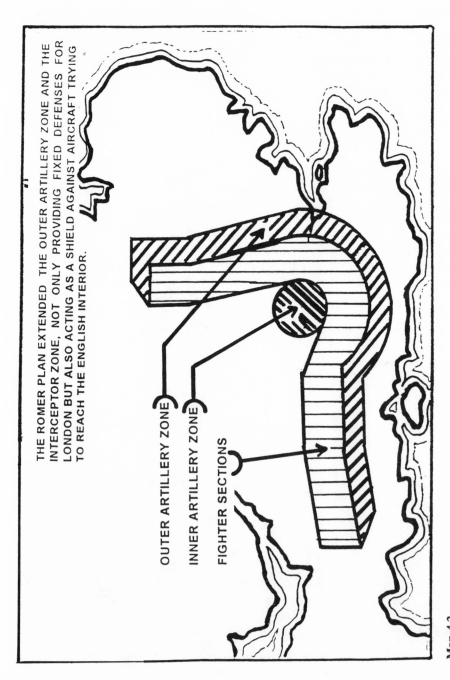

THE ROMER PLAN EXTENDED THE OUTER ARTILLERY ZONE AND THE
INTERCEPTOR ZONE, NOT ONLY PROVIDING FIXED DEFENSES FOR
LONDON BUT ALSO ACTING AS A SHIELD AGAINST AIRCRAFT TRYING
TO REACH THE ENGLISH INTERIOR.

OUTER ARTILLERY ZONE

INNER ARTILLERY ZONE

FIGHTER SECTIONS

Map 4.2
Romer Plan, 1925

the abolition of the Garrison Artillery branch of the Royal Artillery. The air defense units that belonged to the Garrison Artillery were transferred to the Field Artillery.

As modest antiaircraft forces were being built up, new equipment started to come into production for RA units. This included the Vickers Predictor, a single-unit mechanical computer meant to provide firing angles for antiaircraft guns.

World War I antiaircraft prediction had mainly been done on prediction boards or some other kind of two-dimensional plotting device. These were of limited usefulness because they were attempting to solve a three-dimensional problem. The Vickers Predictor used data obtained from observation devices, like target binoculars, fed into the device by way of knob settings. The knobs were attached to three-dimensional cams that translated the mathematical equations into values that interacted with each other in the machine to get new azimuth and elevation values, which were given back to the gun.

Such mechanical devices were the forerunners of modern computers. They gave almost instantaneous answers and would grow more and more sophisticated before their use ended in the 1950s. Later models sent their azimuth and elevation readings to dials on antiaircraft guns; when the true elevation and azimuth indicator needles matched the predictor needles, the guns were correctly aimed.

Light machine guns were the primary automatic weapon for low-altitude air defense, and little need for a heavier such weapon was foreseen until the mid-1930s. A Vickers 2-pounder gun was briefly considered for use, but instead the Bofors 40mm was adopted after its superior performance and design were demonstrated in Sweden to a team of British officers.

Vickers did not get the contract for the automatic antiaircraft gun, but it did fill the need for a heavier, more modern gun design with its 3.7-inch gun. Acquisition of this weapon would be slow until the outbreak of World War II.

To provide high-altitude air defense, the 4.5-inch gun was adopted from the Royal Navy. The weapon was heavy, requiring a semipermanent firing position. Construction of the gun sites delayed 4.5-inch deployment. Meanwhile, Britain's experiments in armor warfare led to the development of the 18 pdr Mk5, a self-propelled antiaircraft/antitank gun. The "Birch Gun" would have been able to provide forward-area heavy antiaircraft fire, but it was obsolete by 1934. No weapon was acquired to replace it, and the need for a self-propelled antiaircraft gun would remain unfilled until the war.

Experiments in 2-inch and 3-inch antiaircraft rockets were also conducted, but the British ran into technical problems. The main difficulty was the requirement that the rocket system "look and act" like a standard antiaircraft gun, ensuring that the potential for such a system to launch a large volume of projectile in a short period of time would not be exploited. Firing tests in Jamaica expended 2,500 rockets but did impress British authorities enough to push development. The rocket program was put on hold in 1939.

For British air defense, 1935 was a pivotal year. Antiaircraft strength was finally great enough for the activation of the 1st AA Division, in December. Its four groups were placed in southeastern England, where the bulk of enemy air attacks had taken place during World War I. Air defenses were extended northward, as seen in Map 4.3.

Meanwhile, the Abyssinian Crisis posed one of the first serious threats to England's overseas empire. The 1st Air Defense Brigade was deployed from England to Egypt, protecting that English protectorate against a possible Italian air attack. The Italians turned out to be more concerned with securing their enlarged empire than attacking Alexandria or the Suez Canal. The unit was withdrawn back to the Home Defence without having to fire a shot.

The same year, an experiment on behalf of the Committee for the Scientific Study of Air Defence proved the concept of radio ranging, or radar. As experiments with radar improved the new technology, England quietly phased out sound mirrors and the larger sound detectors. Sound detectors would remain in service only for fire control and searchlight guidance purposes.

The following year, ADGB was broken up, and the RAF was reorganized into Fighter, Bomber, and Training Commands. These separate commands, based on unit function, would work in conjunction with the Observer Corps, the new radars, and the antiaircraft guns to defend England.

In 1938 the Munich Crisis precipitated a call-out of the air defenses; another European war seemed imminent. Territorial Army antiaircraft units were activated and manned their guns. Appeasement averted war, temporarily, but the emergency brought to light technical problems not obvious during the many interwar exercises. The telephone warning system was found wanting, and other weaknesses were identified. Extension of the telephone lines, new observation posts, and a few clever technical innovations would provide fine tuning for England's national air defense. They would come none too soon.

The Antiaircraft Service of the AEF ceased to exist by the spring of 1919. All Coast Artillery Corps personnel were reassigned back to the United States, where their air defense experience was considered unnecessary. They were soon back to their old job of watching for ships off the shores of the continental United States, because to the American public the thought that the primitive machines used in World War I could attack the United States was absurd. The Atlantic Ocean and the Atlantic Fleet were more than adequate to defend America.

In 1920 a special committee chaired by the Army Chief of Staff saved antiaircraft regiments from total oblivion. The committee evaluated future needs, and among its projected improvements was a recommendation that an antiaircraft regiment be assigned to each corps and that an antiaircraft brigade be assigned to each field army. Antiaircraft regiments were composed of a gun battalion, a machine-gun battalion, and a headquarters element.

Gun battalions were to possess three firing batteries of four 3-inch guns plus a battery of searchlights. Machine-gun battalions were to consist of four batteries of three platoons. Each platoon was armed with four .50-caliber machine guns.

Even though the decision had been made for a relatively strong and dedicated

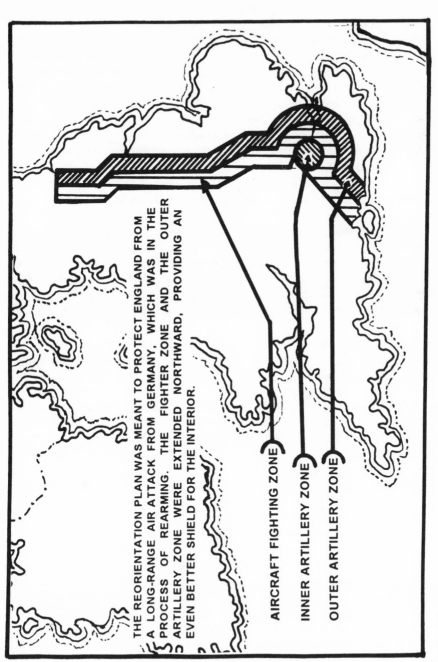

THE REORIENTATION PLAN WAS MEANT TO PROTECT ENGLAND FROM A LONG-RANGE AIR ATTACK FROM GERMANY, WHICH WAS IN THE PROCESS OF REARMING. THE FIGHTER ZONE AND THE OUTER ARTILLERY ZONE WERE EXTENDED NORTHWARD, PROVIDING AN EVEN BETTER SHIELD FOR THE INTERIOR.

AIRCRAFT FIGHTING ZONE

INNER ARTILLERY ZONE

OUTER ARTILLERY ZONE

Map 4.3
Reorientation Plan, 1935

air defense, equipment shortages hindered the deployment of antiaircraft regiments. Many of the weapons possessed by the AEF's air defenses had been sold for scrap or otherwise turned over to the Allies. Indeed, almost all of the 75mm guns had been owned by the French government and were returned to them after the Armistice.

This left the Coast Artillery with a few obsolete 75mms, the M1917 3 in. gun, and the M1918 3 in. gun. The 75mms were all but useless because of their limited elevation and azimuth capabilities. The M1917 could fire up to 7600m, but it had an automatic breechblock that limited the rate of fire and made it difficult to use for barrage fire. In contrast to the fixed-mount M1917, the trailer-mounted M1918 had serious stability problems stemming from the trailer's poor design, as well as from the problems inherent from the M1917 gun itself.

Tight postwar defense budgets limited what could be provided for the Army. Only through intense lobbying was the obsolete equipment of World War I replaced prior to World War II. In the meantime, the CAC had to be satisfied with theoretical studies about how best to deploy the types of weapons that were available and to help develop new ones.

A new-model gun, the M1925, was designed to keep the best qualities of the M1917 while equipping it with an automatic breach. This allowed it to reach a high rate of fire. The M1925 (also known as the M3 3 in. mobile or the M4 3 in. fixed) remained the primary gun of the antiaircraft artillery right up to World War II.

A remote-controlled 60-inch searchlight was also developed, the MV-1. Searchlights made easy targets, and allowing the crews to operate them remotely gave them survivability. A new sound locator was developed that also could be operated by remote control. An acoustic corrector developed for use in conjunction with the sound locator provided for some correction ability, but the use of sound locators had all but ended by the time U.S. forces were committed to World War II.

The Director M1A1 became the standard mechanical predictor in 1928, although for some troops the old M1 models were not replaced until 1931. The M1A1 was a superior design, better thought out than its predecessor, but it would be replaced by newer models, the M2, M3, and M4, by the end of the 1930s. The newer versions relied on electrical data transmission between data acquisition equipment and, in turn, to the guns. Note predictor operation as illustrated in Figure 4.1.

The Coast Artillery Corps's newest weapons represented a systems approach to antiaircraft defense: Guns, searchlights, and directors were all designed to work with each other, becoming more effective together than they would have been working individually.

But while antiaircraft tactics and doctrine was studied in Coast Artillery publications, actual antiaircraft materiel was lacking. With the situation in Europe deteriorating, antiaircraft weapons were given top place in War Department priorities in 1937 and 1938 in an effort to make up for years of neglect.

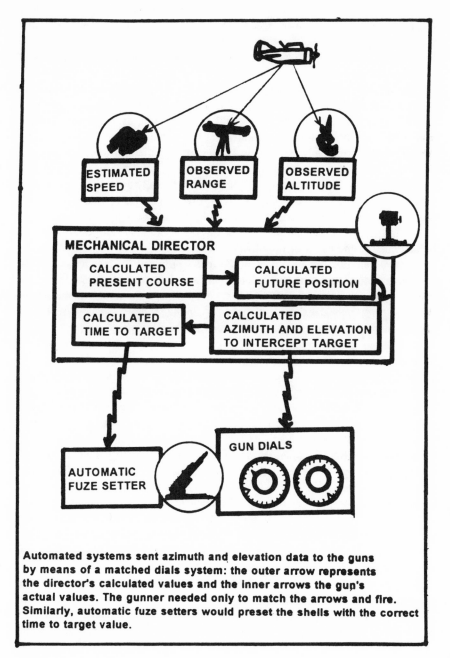

Automated systems sent azimuth and elevation data to the guns by means of a matched dials system: the outer arrow represents the director's calculated values and the inner arrows the gun's actual values. The gunner needed only to match the arrows and fire. Similarly, automatic fuze setters would preset the shells with the correct time to target value.

Figure 4.1
Fire-Control Principle with Mechanical Director

A late addition to the Coast Artillery was the 37mm automatic gun. Extensive testing in the 1930s led to its acceptance, but the first models would not enter service until 1940. In adopting the 37mm, American antiaircraft forces would effectively fill the gap between the altitude of the machine guns and the reach of heavy guns.

Another new weapon was the 90mm Gun M1, operated on the Anti-aircraft Mount. Modifications would result in an improved design, the M2, in 1943. After World War II the weapon would become Gun, Anti-aircraft, Towed: 90mm; M118. The 90mm became known as the Triple Threat, for its versatility: the gun could effectively be used in the antiaircraft, field artillery, or antitank role.

Unlike most of the other powers, France did not totally disband its antiaircraft artillery but did reduce the size of its force. Five *Regiments d'artillerie de DCA* (RADCA) were all that remained from the wartime antiaircraft forces, which would later be organized into three brigades. Reserve units were established, to be activated in the event of mobilization.

Light antiaircraft fire would continue to be provided by Hotchkiss and St. Etienne machine guns, although some innovative new mounts were adopted for use. Observation of the Spanish Civil War convinced French air defenders of the need for a heavier-caliber antiaircraft weapon. Several models were available, but none was adopted for use before war broke out.

The 75mm guns would continue to provide the bulk of heavy antiaircraft artillery. Studies were made of 82mm and 90mm guns, but neither would be available to the army before the war. Instead, the 75mm guns were upgraded with new barrels. The longer barrels improved performance, increasing the gun's range to 8000m. Retrofitted 75mms would only delay the inevitable. The M1932 entered service as an improved 75mm, requiring only 20 minutes to emplace. The guns' rate of fire was increased to 25 rounds per minute.

To supplement the 75mms, World War I–vintage 105mm guns continued in service. The Navy had 90mm and 100mm guns that would be added to the French air defenses.

Strategic and tactical air defense continued to be distinguished through the designations of DCA and DAT, with both types of units operating with each army. In 1940 DCA would be renamed *Forces Terrestres Antiaeriennes* (FTA). In 45 days of combat, the French air defenses would account for over 200 German aircraft. It would not be enough to forestall defeat.

Germany's development of air defense weapons suffered far worse than that of any of the allies of World War I. Whereas the Allies eliminated their anti-aircraft forces by choice, Germany's were eliminated by mandate, under the terms of the Versailles Treaty. The number of weapons allowed to the meager *Reichswehr* were meticulously spelled out. It was permitted 204 field guns and 84 howitzers. The *Reichswehr* was to have no heavy artillery, and antiaircraft guns were not on the list of permissible weapons. That theoretically left the 100,000-man army with only machine guns for close-range defense, and even these were meticulously numbered. With the relatively small ammunition reserve allowed by the treaty, they would not have been useful even in that role for long.

But Germany did retain a minimal antiaircraft capability by equipping some of its permitted field artillery batteries with antiaircraft guns. The remaining German naval vessels had some antiaircraft guns still on board, and German Army officers assigned to the so-called field artillery batteries trained on them.

But in collusion with the *Reischwehr*, the firm of Krupp began to circumvent the terms of the treaty. Prohibited by the Versailles Treaty from using his own German factories to produce large numbers of weapons for the *Reichswehr*, he used a number of loopholes to develop and build new military equipment.

Though the treaty prevented the manufacture of weapon prototypes by the Germans, it could do nothing to prevent paper designs of new weapons from originating from Krupp's engineers. Nor could it do anything about companies that had been set up outside of Germany for the design of U-boats and other such equipment. Some weapons officially manufactured for export instead ended up in Germany's arsenal. But the maneuver that would prove most helpful in the building of new antiaircraft weapons would be Krupp's involvement in Bofors.

In the coming war, the Swedish firm of Bofors, to this day a well-known military manufacturer, would supply antiaircraft guns to several nations on both sides. In the 1920s Krupp began to influence the company by buying into its stock; by 1925 Krupp owned a controlling interest in the firm. While maintaining influence there, Krupp allowed *Reichswehr* officers to tour Bofors plants and see the latest developments in military technology. Swedish neutrality laws eventually stopped such blatant violations of the spirit of the treaty, but Krupp remained in control of Bofors.

The antiaircraft-equipped field batteries were secretly reequipped in 1928 with Krupp 75mm guns that had supposedly been exported out of Germany. These units were sent to underpopulated regions to keep them out of sight of international observers. There was a further expansion of flak units in 1932, with antiaircraft batteries being formed with the designation of "transport units." Antiaircraft machine-gun companies were formed and trained under the auspices of the *Deutsche Luftsports Verband* (German Air Sports Association).

With Hitler's rise to power, rearmament no longer needed to be hidden. Germany immediately expanded the size of its Army and Navy and created an air force, the *Lutfwaffe*, to control the air. In 1936 the new force was made responsible for air defense artillery units; it was now in command of both offensive and defensive air elements, providing antiaircraft weapons for the protection of *Luftwaffe* bases, units in the field, and home defense. The German Army maintained antiaircraft units of its own, organic to its combat formations.

The *Luftwaffe* and the German Army soon had new and effective antiaircraft guns. The Flak 30 2cm and Flak 18 3.7cm antiaircraft guns rapidly entered service as short-range weapons, and the 8.8cm Flak 18 would become the mainstay of high-altitude air defense, reaching up to 9900m. The Flak 18 was an excellent gun that would gain a fearsome reputation during World War II. The *"acht-acht"* would soon get a chance to prove itself, during the Spanish Civil War, when Hitler sent it as part of the Kondor Legion.

The first German fire director came into service, the *Kommandohilfsgerat 35.* The Germans would continue to work on their fire-control equipment and methods, improving them into the effective system that would defend the skies of central Europe during the coming war.

Germany recognized the potential of radar and did much work on it in the 1930s. By 1935 they had two models: Freya and Wurzburg. Freya was an acquisition radar, its large antenna providing 360° coverage as it rotated. It had a range of 120km and was fully mobile.

Wurzburg had a range of about 20km. It was directional radar and as such had great potential as a fire-control and intercept radar. But because Germany's war machine was being molded toward Lightning War, based on offensive strategy, neither radar inspired any interest among German leaders. Freya and Wurzburg would not begin mass production until 1939.

During World War I, Japan was isolated in Asia while England and Germany were learning firsthand the lessons of strategic bombing and tactical air support. The Japanese Empire did participate in the war and succeeded in taking most of Germany's Asian and Pacific colonial possessions but largely remained unaffected by developments taking place in air defense technology and tactics. Japan would follow other military powers slowly if at all in air defense.

It should not be surprising then that the first true Japanese antiaircraft gun was not produced until 1921, and not until 1924 was the first air defense regiment formed. There was simply little interest in protecting the home islands or the Imperial Army against air attack. This oversight was not due to a lack of technical ability; Japanese industry had developed many weapons on a par with European and American technology and had proved it could make almost anything the armed forces required. To understand fully Japan's disinterest in air defense, one has to look at Japanese history and geography.

Geographically, Japan saw little threat to its Home Islands off the east coast of Asia. China and the USSR were the only two countries within aircraft range of Japan in the 1920s and 1930s, but China's air arm was virtually incapable of causing militarily significant damage in Japan. As for the Soviets, they indeed had heavy bombers capable of destroying targets in Japan but they had few bases in the Soviet Far East and seemed more concerned with activity in Europe than in Asia. After 1941 the USSR was locked in a life-and-death struggle with Germany and also ceased to be a concern in Japanese planning until late in the war.

Historically, Japan had never been successfully conquered. This resulted in a mentality that the Home Islands were somehow invincible, that they could not be invaded and certainly not bombed. And so, antiaircraft strength and development were always given low priority during the interwar period.

Antiaircraft training was poor when compared to other contemporary branches of the Imperial Army. As few resources were allocated to the antiaircraft artillery, units rarely participated in live-fire exercises. Many batteries never fired on a moving target until they found themselves in combat; they were considered combat-ready when they received their requisite personnel and equipment.

The Chiba Antiaircraft School was established and trained officers, cadets, and NCO candidates in the art of air defense. No specialists were trained; instead, all students were taught "a little bit of everything" as part of their overall course. Antiaircraft personnel were given gunnery lessons in automatic weapons and heavy guns, were trained to operate searchlights, sound detectors, and radios, and were taught some tactics.

The Japanese did develop a sophisticated way of training antiaircraft personnel in searchlight deployment and gun laying. Chiba possessed what was called the Gun and Searchlight Commanders Training Room. Inside, lighting controls could simulate nighttime conditions from dusk to moonless darkness. Light projectors could paint "clouds" on the ceiling, while models of aircraft flew through the simulated sky by means of wire.

Students were to deploy miniature searchlights to solve all defense problems. Range section personnel were trained by means of special directors, which were calibrated to engage the simulated planes. This was in advance of other countries' training methods at the time.

Progress was slow in the 1920s and 1930s. In addition to traditional Japanese overconfidence and newfound German military assistance, the Imperial Army was influenced by the nature of the long-term war it ended up fighting against the Chinese. The conquest of Manchuria and the invasion of China saw little use of airpower by Japan's enemies, reinforcing the belief by senior officers that air defense was not a serious need of the field forces. Though Japan did have antiaircraft brigades, regiments, battalions, and companies, in the field the antiaircraft was assigned primarily to the division at battalion strength (if available), with the division commander deciding on deployment.

While the Japanese Army stressed integration of fire to maximize the effects of air defense, it also continued to rely on small arms to defend individual units against air attack. The Model 99 7.7mm rifle was designed with a rear sight that provided the infantryman with an approximate lead when engaging enemy aircraft. If a large enough unit, a battalion or regiment, fired all of its rifles at a single target, there was a good chance of two or three hits.

The Japanese had three designations of their dedicated air defense weapons: *kosha kikanju* (antiaircraft machine gun), *kosha kikanho* (antiaircraft machine cannon), and *koshaho* (antiaircraft gun).

The Model 92 7.7mm "Lewis-type" machine gun employed in small units could be equipped with special mounts and adapters that allowed them to be used in the air defense role. Similarly, another Model 92 machine gun that became the standard MG of the Japanese Army could also be fixed in the air defense role.

The Model 93 13mm machine gun could be deployed in single or dual mounts in the antiaircraft role. The dual mount included a sophisticated sight that allowed accurate tracking of an aircraft flying up to 500 kilometers per hour, at ranges between 200 and 3,000 meters.

Yet another light antiaircraft weapon provided to the Japanese soldier was the 70mm Barrage Mortar. The launcher consisted of a simple tube and block design; the shell it fired contained several charges that would float back down to the ground, each under its own parachute. The intent seems to have been to fire a large number of charges into the air, where an aircraft might possibly collide with them. The charge would then explode, causing at least some damage to the plane. Unexploded charges could theoretically be recovered and reused. The barrage mortar was largely ineffective. There is no Allied record that any aircraft was shot down by one.

The Model 96 Type 2 25mm antiaircraft/antitank automatic cannon could be found in both dual and triple mounts. With a formidable 300 round-per-minute per barrel firing rate that was slowed only by how long it took gun handlers to replace the 15-round magazines, the Model 96 could put out a respectable curtain of steel.

When it came to heavy antiaircraft guns, the Japanese were at a distinct disadvantage. The Model 88 75mm gun provided the backbone of the Japanese antiaircraft artillery, even though it had been in service since 1928 and in fact was closely modeled on the French 75mm antiaircraft gun in wide use during World War I.

The Model 88 was a good design and as such was able to continue in service right up to the end of the war. The weapon was towed to its position by truck, then emplaced on its highly stable five-outrigger platform. The gun had a respectable theoretical altitude of 10,000m but, because of the manner in which Japanese gunners used it, the effective ceiling was closer to 7000m.

Like all the heavy Japanese guns, the Model 88 suffered from poor fire control. Corrections were still being transmitted vocally, which was adequate for the low ceilings and speeds in use in 1928 but was not up to taking on the high-performance planes of the 1940s. Later, a system was devised for the Model 88 to make corrections electrically.

The Model 14 105mm gun was the heaviest gun in use with the Japanese Army. It took 30-45 minutes to emplace the weapon, and the gun had many technical problems, which were addressed only after America entered the war. Like the Model 88, it used a hydropneumatic recoil system. The design also included an automatic fuze setter.

Fire-control equipment remained primitive, even though the Japanese recognized the need for improvement. Automatic weapons relied entirely on mechanical and optical sights. The Model 88 had fire control apparatus that included a 2-meter-base height-and-range finder, a target-speed and course-angle calculator, a corrector scale, and spotting binoculars. While the quality of these devices compared favorably to that of their American and European equivalents (when still in use), they represented a five- to ten-year lag in technology and doctrine.

The Japanese had designed and deployed a computing director in small numbers for use with the Model 88. Even such a mechanical device required precision machining, and Japanese industry never seemed to produce enough of the machines. Japanese director technology would remain 10-15 years behind other world powers.

In 1939 the Antiaircraft Artillery became a separate branch of the Artillery Corps, on par with the Field Artillery and Seacoast Artillery branches. But most Antiaircraft Artillery funds went to operations and acquiring more weapons, with little for research and development. No serious radar research was done prior to the war, and Japan would find itself at a distinct technological disadvantage when it came to air defense.

The Soviets have had some sort of air defense capability from its very beginnings. Spurred during World War I by the bombing raids of the huge German Gotha bombers and unhindered by the traditionalist czarist officers, the military leaders of the Red forces were open to new concepts of warfare.

According to Russian tradition it was on 29 October 1917 that the Putilov Works in Petrograd formed an armored antiaircraft battalion on Lenin's direct orders. This is supposed to be the very first air defense unit formed by the Red Army, and the predecessor of the USSR's elite Order of Lenin Guards Putilov-Kirov Air Defense Missile Regiment. This show unit participated in the May Day parade every year in Moscow. 1924 is the year given by other sources, when the 1st AAA Regiment was established in Leningrad.

In any case, the Bolsheviks took air defense seriously enough that by 1927 the antiaircraft artillery had its own special detachment on the Red Army Staff in Moscow. Air defense came under the heading of *PVO*, *Protiovozdushnoi Oborony*, a designation that would remain with the service even through its changes.

PVO regiments were deployed in sectors to defend the Motherland, with three or four in each of the border military districts. Thee sectors were usually under the command of an aviation officer, rather than an artillery officer. Neither aviation nor antiaircraft artillery were considered separate services, and both were subordinate to the commander in the field; the placing of an aviation officer in charge of air defense sectors reflected the emphasis on fighter interception of enemy aircraft and the use of antiaircraft artillery as a last-ditch effort to stop an air attack.

A primitive early warning network was organized to aid the sectors in detecting, identifying, and engaging intruding aircraft. It consisted of observation posts manned by both Red Army and *Militsia* personnel and was known as the Aerial Observation, Warning, and Communications Service, or by its Soviet acronym, *VNOS*.

In 1932 the Red Army formed the Air Defense Directorate and reorganized and expanded the units and organizations under its control. The Directorate was semi-independent of the Red Army, as its emphasis was on strategic, rather than tactical, air defense.

Under this new organization, VNOS was made a full-time service by discontinuing *Militsia* participation. VNOS was made more "military" by the formation of companies and battalions. Air defense divisions were likewise formed, and support units were allocated to them. In addition, several squadrons of interceptors were placed under the directorate's control for the express purpose of air defense.

The growing air threat from Germany prompted further growth of the air defense forces, and in 1937 several independent air defense corps were organized around Moscow, Leningrad, and the vital oil center at Baku in the Caucasus. These corps controlled all air defense assets in their defense zone, with the exception of aviation units.

Efforts were made to supply the Air Defense Directorate with improved weapons. A whole new series of antiaircraft guns was designed and deployed at this time, as well as such support equipment as new-model searchlights, sound detectors, and for the first time, radar. The disastrous Russo-Finnish War, which should have been a walkover for the Soviets, instead turned into a fiasco. The entire Red Army was reorganized as a result, including the PVO.

These weapons would see combat for the first time during the Great Patriotic War. Germany would throw the weight of its entire war machine, including its Luftwaffe, against the USSR. Air defense units would prove the only protection against some of the Germans' more determined raids.

During the two decades between the world wars, aircraft technology improved enormously. Fabric and wood construction gave way to metal. Biplane designs were phased out in favor of monoplanes. Radial engines were largely replaced by water-cooled in-line models.

Aircraft became more specialized. Swift single-engine models were designed as pursuit, or fighter, aircraft. They would destroy the enemy's planes in defense or as escorts of an attacking force. Fighter-bombers could engage in air-to-air duels or carry a modest bomb load. As a result, fighter speeds rose from the late World War I standard of 190kph to over 500kph.

Aircraft carriers were built by most major powers and equipped with their own specialized aircraft. Naval fighters and fighter-bombers were designed to operate off carrier decks, along with torpedo-bombers.

The most impressive development was in bomber technology. Multiengine bombers capable of carrying 2,500kg of bombs at a range of over 2,000km were used during the Spanish Civil War. The potential devastation of strategic bombing was demonstrated on a small scale and captured the imaginations of military planners, in both defensive and offensive thinking. With the technology on hand and strategic theory to use it, World War II would see aerial warfare on an unprecedented scale and, in turn, air defense of increasing sophistication and scope. Each major power would develop air defenses that reflected their past experience and their view of future air developments.

5

England: From the Battle of Britain to NATO

Thanks to her prewar experiments in air defense–related technologies, Britain was probably better prepared than any other country when it came to aircraft detection and flak. However, these resources would become heavily strained by one of the fiercest strategic air campaigns ever mounted: the Battle of Britain.

The ground war had gone badly for the Western Allies in 1940. German *Blitzkrieg* campaigns had resulted in the occupation of Denmark, Norway, the Netherlands, Belgium, Luxembourg, and most of France. England stood alone, separated from Nazi Europe by the North Sea and the Channel and within range of *Luftwaffe* bases in western Europe and Scandinavia. A German invasion of England was imminent, but the Germans knew that to invade the island successfully they would have to gain control of the air.

Great Britain's air defense organization had gone through several different designs during the interwar period, but the air defense network adopted during wartime protected (in theory) the entire United Kingdom. Fighter Command Headquarters outside of London coordinated overall defense; in turn, it divided England into four RAF fighter groups. Group headquarters plotted incoming enemy aircraft and formulated a response, scrambling interceptors and alerting guns. RAF and army resources were allocated among sectors within group boundaries. Plotting was improved, but the technique was largely the same as that practiced during World War I.

Prior to the war, most antiaircraft artillery units were organized into Air Defence Brigades or independent batteries. An Air Defence Brigade consisted of three to four heavy batteries and a single light antiaircraft battery. The 1st AA Division was formed in late 1935 to protect the most likely area of an enemy attack, southeast England. More divisions were activated throughout the war, absorbing the Territorial Army Brigades brought into active service. All ground-based weapons would be placed under the British Army Antiaircraft Command after the war began. The stage was set for Air Defence Great Britain (ADGB) to be established as a combined command organized as shown in Map 5.1.

As well-organized as it was, England had scarcely 695 heavy antiaircraft guns and 253 40mm Bofors guns, with 2,700 searchlights to support them, when the war began. However, there were many excellent weapon designs and prototypes, including the antiaircraft rocket project, and British war production rapidly began to turn these out.

Later gun designs included a 4.5 in. adapted to fire 3.7 in. ammunition, which resulted in higher shell velocity. Naval 5.25 in. guns were adapted for Army air defense role in a powered static model; such weapons were used to protect vital areas.

Lewis light machine guns were issued as a stopgap measure, but the only practical result of the obsolete guns was a lift in morale; initial German attacks were too high to be hit by machine-gun fire. Later in the war, Luftwaffe aircraft turned to low-level attacks to avoid heavy flak, only to run into the excellent Bofors guns, the issued machine guns, and other light weapons.

But at least as important to the defense of Great Britain was radar. The new technology was a force multiplier, to use a modern military term. While England lacked sufficient air defense resources to cover all possible enemy approaches, radar permitted the British to concentrate their aircraft and to give sufficient warning to their guns.

Following radar experimentation in the 1930s, a permanent network of radar stations was constructed along England's southern and southeastern approaches. Called Chain Home (CH), the system consisted of towering fixed antennas, anywhere from 60m to 90m tall. The antenna emitted a radio signal, which would bounce off an airborne object and return as a second signal. By measuring the time between the signal's emission and the receipt of a return signal, the distance to the object could be calculated. An approximate location for an aircraft could be ascertained by comparing two different ranges from two CH stations for the same aircraft.

The radar "fence" would continue to be expanded around the island's perimeter; the southeastern approaches would be supplemented by new stations along the east coast, all the way north to Scotland. Once in place, the radar net provided early warning of German attacks whether they originated from German-occupied Norway, Netherlands, Belgium, or France.

The British realized that the Germans would rapidly change their tactics and fly below 1500m to sneak through the defenses. Work on Chain Home, Low-

Map 5.1
Air Defence Great Britain (ADGB)

flying (CHL), began almost immediately after war broke out. Radar research had been underway to provide a closer range-detection capability for the Navy and Army. This was adapted for CHL; unlike the fixed transmitter for Chain Home, the CHL antenna rotated in azimuth, eliminating the need to corroborate data with a second station. Rotation was achieved by the simple expedient of having an airman pedal a bicycle frame adapted for this use.

With both sets of radar in operation, the British were able to detect formations almost as soon as they began assembling over France for raids. Filtering centers analyzed the size and probable targets, relaying data to control centers that in turn were able to plot their range and altitude. Success in combat ensured radar's place in the future of air defense.

The Germans were quick to appreciate radar. In August 1940 the Luftwaffe singled out British radar installations for destruction. The Chain Home antennas, towering above the surrounding countryside, probably made the Germans realize that the British were using some sort of radio direction-finding. But for the most part their attacks only caused some relatively minor equipment damage that was quickly repaired. For a time, the Germans concentrated their attacks on the buildings that housed skilled radar personnel, a resource not so easy to replace.

One exceptional radar raid was the 12 August attack on Ventnor Station. The station was destroyed, creating a radar gap 16km wide. As the air defense net at that time was of a perimeter design, with little or no depth, the breach presented a serious threat to England's survival.

But apparently the Germans never realized their success. Signal intelligence was in a primitive state at that time, and the Wehrmacht may not have been geared toward monitoring and analyzing Britain's radar system. The gap was plugged before the Germans discovered it.

Then the Germans switched to attacks on the RAF's airfields and English aircraft factories and supply depots, in fact, on the entire air capability of the United Kingdom. *Adlerangriff* (Eagle Attack), launched in mid-August, was meant to eliminate British air power once and for all.

To accomplish its task, the Luftwaffe was equipped with twin-engine bomber models like the He111, the Ju88, and the Do17. These aircraft had relatively small bomb loads, especially when compared to the strategic four-engine bombers of the United States Army Air Corps and the RAF Bomber Command. Although they would be used to their maximum capabilities, German bombers were really meant to support the armies in the field and not to wage a lengthy strategic bombing campaign.

In just a few days of intense fighting, both sides suffered heavy losses, although the British could afford them far less than the Germans. The British had several advantages in defending their own country: Downed RAF pilots could be recovered to fly again, while Luftwaffe pilots shot down over England were lost to Germany forever. And British fliers knew what would happen to their country if they were defeated.

Yet, the sheer intensity of constant combat was taking its toll; every day RAF pilots were taking to the sky in one-on-one duels to the death, surviving, landing, refueling, getting something to eat, and then scrambling yet again. The weight of England's survival was coming to rest on just a handful of fighter pilots.

They were equipped with first-rate aircraft. The Hawker Hurricane was capable of flying 529kph and of reaching an altitude of 10,850m above sea level. The "Hurry" was the mainstay of Fighter Command, but it was the Supermarine Spitfire that became almost legendary during the Battle of Britain. The Spitfire could fly 50kph faster than the Hurricane and, more important, was 100kph faster than the Me109, the primary fighter of the Luftwaffe.

Some interceptor aircraft (light bombers) were equipped with small radar sets for night-fighter purposes. But as the sets were only practical at a range of perhaps five kilometers, to find the enemy bomber formations effectively the night fighters, as indeed the day fighters to a lesser extent, required direction from the ground.

The radio sets sought by the RFC during World War I were standard equipment aboard the fighters of the RAF. The ROC (the Observer Corps was graced with the title of "Royal") reports and radar tracks were analyzed, and vectors were given to alerted fighters.

Improved radars known as Ground Control Interception (GCI) models were operational by 1940. The improved display scopes made it easier to assign intercept vectors to airborne fighters. Radar-assisted GCI would become a standard feature of all postwar national air defense networks.

The Germans were convinced that the British were down to only 150 fighter aircraft; in fact, they still possessed 750, despite almost 25 percent losses. *Reich Marshal* Hermann Goring, commander of the Luftwaffe, planned night and day air attacks concentrated on Fighter Command and its airfields. Fuel storage would also be targeted. Once Fighter Command was knocked out, the Luftwaffe would be able to attack England at will.

The Germans were able to thwart radar to a slight degree by flying formations on the edge of Britain's radar coverage, sometimes merely patrolling along the coverage before turning back to base and other times suddenly turning towards the British coast to attack. Though the British could "see" the enemy formations, their mere presence could no longer be used to justify scrambling RAF fighters.

Fighter Command found itself fighting for its very existence. Casualties rapidly left it 200 pilots short of manning all its fighters, despite the use of volunteer pilots from Poland, France, Czechoslovakia, and other occupied countries and from Canada, the United States, Australia, and other free countries. During *Adlerangriff* the RAF's loses were always far lower than the Luftwaffe's; during the second phase their losses were much higher and even went above those of the Germans a few times. An overconfident Hitler set the date for Operation Sealion, the invasion of England, for 21 September.

But the Germans saw no sign that the British air defenses were weakening, and in the meantime they were suffering high numbers of bomber and fighter losses at the hands of RAF pilots and antiaircraft gunners. The pilots had earned the admiration of Prime Minister Winston Churchill, who stated, "Never was so much owed by so many to so few."

The Luftwaffe switched to night attacks, using radio beams to ensure accuracy. They also concentrated on bombing population centers, rather than purely military targets. This was the start of the so-called Blitz. It began with a particularly heavy raid on the night of 7 September, one that met with only slight resistance as the defenses were still geared toward dealing with attacks on the fighter bases. Over 350 bombers escorted by 600 fighters succeeded in reaching London, setting fire to several areas. A second wave of bombers flew in around 10 P.M., guided by the first fires. Bombs would fall continuously until 4:30 A.M. the next morning. Despite efforts to get the fires under control, some were still burning that night when the Germans returned.

General Frederick Pile, AA Commander, decided to abandon the idea of fixed azimuth firing, of presetting the guns to cover the entire sky and only firing guns when an aircraft was approaching or inside the preset azimuth. Though the resulting fire was not as effective or as sparing of ammunition, it was heartening for the people of London to see the skies lit up with defensive fire. Antiaircraft served to build morale in this case.

Even some obsolete truck-mounted 3-inch guns were sent around the city during raids, stopping in front of air raid shelters and giving the occupants a morale-boosting show of resistance. The chances of actually hitting an aircraft with such a haphazard emplacement and engagement was extremely low, but one of the navy crews manning the guns did manage to bring down an enemy plane.

More guns were brought into service in London from all over England. The British took advantage of the bomb destruction to create gun positions on top of the debris, deep inside the city. It would have been difficult to find emplacements for them otherwise in an area as built up as London. Churchill himself ordered batteries into Hyde Park, where the people could hear them shooting off.

English gunners were pushed to their limits as the rigors of actually firing the guns, a physically demanding job, and of cleaning and maintaining their weapons took their toll. Many crews stayed at their posts around the clock, replenishing ammunition stocks between raids and sleeping when they could in the daytime. At night, the crews would return to firing at the enemy.

In addition to TA and RA gunners, women of the Auxiliary Territorial Service (ATS) began to take their place among the British air defenders. The ATS was established in 1938, the same year that it was determined that, in the event of war, women could perform all the duties involved in antiaircraft gunnery except for handling the heavy shells.

Before the end of 1941 women were being drafted into the ATS and so-called integrated batteries were seeing action in the defense of London. Known as "ack girls," enlisted women were placed in charge of fire control aspects, while men operated the guns. Female officers at first had no military duties to speak of and were left out of the chain of command. In time ATS officers would take their places supervising fire control, and some would even take command of some units.

The British use of women in air defense might have preceded the Soviets' doing the same. British women bravely manned their weapons in the open during bombings, some of them dying at their posts. But the British used women out of necessity, not because they sought to further the cause of female equality. In doing so, they may have beaten the Soviets to such expediency.

Guns could be controlled at the Group level, with a Gun Liaison Officer (GLO) watching the plots of enemy aircraft approaching England and determining what gun action would be most appropriate. The GLO would then get in contact with AA Operations Rooms within the Group Area, giving them a "hold fire" or "free to fire" command for their local areas, depending on whether friendly aircraft were present. This was controlling air defense by volume, as each gun zone was given a simple command that determined how its weapons would be used.

The lethality of the antiaircraft artillery increased as gun-laying (GL) radars became available to give precise height, range, and bearing information to the predictors. Some technical flaws limited the usefulness of the early sets when they were first deployed, but this was overcome by laying a level field with, of all things, chicken wire. In this way, one of the most sophisticated weapons of war England then possessed was aided by use of a humble material that could be found on almost any farm.

The standard GL3 radar set was supplemented by the SCR-584 from the United States, which could track targets automatically, without needing the operator to guide it. This was especially useful during the V-1 attacks.

For 65 nights the Luftwaffe tried to break the back of British resistance by destroying the city of London. Physical damage and casualties were high, but the Germans never came close to knocking England out of the war or to destroying the RAF so that England could be invaded, or even to causing England to ask for a separate peace. Hitler at first postponed and then finally canceled Sealion and prepared to attack the USSR.

German air attacks would continue, but they would rarely reach the intensity of the Blitz. Though they caused little damage when compared with the massed bomber attacks early in the war, so-called tip-and-run attacks of single or paired fighter-bombers would prove to be most troublesome, as they flew under the radars at high speed, appearing over coastal targets without warning.

During the Blitz British authorities practiced many passive measures meant to minimize the bomber damage. An evacuation of children to the countryside was begun, to save them from the bombs. Those who remained behind took to the Underground, the subway system under the streets of London. Anderson shelters provided a minimal shelter for family homes, and other shelters were prepared by Air Raid Precautions, the ARP.

Other passive air defense measures included fake airfields, "K sites," which were constructed to draw the Germans away from legitimate targets. These were complete with dummy fighters and bombers built by the British film industry. "Q sites" were also built for nighttime deception and consisted simply of lights laid out to look like flare paths and circuit lights. Sometimes these were deployed in conjunction with the K sites, but often they were simply laid out in remote areas.

Electronic spoofing was initiated, the first electronic countermeasure. The Germans used a dual beam system to increase the accuracy of their bombing, and the British jammed it or sent spurious signals to cause the Germans to drop their bombs prematurely.

The British continued to improve the air defenses even as the intensity of German attacks slackened for a time. They experimented with balloon mines, a scheme that proved difficult to implement. As for barrage balloons, they proved still to have some usefulness. Instead of deploying balloon aprons, as in World War I, the British deployed balloons individually, varying height and positions to confuse the Germans who might try to navigate through the pattern.

Along the coasts and in the vulnerable Thames estuary, shore batteries of antiaircraft guns were augmented by Maunsell Forts. These large structures were built in dry dock. Once afloat the forts were towed to their positions along the coast or in ports. Once sunk into place they provided an excellent platform for antiaircraft artillery. Each was equipped with two 3.7-inch guns, two 40mm guns, radar, and quarters for 120 men. Each was a self-contained unit.

A variation of the Maunsell Fort was the Army pattern, in which several towers were set up in a group, in order to provide concentrated firepower in the same manner as an Army antiaircraft battery would. Some of these were especially helpful in the last year of the war.

The British continued to strengthen their electronic frontier. The Germans continued their tip-and-run raids, flying just above the waves of the Channel to get under the CHL network. A supplementary system named Chain Home, Extra Low, was installed. It used a newly developed centimetric radar, which the British were able to "point" between the water and CHL's lowest acquisition level.

The British also began installing transponders aboard their aircraft. Called Identification Friend or Foe (IFF), the system operated with the radars, sending a coded signal towards a radar "blip"; if the aircraft was friendly and equipped with an IFF transponder, it would send the coded reply. As radar made aerial warfare an affair of greater and greater distances, IFF would become absolutely vital to prevent fratricide.

British radar research resulted in yet another technological breakthrough, the proximity fuze. Most shells were by this time automatically set with a time to detonation before being fired by the gun. While this time was estimated using the best predicting instruments then available, it was still a guesswork method.

Proximity fuzes took the guesswork out of the equation. The fuze consisted of an electronics package small enough to fit in an antiaircraft shell and yet resilient enough to survive the stress of being fired out of a gun. It emitted a doppler signal; if the signal bounced off a target, the shell's receiver would detonate the explosive as soon as the signal indicated that the shell was passing the target. This ensured that antiaircraft shells would detonate as close as possible to the target.

But when this breakthrough was made there was little hope of exploiting it; England was already producing as much as its industry could. The supply problem was solved by giving the secret of the proximity fuze to the United States, which in turned copied it, mass-produced it, and supplied large quantities to Great Britain.

Designated VT, T98 (for the 3.7-inch gun version), the proximity fuze was purposely given the misleading designation "Variable Time" in order to hide its existence. Extraordinary measures were also taken to prevent the VT fuze from falling into German hands, including withholding the device from Allied antiaircraft units on the continent.

In response to British strategic bomber attacks on Germany, Hitler ordered the so-called Baedeker Raids in April 1941. The attacks were directed not at military targets, nor even at industrial urban centers. The raids were mounted against sites of historical and cultural importance (the name came from a popular tourist guidebook); many were not even defended by antiaircraft artillery. The purpose of the attacks was simply terror and revenge.

Meanwhile, the English were not just committed to defending the skies over Great Britain but also were responsible for air defense of their wide-flung empire as well. British antiaircraft units would see action in southern Asia, Iraq, and North Africa, among other areas of British influence.

The island of Malta lies in the center of the Mediterranean, near Sicily. Its location was a perfect base for securing Allied supply lines to Egypt, and for interdicting the supplies going to Rommel's *Afrika Korps*. The Germans decided to seize the island by airborne assault, which meant destroying or at least nullifying the air defenses of the island. Intense attacks by the Luftwaffe and the Italian *Regia Aeronautica* began in early 1941.

When war began, there were scarcely any aircraft or antiaircraft guns. Prewar plans projected a need for four fighter squadrons and 112 heavy and 60 light antiaircraft guns, but because of budget constraints only a few old Sea Gladiator biplanes and some heavy antiaircraft guns were assigned to an RA regiment. The obsolete biplanes, the sole RAF presence in Malta, were given the nicknames Hope, Faith, and Charity and were able to hold off Italian attacks during the first months of the war.

Early needs in other theaters delayed a buildup of defenses, even though it was clear that Malta's position was becoming more and more untenable. A single squadron of Hurricanes, with 72 heavy and 34 light antiaircraft guns, was ready for the onslaught when it began.

British aircraft losses were intense. Fighter aircraft were sent to the island by aircraft carrier and from Egypt, but finally losses were high enough that British bombers were withdrawn from the island, reducing Malta's interdiction value.

Malta was transformed into an air defense fortress as soon as German pressure abated, and bombing was left mainly to the Italians. Airfields were constructed and enlarged, and a dispersal system was established to protect parked aircraft from sudden attack. Gun defenses were dug in.

This was opportune, as the Germans again turned their attention to Malta in December. By the end of January 1942 only 28 Hurricanes remained operational; two weeks later they were down to 11. The civil population went underground, and attacks on shipping virtually cut off supplies. Even submarines had to stay submerged while in port.

The first Spitfires were shipped to Malta and, as in the case of Operation Sealion, the air defenses proved to be too stubborn to allow for invasion. HRH King George VI awarded the Maltese people the George Cross, England's highest civilian award for gallantry, for their courageous defiance of the Axis.

There were other cases of British air defenses throughout the Empire during World War II: failures like Crete and Malaya, successes like Iraq and Egypt. In other instances, elaborate defenses were built but were never seriously attacked (as in the case of Gibraltar).

On all fronts, Axis attacks were growing in intensity and improved technique. German air raids were occasionally mounted against the radar stations, but of course antiaircraft weapons sited nearby made the radars hard targets to knock out. Also, the very design of the radar antennas, large-scale metal structures set in concrete, made it difficult to cause lasting damage.

Building on their success with guided bombs, the predecessors to modern-day "smart weapons," the Germans looked into the development of antiradiation weapons. A passive seeker, Radieschen, was mounted on SD 1400 X and Bv 246 bombs and tested in late 1944 and early 1945. Although research was promising, failure rates were 80 percent in the test drops at an artillery range. The program was canceled, and the German "ARM" never saw action. But other German secret weapons would.

Just as Germany had switched from zeppelins to bombers in World War I, increasing air defenses caused Germany to switch from a bomber offensive over England to a campaign using unmanned air weapons. The first of these "vengeance weapons," the V-1, was launched against Britain in early June 1944. The nature of the attacker demanded a new approach to air defense.

The V-1 was a small pilotless aircraft propelled by a pulse jet, in effect, a flying bomb. It is interesting to note that while the V-1 was in the developmental stage it was designated a *Flak Ziel Gerat*, or antiaircraft target apparatus, for security purposes. The FZG 76 was further deployed in flak regiments and flak detachments, all in an effort to hide this new offensive weapon from Allied intelligence.

The Allies did know that a new German secret weapon was in the offing but were at first unsure of the nature of it. Much of the photographic evidence being gathered and the intelligence being analyzed seemed contradictory at times. In fact, what the Allies were looking at were two different weapon systems in development for the same purpose: the V-1 (originally FZG 76), which was the Luftwaffe's unmanned jet, and the V-2 (originally A-4), which was being built by the German Army as a sort of long-range rocket artillery system.

Even as the war in Europe was entering its final stages, Allied photo interpreters began to note the presence of "ski ramps" being constructed along the channel coast of occupied France. Straight lines drawn along the ramps' axes ominously converged on the primary German target: London. That England was about to be the subject of another air campaign was confirmed when an earlier photograph of the German experimental area in Peenemunde was examined and a similar ramp identified—with a cruciform-shaped aircraft seemingly ready for a test launch.

In November 1943, RAF Fighter Commander was officially renamed Air Defence Great Britain, reviving the title used by England's interwar scheme, and placed under the control of the Allied Expeditionary Air Force. ADGB was under the command of Air Marshal R. M. Hill and consisted of Balloon Command, the Royal Observer Corps, Antiaircraft Command, and three RAF groups. In addition to the defense of England itself, ADGB was also responsible for the nighttime air defense of the beach heads. Coincidentally, this reorganization placed the air defenses of Great Britain in a much better position to intercept and destroy the theoretical threat of robot bombs.

The following month Allied Expeditionary Air Force considered what measures could be taken to protect Britain against the flying bombs. One of the biggest problems facing the air defense planners was the lack of firm intelligence on the capabilities of the new weapon. Initial estimates placed the aircraft's speed at between 250 and 420 mph (402kph to 676kph), flying at an altitude between 500 and 7,000 feet (152m to 2,128m). The actual maximum speed was 654kph, with a 3,000m ceiling.

The Diver Plan was written as the most effective way of countering the proposed threat. It gave the primary responsibility for destroying the flying bombs to interceptors, with a gun zone providing a last line of defense. Because this was a drastic rearrangement and reallocation of air defense resources, including some earmarked for a future invasion of the continent, the plan was put on standby: It would not be implemented until the phantom secret weapon made its appearance.

Meanwhile, one V-1 countermeasure that was briefly considered was to build magnetic coils that would generate magnetic fields capable of throwing the robot devices off course. The idea turned out to be impracticable, as it would have required enormous amounts of electricity and scarce copper out of a wartime economy already stretched to its limits. Measures were also taken to interfere with radio signals for the V-1, under the mistaken assumption that the new weapon would use command guidance. But there was a practical countermeasure that was also exceedingly simple in conception: mount preemptive strikes on the V sites.

Preemptive strikes were made against identified launch sites in April, May, and June of 1944, and afterwards most of them appeared inactive. A new type of site, less distinct than the original ones, was then constructed. They were not built with easily identifiable launch ramps; instead, concrete was laid so that a simpler ramp could be put together rapidly just before the site was ready to become operational. The modified sites were not immediately connected to the flying bombs by Allied intelligence, and there were few bombing resources to commit to the new installations: Operation Overlord, the invasion of Europe, took precedence after 6 June 1944.

Once the construction of the modified sites was complete and the V-1 missiles were available in quantity, the Germans launched their first attack on 13 June, shortly after the Allied landings at Normandy. Colonel Wachtel, in command of the V-1 units, intended to fire 500 missiles a day at England. Only ten were launched the first day, and of those only four made it to the English coast.

At first, the defenses of the Diver Plan were not implemented by the Chiefs of Staff; considering the poor showing of the first bombs the military wanted to wait and see just how many daily launches the Germans could sustain.

But as the number of "buzz bomb" launches escalated daily, it was clear that some specific air defense countermeasures would have to be implemented. But the initial experiences with the V-1 led to new thinking, and a variation of Diver was put into operation: Every gun and gun-laying radar available would be transported to the coast to form a Diver belt, a gun zone through which the V-1s would have to fly to reach their targets. The American and British gun-laying radars would have clearer fields of fire over the channel and the countryside, free of clutter. Interceptors would then have the whole of southeastern England between the Diver Belt and the city of London itself as a huge fighter zone. The V-1 defenses at this stage are illustrated in Map 5.2.

The mass relocation of the guns was an enormous task—and a huge risk. Antiaircraft guns in transit could not do their job, and once on the coast the batteries had to find suitable positions. Heavier guns normally required concrete emplacements, but waiting until such emplacements could be built was unthinkable. An improvised type of position called a "pile mattress" was engineered. Once in place, British and American units in the Diver Belt took a toll on the incoming bombs; the overall effectiveness of gun defenses rose dramatically.

The Germans experimented with launching their flying bombs from airborne bombers over the North Sea, skirting the Diver Belt defenses. These were dealt with by creating a Diver Strip to protect the eastern approaches to London, which would be supplemented by other Diver emplacements over time.

The fighters were also enjoying success. Interceptors like the Spitfire had a hard time shooting down the flying bombs. Their speed was very close to the Spitfire's, making a pursuit of the bombs useless unless the range was very

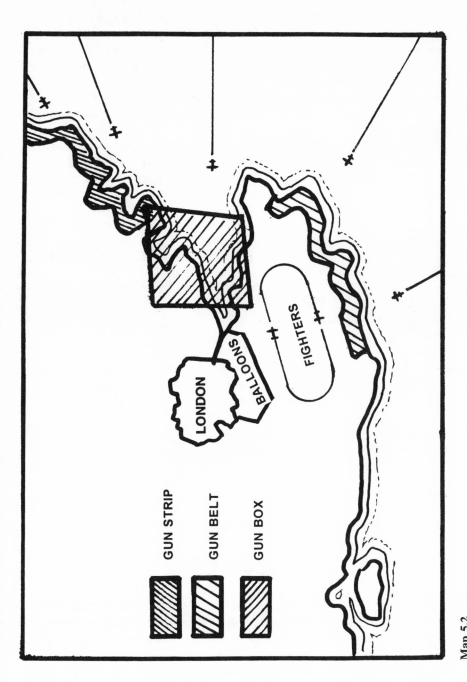

GUN STRIP

GUN BELT

GUN BOX

LONDON

BALLOONS

FIGHTERS

Map 5.2
V-1 Defenses around London

short. Interceptors had to approach from the rear because making passes at bombs from other quarters gave the pilot only one slight chance to hit it.

Once on the tail of a V-1, the pilot had two options: shoot it down with cannon fire or tip it. By placing one of the fighter's wings under the stubby wing of a buzz bomb and then executing a slight roll a pilot could throw off the delicate gyroscopic guidance system of the bomb, making it plunge to earth. Some pilots preferred tipping to using cannon fire because pursuing the missiles at high speeds inevitably meant flying through the fireball of a successfully destroyed V-1.

Even as the V-1 attacks reached their height, another German "wonder weapon" reached operational status. While the Luftwaffe was working on a flying bomb, the German Army was working on the development of a liquid-fueled rocket that would serve as an adjunct to long-range heavy artillery. Begun as the A-4, the V-2 rocket was partially the reason for Allied intelligence's confusion in assessing a future air threat: Information gathered about both weapons was assumed to concern the same project.

The V-2s needed no launch ramps, just a level, circular launch platform. The German Army eventually developed mobile equipment that required the barest minimum of support and eliminated the need for the circular position. A battery could fire a missile from almost any accessible clearing, making its prelaunch detection almost impossible.

V-2s were let loose against England beginning in September 1944. Unlike the previous bombing campaigns and the V-1 campaign, there was no obvious solution to the defense problem posed by the missile. It flew in a ballistic arc that brought it to the edge of space and then almost straight down over its target, and it traveled at over 6,000kph, several times the speed of sound.

The only practical plan was one of presetting large numbers of guns to fire simultaneously into the missile's path, as determined by radar. But the number of guns required would have been prohibitive, and the chance that a shell would detonate the warhead of an incoming V-2 astronomically small. There was little to do but let the missiles come and minimize the potential damage done by them.

Radar stations were set up along the southeast coast of England to monitor V-2 launches in their initial stages in Occupied Holland. This gave early warning for civil defense.

Air patrols searched for V-2 batteries set up for launch or on the move, but the missiles were frustratingly hard to find. The missiles would continue hitting England until the end of March 1945.

After the Allied invasion of France and the opening of a second front in the west, the German air attacks on England slackened as their bases were captured. By October 1944 most of France, Belgium, and Luxembourg had been liberated. German V-1 and V-2s were being pushed out of range of England but were still able to reach continental cities in Allied hands.

The Germans opened their new V-1 offensive from the Netherlands with attacks on Brussels, then a few days later turned their attention to Antwerp. The Belgian city of Antwerp was vital to the Allied armies because of its port facilities. The ports already in Allied hands were of limited value and working to capacity.

Few aircraft could be diverted to the defense of Antwerp, and as a result the city's defense was left almost solely to ground weapons. Antiaircraft batteries with the British Army were pulled from the front and positioned along the probable routes the V-1s might take to hit the city. Attacks became so intense that some batteries were withdrawn from England itself to help shield Antwerp. Some U.S. 90mm battalions were also added. The positioning of antiaircraft units around Antwerp is shown in Map 5.3.

The result of these measures was impressive; few buzz bombs ever reached Antwerp. But when V-2s were also unleashed against the city (over 900 of them), the damage reached appalling levels. The antiaircraft gunners could do nothing but watch the sudden explosions of the missiles while they waited for the next V-1 attack. But the V-1 was defeated, as surely as Germany itself was defeated.

Some postwar critics pointed to the enormous damage the Luftwaffe inflicted on some parts of England and questioned why so many resources and personnel were committed to air defense when clearly "the bomber will always get through." In response, air defense advocates pointed out that the bombers did not always get through; thousands of them were shot down. These bombers never returned to their bases to refuel and reload. The destruction was bad enough but imagine, the advocates would say, what would have happened without the guns?

Following the war, Great Britain maintained its air defenses, although it was impossible to do so at the same strength in peacetime. By 1950 the Cold War had begun; the USSR was the new enemy, and nuclear bombers were the newest threat.

Propeller aircraft were replaced by British jets. New and improved radars searched the skies for unknown aircraft. The ROC went underground, literally. Its observer stations were built beneath the surface, and corps members were given the task of atomic survey, that is, reporting nuclear fallout. Although still trained in aircraft recognition, ROC members were largely superseded by radar; the ROC was inactivated in 1975. The ROC Medal was instituted for members who completed 12 years or more of service.

American gun units were stationed in England for a number of years to defend USAF units stationed at RAF bases. British gun units would also continue service as new and improved guns were sought.

Attempts were made to increase the rate of fire of the 3.7-inch gun. Many experimental models were tried, but the Ratefixer CN was the weapon deemed best-suited for British air defense, being capable of firing 75 rounds per minute. But when the weapon was ready for production in 1949, it was already obsolete.

The British also experimented with a taper bore gun, which reduced its bore

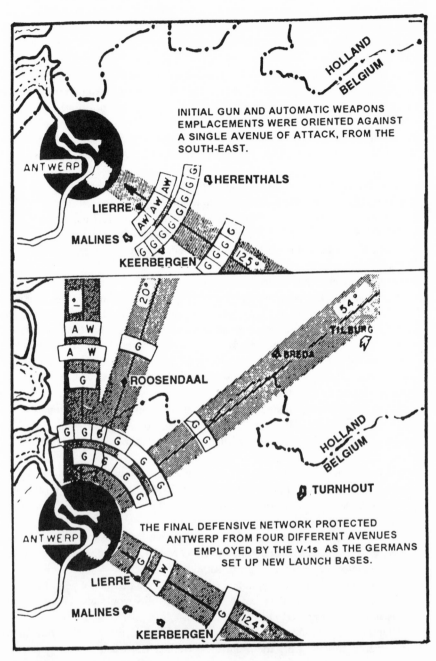

INITIAL GUN AND AUTOMATIC WEAPONS EMPLACEMENTS WERE ORIENTED AGAINST A SINGLE AVENUE OF ATTACK, FROM THE SOUTH-EAST.

THE FINAL DEFENSIVE NETWORK PROTECTED ANTWERP FROM FOUR DIFFERENT AVENUES EMPLOYED BY THE V-1s AS THE GERMANS SET UP NEW LAUNCH BASES.

Map 5.3
Allied Air Defenses at Antwerp

width from 4.26 to 3.2 inches along the length of its barrel, increasing shot velocity. But the problem of creating stable shells capable of surviving the reduced width of the barrel proved too difficult to solve. A 102mm gun, the X1, was designed to use the same mounting. It was ready in 1956 but would be scrapped by 1957.

A 5-inch gun called Green Mace was tested in 1956, but the design would also be abandoned. It was just as well; a single Green Mace weighed 28 tons.

Like other countries, Great Britain turned to missiles to provide air defense. The wartime Stooge missile project never resulted in a usable weapon, but postwar studies of German surface-to-air missiles and the Soviet and American successes in the field helped to influence British defense planners.

The 1957 White Paper determined that manned aircraft were obsolete. Great Britain turned to creating its own nuclear deterrence force, leaving the defense of the United Kingdom to SAMs. This political decision was quite premature. British fighter aviation, once at the forefront of world technology, would find itself lagging further and further behind that of other nations. The damage caused by the White Paper would take decades to fix.

While turning to SAMs for air defense, the British never committed themselves to them in great enough numbers or enough types to provide a serious defense in depth. The Bloodhound ramjet-propelled guided missile entered service with the RAF in 1958, while the Thunderbird rocket-propelled guided missile entered service with the Army. Both weapons were similar in appearance, but neither were ever available in large numbers. Both systems were best suited for defeating high-altitude jet bombers. Low-altitude systems, such as Rapier and Tigercat, would be adopted later on.

During wartime, Great Britain's air defenses would be linked to NADGE, NATO Air Defense Ground Environment. Theoretically this system gave unified control over all air defense assets regardless of type or nationality. In this way, a Norwegian radar might provide early warning of a Soviet bomber formation, transferring the information to a Thunderbird missile battery, which might in turn request German Starfighters already on patrol over the North Sea to be vectored in by GCI.

This integrated air defense system would make NATO's forces into a unified whole in the face of Soviet attack, but a problem developed when the French insisted on retaining absolute control of their own forces within the system. Interestingly enough, however, most of the components, jet fighters and surface-to-air missiles, were pioneered into practical weapons not by the United Kingdom but by its bitterest enemy during the Blitz, the Third Reich.

6

Germany: Air Defense in Festung Europa

Germany, after its initial sweeping victories during World War II, found itself on the defensive in its own skies. Allied heavy bombers could reach to almost any corner of Germany's new empire, even into its industrial heartland. Germany would face the challenges of defense much in the same way it had faced the challenges of creating an offensive war machine: through organization and technical innovation.

The air defense armament of the Luftwaffe and the German army were at the beginning of the war conventional, fitting in with the mainstream of military theory. Though a good civil defense network was in place, the large number of airmen and soldiers in air defense units were either defending the ground forces or a few strategic installations. The arsenal being shaped in the crucible of war was similar to those of other powers.

The 2cm Flak 38 supplemented Flak 30. The 2cm antiaircraft guns were deployed in many different variants, including single-, twin-, and quadruple-barreled guns and towed, motorized, and armored weapons, including the Wirbelwind antiaircraft tank. Such 2cm weapons could reach aircraft at 4800m away and at up to 3800m in altitude. Their rate of fire of up to 220 rounds per minute per barrel made them very effective for close-range defense.

The 3.7cm Flak 18 was further improved into the Flak 36, Flak 37, and later Flak 43 models. These guns could fire at a range of 7200m and up to 1600m altitude, using high-explosive shells. A similar weapon of higher caliber, the 5cm Flak 41, was also developed in order to provide coverage of an air defense "blind zone" between 1800m and 2750m. These two altitudes represented the upper range of automatic weapons and the lower range in which it became impractical to use heavy antiaircraft, respectively.

The 8.8cm Flak 18 was modified into the Flak 36, Flak 37, and Flak 41 models. The 8.8cm saw service on all fronts, from the Arctic to North Africa, from France to Russia, and all across the heart of Germany itself. The "88" became well known among Allied airmen, gaining a fearsome reputation for itself.

Just before the war began, a new heavy gun came into service, the 10.5cm Flak 38. With 12,000m vertical reach and 19,000m horizontal range, the 10.5cm gun provided excellent supplemental coverage for the 8.8cm in the air defense battles over Germany. The 10.5cm was available in both static and mobile models. Later, the 10.5cm was itself supplemented by the 12.8cm Flak 40, increasing the horizontal range almost 23,000m and the engagement ceiling 16,000m. Despite differences in caliber, heavy antiaircraft guns had many common features, as seen in Figure 6.1.

As the war continued, the Germans also pressed captured antiaircraft artillery into service, in some cases retaining them in position where they had been placed by the enemy. These weapons included excellent 40mm Bofors guns, captured or built in a number of countries the Germans overran and known to them as the 4cm Flak 28. The enemy weapons either fired captured stocks or were modified to accept standard German rounds. Thus many British, Free French, and Russian pilots found themselves being engaged by 9.4cm Flak Vickers (e)s, 7.5cm Flak (f)s, and 8.5cm Flak (r)s.

Crewman kept score of victories by painting rings on the barrels of their guns. These markings could vary from piece to piece and kept track of antitank and antiaircraft victories.

To aim the heavy guns Germans used several directors, or *Kommandogeraten*. The Kommandogerat 36 replaced the Kommandohilfsgerat 35 as the primary gun director, the smaller 35 becoming an auxiliary director thanks to its smaller size. The Kommandogerat 40 followed, with electrical data transmission to the guns and a reduction in crew size from 11 to 5.

The Luftwaffe usually employed the 150cm Flakscheinwerfer 37 to provide searchlight illumination. When the more powerful 200cm Flakscheinwerfer 40 entered service, it was frequently used as a master light that would search out a target, with the aid of a sound detector or radar, lock on to it, and then pass it to other, nonguided searchlights.

Barrage balloons were frequently deployed by the Germans. There were two main types, the larger being flown from 1800m to 2500m and the smaller at altitudes of less than 900m. The cables on barrage balloons were sometimes armed with explosives. The German populace got so used to the sight of balloons over their cities that they nicknamed the balloons "rubber flak."

Sound locators were the initial means of aiming searchlights and guns in

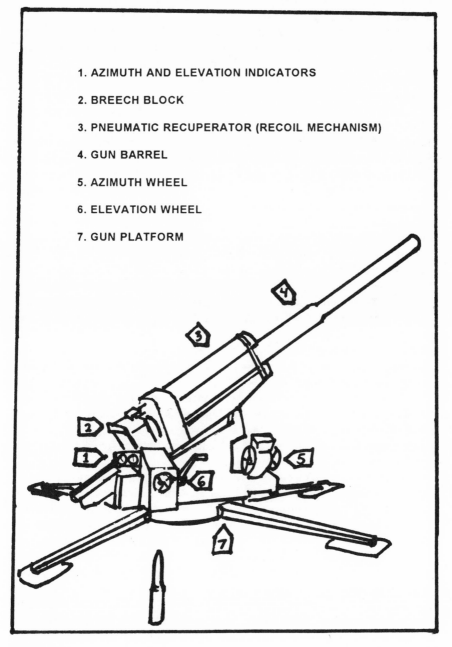

1. AZIMUTH AND ELEVATION INDICATORS

2. BREECH BLOCK

3. PNEUMATIC RECUPERATOR (RECOIL MECHANISM)

4. GUN BARREL

5. AZIMUTH WHEEL

6. ELEVATION WHEEL

7. GUN PLATFORM

Figure 6.1
A Typical Heavy Antiaircraft Gun

inclement weather or at night. These would be used less and less as far more reliable radars became available.

Designs for Wurzburg and Freya radars were placed into production. Wurzburg was improved into the *Reise* ("giant") Wurzburg, with a range of 64km. Reise Wurzburg was better suited for interception duty, while the "small" Wurzburg remained in use directing flak and searchlights.

As manpower resources in Germany diminished, the flak arm of the Luftwaffe struggled to maintain and even increase its strength. *Flak Wehrmaenner*, defense workers called to serve in a home guard capacity, and *Luftwaffehelfern*, 15- and 16-year-olds not yet drafted into service, were pressed into air defense duties in German cities, helping to load and operate the heavy guns.

At least 100,000 *Flak Kampfhelferinnen*, female volunteers, also served in noncombat air defense roles, most notably as controllers, searchlight operators, communication specialists, and sound locators. Many *Kampfhelferinnen* saw duty outside Germany with the flak arm, nicknamed *"Blitzmadchen"* or sometimes *"Flintenweiber."*

Units in Germany were further augmented by non-Germans. Laborers from Axis countries like Italy and Croatia helped to man the guns, as did Russian POWs given a choice between starvation or collaboration. These non-Aryans were usually trusted only to help handle ammunition, but some "reindoctrinated" Soviets manned other positions on the guns, even firing them on rare occasions.

The SS, Army, and Navy all possessed air defense units of their own. The *Reichsarbeitdienst*, the official German labor organization, also manned guns of its own for home defense.

The air defenders of Germany were recognized with distinctive combat badges. The Luftwaffe and the Heer each had a distinctive Flak Badge that they presented to their gunners. The Flak Badge was awarded on a point system, 16 points being required to win the award. Points were awarded for each air defense engagement.

Both badges featured a heavy antiaircraft gun pointing skyward, surrounded by an oval wreath and graced with either an Army or a Luftwaffe eagle. The Luftwaffe also had embroidered qualification badges, worn on the left forearm of the uniform, for such specialties as sound location operator, rangefinder, and antiaircraft artillery.

Germany had effectively knocked the western Allies off the Continent in the first year of the war. As an Allied invasion of Europe with land forces was out of the question for the immediate future, what evolved instead was a strategic bombing campaign that had the twin objectives of destroying Germany's capacity for war and preparing for the return of Allied ground forces in the west.

Germany had a massive problem in air defense. It had to protect not only the Fatherland but the whole of Nazi Europe. This included Norway, Occupied France, the Low Countries, and much of the Balkans. Germany had to defend its Axis allies and fight a war in North Africa as well.

Axis resources were not immediately stretched to their breaking point because of Allied limitations. After the fall of France and the invasion of Yugoslavia and Greece, there were only two practical bases from which to launch attacks: England and Egypt. Egypt provided a jumping-off point for Allied Mediterranean strategy, but it was from England that planes would come, in ever-increasing numbers.

First, they came from RAF Bomber Command. Unlike Germany, England had developed many heavy bombers designs prior to World War II. These included twin-engine Whitleys, Hampdens, and Wellingtons. Four-engine Lancasters, Stirlings, and Halifaxes soon followed, aircraft better suited to take the war to the enemy.

Bomber Command was steeped in the doctrine of strategic warfare—the concept of defeating an enemy by destroying the factories that make his ammunition, the refineries that produce his fuel, the trains that bring his food—to make the homeland that supports the war effort the target.

The original doctrine relied upon daylight bombing, with defensive armament aboard the bombers providing protection for the planes. Daylight bombing promised a high degree of accuracy, but losses were too high for the RAF. Bomber Command switched to night bombing, accepting a loss in accuracy for lower loss rates.

These raids were ineffectively met at first. German night fighters could rarely find the bombers unless they were illuminated by searchlights. As the searchlights were located in the target cities, night fighters often found themselves illuminated by the seachlights and engaged by their own antiaircraft artillery. Effectiveness would improve as air defenses became better organized and better equipped.

America's entry into the war brought the United States 8th Air Force into the fray. The United States Army Air Force had reluctantly followed the doctrine strategic warfare as laid out by Brigadier General Billy Mitchell and had developed the four-engine B-17 Flying Fortress and B-24 Liberator bombers. Both planes would see heavy action over Europe.

In contrast to the RAF, the USAAF did not abandon the idea of daylight bombing. American war planners believed that with fighter escorts, tight bomber formation, and high-altitude bombing raids, losses would be acceptable while they inflicted pinpoint damage to the German war machine.

The overall result was what was termed "round-the-clock" bombing: American bombers by day and British bombers by night. This placed the Reich under constant attack from the air, with respites only when the weather was too bad to fly.

The first line of Germany's defenses was the German flak units and fighters based in occupied France, Belgium, and the Netherlands. Electronic surveillance units listened for radio clues that hinted at a raid. Later in the war, radars would be positioned along the channel coast to detect Allied planes as they became airborne.

Ju88 and Do17 bombers converted to night fighters would rise to intercept and blood the British bomber units as they rose from their English bases for a mission. But these were mere nuisances compared to what awaited the bombers when they reached the German frontier and the Kammhuber Line.

Named for Major General Josef Kammhuber of the Luftwaffe, the line consisted of several elements that worked in unison to counter the bomber streams entering Germany. Against the British night bombers, searchlight batteries were pulled out of the cities and placed in a defensive belt on the frontier, in some areas 20 miles wide. The belt defense provided a wall for the Reich, as shown in Map 6.1.

As aircraft entered the belt they would be "locked on" by a searchlight, then passed on to another as they proceeded across the belt. At first the searchlights relied upon sound or luck to acquire an aircraft, but later a radar-guided master light would make it virtually impossible for Allied planes to enter the belt without being illuminated.

Once illuminated, the incoming aircraft were prey for night fighters, mostly twin-engine Me110 Zerstorers. The searchlight belt was a fighter engagement zone, allowing the night fighters freedom to engage the enemy without fear of engagement by friendly flak, a very real possibility over the target cities.

As Wurzburg radars became available, some were dispatched to the Kammhuber Line as part of a ground-control intercept scheme. The radars were placed in front of the searchlight belt in a new line composed of boxes 32 kilometers on a side, roughly the range of a Wurzburg radar operating from the center of the box.

Each box had a Freya radar for long-range target detection, at least one airborne fighter, a control center, and two Wurzburg tracking radars. The Freya would detect incoming aircraft, and one of the Wurzburgs would lock on. At the control center the airplane would be indicated on a glass map by a green light. The night fighter being tracked by the second Wurzburg was indicated by a red light. The controller would call instructions to the fighter based on the positions indicated on the map until intercept was achieved. This was called *Himmelbett*, the German word for a four-poster bed, which the boxes resembled.

The British responded with saturation tactics, sending huge bomber streams through a single *Himmelbett* box. Kammhuber in turn equipped the boxes with more radars, allowing the control of more night fighters.

Once past the Kammhuber Line, the British bombers met a new threat beginning in 1943. German interceptors, working alone and roaming at will behind the Kammhuber Line, practiced what were effectively guerrilla tactics against the bombers. Called *Wilde Sau* (Wild Boars), the fighters were not controlled from the ground and were free to go wherever they judged the best point of interception to be. The *Wilde Sau* relied upon a silhouette of enemy bombers against the burning target or the glow of searchlights. They took a toll on the bombers during what might have otherwise been a respite: the flight between the German frontier and the point defenses of the target.

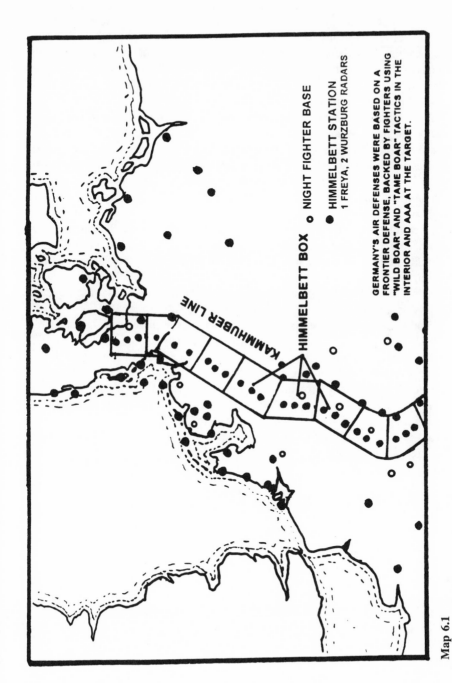

Map 6.1
Western Air Defenses of the Reich

These were followed by *Zahme Sau*, Tame Boars. The *Zahme Sau* were directed by one of five divisional control centers using radio beacons scattered across western Germany. At the control centers female auxiliaries would mark the location of bombers, as reported by radar, observers, and other sources, with beams of light on a glass map. This lent the auxiliaries their nickname, "*Leuchtspucker*," Lightspitter. Probable courses were plotted, and the map was photographed every five minutes for later analysis.

The controller, watching the action on the map, would dispatch the *Zahme Sau* at the best possible time for interception and in the path of the bombers' likely course. This was a tricky business; often, the bombers would fly deceptive courses while decoy forces went to targets that were not to be bombed that night. A right decision meant an interception that gave the pilot plenty of fuel and ammunition with which to fight the enemy; the wrong decision a pointless flight with no chance of success.

To counter the American day raiders, Luftwaffe interceptors had ample time to strike. The bomber stream was easy to follow as the big bombers' engine contrails pointed to the planes. For raids on targets in eastern Germany, like Berlin, the bombers' escort fighters had insufficient range to follow all the way. The Fw190s and Me109s would pounce on the bombers after the first wave of escorts turned back and before they entered the flak.

Finally, the bombers had to face the flak batteries in place at the target. Here, 8.8cm, 10.5cm, and 12.8cm guns reached into the sky for the enemy. Some of the static guns were placed in dual mounts, simplifying gun laying. At first the gunners relied upon searchlights or sound detectors for their targets, but later radar took up the fight, providing azimuth and elevation for the weapons.

At first, batteries were positioned in the open where the guns might have a good field of fire. Between alarms the guns were kept ready in walled enclosures meant to minimize blast effects from bombs, their barrels aimed in the likely direction of an enemy approach. An ideal layout would place three batteries within three kilometers of the Vulnerable Point, a potential target. An imaginary circle was drawn 4400m from the Vulnerable Point; this was the Line of Bomb Release. Another circle was drawn at 10 kilometers; the area between this circle and the Line of Bomb Release was the Flak Engagement Zone. Another 2200m out was the Zone of Preparation.

As defenses improved, flaktowers were built by the Todt Organization, the OT, to provide elevated antiaircraft emplacements with clear fields of fire, in some cases rising twelve stories above the ground. Designs varied, but for the most part the towers provided a top gun platform on the roof for heavy weapons and a gallery around the roof for lighter automatic weapons. Interior space provided ammunition storage and crew quarters.

The Luftwaffe constructed flaktowers around vital military installations like factories and ports. Towers were usually mounted in pairs, with one tower providing fire control by replacing its heavy guns with a gun-laying radar. Their heavy construction usually isolated them from the effects of the bombs, making them difficult to knock out. Supporting the guns, searchlights were set up in a checkerboard pattern outside the Flak Engagement Area, within the Zone of Preparation.

On a typical night mission, the bombers had to run the gauntlet twice, once on the way in and once on the way out. The long-range night fighters were particularly effective, hitting bombers as they were "stacked up" over England waiting for permission to land. Sometimes the bombers' machine guns would be empty of ammunition, having expanded it in the life-or-death struggle over Germany. The Allies were fortunate that Hitler decided to transfer these aircraft to the Mediterranean theater, providing the bombers a respite before and after crossing the Kammhuber Line.

Antiaircraft artillery strength was particularly high in the Ruhr Valley, and for two good reasons: the area was the source of much of German's industrial might, and it was easily within range of the RAF's heavy bombers. RAF crews facing the German air defenses gave the Ruhr the ironic nickname "Happy Valley."

To avoid flak, British pilots would dodge the oncoming bursts to avoid them. They added a new word to describe this tactic, "jinking," that would still be in use among American pilots in Vietnam thirty years later to describe antiflak maneuvers.

Germany employed decoys to lure Allied bombers off target, some quite simple and others extremely sophisticated. The simplest were fires set by the Germans after the first wave of a night bombing force had passed; the intent was to make the following waves believe that the German fires were the actual target set ablaze and drop their bombs in an uninhabited area. To fool daylight bombers, fake towns of papier mâché were built.

The appearance of cities were changed, roofs painted, and camouflage nets spread to make streets disappear, in order to confuse bombardiers. This did little good against alert bombing officers and was totally ineffective against the radar bombing that appeared late in the war. The most effective protection for factories and other war facilities was to move them underground, if possible, or divide war production into many small subassemblies.

The *Reichsluftschutzbund* (RLB), or Reich Air Protection League, primarily concerned itself with civil defense measures. While it numbered some 20,000,000 members in uniform, it had little to do with active air defense measures. The RLB divided Germany into 15 *landesgruppen*, which were further divided into *ortsgruppen*.

The *Luftschutz Warndienst* (LSW), Air Raid Warning Service, served as an aircraft detection, identification, and tracking apparatus. The LSW continued to serve until the very end of the war, even as radars became available to detect incoming planes. The warning service decided when and where air raids would be declared and when it was safe to trigger an "all clear."

While sirens were used to get civilians under cover in the bomb shelters, most Germans relied upon radio. A device attached to a standard set, called a *Draht-*

funk, provided a civil defense warning. Through a continuous transmission, the radio emitted a "tock-tock" sound when there were no enemy bombers over the Reich. When planes crossed the frontier the sound changed to "ping-ping"; a voice would occasionally come on the air to announce the location and course of incoming bombers.

In contrast to the western frontier, Germany's eastern approaches were lightly defended. The exception was Ploesti, and for good reason.

The Romanian city of Ploesti was the primary source of oil for Germany's war machine, thanks to the fascist dictatorship of Ion Antonescue. Romanian oil found its way into the Wehrmacht's panzers as they rolled through a dozen countries and fueled the Luftwaffe's bombers as they bombed much of Europe. One-third of Germany's petroleum needs came from Ploesti. In Winston Churchill's words, Ploesti was "the taproot of German might."

Colonel (later Major General) Alfred Gerstenberg was sent to Bucharest in 1940 as part of a German military assistance program. Nominally, he was air attache to the German embassy; in fact, he was in charge of keeping the supply of oil flowing from Romania. He was responsible for protecting the oilfields and refineries of Ploesti and intended to take whatever measures necessary to preserve them.

Early in the war there was no threat to the Ploesti oilfields. All of the bordering countries were either German allies or occupied by Germany. Then Germany turned on the USSR and briefly put the oilfields in jeopardy; the Soviets mounted a few ineffective bomber attacks in June 1941 before the front was pushed too far east to reach Ploesti.

While Germany recognized the importance of the Romanian city, there seemed to be no way for any of the Allies to reach such a target deep in Axis territory, until America entered the war. Soon after America's entry into the war, the United States had deployed a B-24 shock force called Halpro to Egypt. Originally, Halpro traveled a circuitous route over darkest Africa on its way to attack Japan from Chinese bases, but that was changed en route after the Nationalist bases were captured. The vital city of Ploesti would be the first European target struck by the Army Air Force.

The Halpro raid rook place on 11 June 1942. Twelve of Halpro's thirteen Liberators reached the target area but caused no damage on the oil facilities. The raid only served notice that Ploesti was vulnerable after all; Gerstenberg began to get much of the aircraft, flak, and personnel he had been requesting all along. As guns and aircraft arrived they were fed into Gerstenberg's air defense fortress, *Festung Ploesti.*

Because of the distance and other difficulties involved, another Ploesti raid was not mounted until 1 August 1943. Trying for pinpoint accuracy against the target (actually, several individual targets in and around Ploesti) and knowing that the enemy expected them to fly at high altitudes, the B-24 crews intently trained for a sophisticated low-level, high-speed attack that would knock out all the refineries in one big bombing mission, code-named Tidal Wave. It was hoped that the low-level tactics would take the Germans by surprise, saturate the air defenses, and prevent the flak from concentrating on any single formation. Five heavy bombers groups would be mounting the raid, including three sent from the 8th Air Force in England; 178 B-24s lifted off from bases in Libya on their way to Ploesti.

The element of surprise was lost when a coded alert message sent out to Allied units was intercepted; the Germans were unsure of the exact target, but they were aware of the possibility of an attack somewhere in the Balkans. This was confirmed by aircraft observers on the occupied island of Corfu, who reported the bombers changing course; the target was further narrowed to Ploesti, Sofia, or Bucharest. Wurzburg radar tracked the planes as they passed through Bulgarian airspace without dropping bombs; the target was narrowed to just Ploesti or Bucharest.

Gerstenberg had several nasty surprises waiting for the Americans, the biggest being the actual strength of the air defenses in and around Ploesti. U.S. intelligence had assessed the defenses of Ploesti as consisting primarily of Romanian-manned guns, less than 100. Actually, the Germans had 237 heavy guns, mostly manned by Germans and supplemented by hundreds of automatic weapons. Intelligence believed that most of the air defenses were oriented east, against a Soviet attack. In fact Gerstenberg was convinced that an Allied attack would likely come from Africa and had placed sufficient defenses north, west, and south as well.

The B-24s were suddenly lost to German radar as they dropped to attack altitude. The planes hugged the ground on their approach to Ploesti and soon ran into Gerstenberg's outer flak ring. Mostly consisting of lighter guns and automatic weapons, the outer flak ring contributed to the disruption of the American attack. The German command-and-control network effectively alerted the guns to engage the planes as they entered the defenses.

The guns were mounted in flaktowers and machine-gun pits and hidden in church steeples, water towers, rooftops, and any structure that provided a clear field of fire. Crewmen watched in dread amazement as haystacks parted to reveal yet more hidden guns; it seemed that everywhere they turned there were 2cm or 3.7cm antiaircraft weapons. The Liberators' turret gunners returned fire, with their .50 caliber machine guns raking the antiaircraft guns and suppressing some of them. The first of many planes to explode or crash around Ploesti went down.

Two groups followed a railway line to their targets and ran into Gerstenberg's "Q Train," a mobile antiaircraft platform that had guns hidden in collapsible boxcars. The Q Train just happened to be at the perfect place at the perfect time. It ran parallel to the bombers while its gunners had a field day shooting up the low-flying B-24s, one group flying on each side of the train. The turret gunners managed to hit the locomotive and the train fell to the rear, but not before several planes had been hit.

The bombers entered the inner flak ring of *Festung Ploesti*. Liberators ran into heavier guns, including the dreaded 88s and 105mms. Despite what Allied intelligence believed, the heavy guns were able to traverse fast enough to engage the low-flying bombers, one 88 hitting a group flagship dead in the nose. Barrage balloons claimed more planes as Liberators' wings caught the cables and either set off explosives mounted on the wires or had their wings ripped off.

Interceptors had been misdirected by the Liberators' course changes, and few hit the bombers prior to dropping their bombs. Then the fighters had to wait patiently for the bombers to leave the inner flak ring, reserved for gun engagements only. They attempted to make up for that as huge clouds of dark smoke billowed up from the burning refineries of Ploesti. Ground controllers directed Luftwaffe and Romanian Royal Air Force fighters to find and punish the big bombers before they could get away. Me110s and Me109s took their toll, as well as Romanian-built IAR-80s and -81s.

As the Tidal Wave force moved out of range of the inner fighter ring, they came under attack as they flew the gauntlet over Axis territory. Bulgarian RAF fighters attempted to hit the formations limping out of Romania, its obsolete Czech Avia-534s and Me109s taking out a few more planes. More Luftwaffe fighters based in Greece and Italy completed the outer fighter ring, directed by the air defense network, and took out more of the Liberators. Other B-24s barely made it to Turkey and internment.

Only 33 Liberators were still capable of operations following Tidal Wave. *Festung Ploesti* had devastated five USAAF bomber wings, dealt a blow to the U.S. 9th Air Force that it would never fully recover from, and ensured that there would be no more such raids in the immediate future. In one big raid the B-24s had managed to drop their bombs on most of the targets despite the flak, and in many cased the low-altitude raid caused more damage than a high-altitude raid would have because of shields placed near refinery structures; bombs were dropped inside the shields, compounding the effects of blast.

And yet, despite the accuracy of the bombs dropped, the Allies efforts were thwarted by one final passive air defense measure. Gerstenberg had linked all the refineries together with a pipeline that helped speed damage-control efforts. Crippled facilities could be bypassed and production increased in undamaged refineries. Even though oil reserves at Ploesti had been effectively destroyed, production was back to normal levels within a few days.

Gerstenberg had justified his hoarding of precious aircraft, weapons, and personnel in what was perceived to be a quiet sector. Following the raid he was able to improve *Festung Ploesti* into what was possibly the single most heavily defended city in World War II. More guns were sent to Ploesti and the Axis air forces of Bulgaria and Romania got newer model aircraft from Germany in anticipation of future attacks. Smoke generators were also installed around the oil city to conceal its refineries from attack.

Allied airpower was building in the Mediterranean, and new bases in Italy made conventional high-altitude attacks practical. The smoke screen, alerted by the radars set up on the Ploesti approaches, protected the refineries at first when the heavy bombers returned. Oil production actually increased. Then the Allies began to send a "master bomber" in a P-38 fighter ahead of the main formation, to scout out holes in the Ploesti smoke blanket. The master bomber then directed the attack force to whatever refineries remained exposed, rather than relying on a preconceived bombing plan. The heavy bombers began to take a toll on Ploesti at last, but they were never able to shut it down completely: Production was still at 20 percent when the facility fell into Russian hands.

Antiaircraft defenses throughout the Reich would grow to an organization of seven flak korps of 29 divisions, supported by 13 independent brigades and 160 Abteilungs—an enormous expansion from the 450 antiaircraft batteries available when the strategic bombing campaign began.

The strategic war mounted from bases in Britain and occupied Italy continued to grow in intensity, and with new Allied bomber tactics. The Allies continuously sought ways to skirt Germany air defenses, probing for weaknesses. One raid on the French city of St. Nazaire used several waves of U.S. bombers flying in at different low altitudes; it was a costly experiment, especially for the air crews at the lowest altitude, and the heavy pounding the United States Army Air Force (USAAF) took there earned St. Nazaire a nickname: Flak City.

In fact, the USAAF began a new science in 1943 known as Flak Analysis, the study of enemy air defenses and the best ways to defeat them. The airmen involved in flak analysis monitored recon photographs, debriefed air crews returning from raids over the Continent, and studied technical data on Axis antiaircraft weapons and their associated fire control equipment. This new science allowed Allied bombers to avoid flak weapons (around the perimeter of the Reich, in any case) and minimized USAAF and RAF casualties.

Flak analysis helped to deal with enemy antiaircraft artillery, but it was the increasing range of Allied fighters, augmented by drop tanks, that helped to ward off Luftwaffe interceptors. P-51 Mustangs and P-38 Lightnings were able to escort heavy bombers all the way into the heart of Germany, rather than just part of the way. German pilots could no longer wait until after escorting fighters turned back for England before pouncing on the bomber streams.

As Allied bombs continued to rain on the Reich, German scientists worked feverishly to find new weapons to sweep the skies clean. As in many other endeavors of warfare, Germany became the pioneer in jet interceptors and surface-to-air missiles.

As with radar, Germany had made significant progress in jet technology in the 1930s. As with radar, Germany did not take advantage of its success until after the start of the war. The Me262 reached production in 1944, after political infighting and shortages had caused the project to be delayed.

The Me262 Schwalbe was fast (1000kph), almost too fast to engage the bomber streams effectively. The jet fighter did take its toll on the bombers, but it came too late to stem the tide. Another aircraft, the Me163 Komet, was a short-range rocket interceptor that was placed behind the Kammhuber Line. The Komets were even faster than the Me262, flying at over 1100kph, but had a very short flight time and used an extremely volatile and dangerous fuel combination. The Me163 was a technological dead end.

Not so with missiles. In September 1942 the Inspector-General of Antiaircraft Defenses, General Walter Axthelm, drew up a three-stage plan for the development of antiaircraft rockets. The first stage called for the deployment of unguided barrage rockets that would use existing antiaircraft gun mounts and support equipment. The second stage called for larger missiles that would be guided to their targets by means of existing radio controls. In the final stage, missiles would be sent up with radio guidance and supplemental terminal guidance. Planning was begun on the operation and organization of a future missile-based air defense, and orders were sent out to begin work on these projects.

Several private firms had already begun such missile research independent of the German government, prior to official authorization and despite the demands already placed on the Reich's industrial base. Several prototypes were available by 1944 and were being tested by the Luftwaffe's Flak Training and Research Section 700.

Schmetterling ("Butterfly"), or Hs117, was a dual-propelled antiaircraft missile that initially would have been boosted by two strap-on solid fuel rocket motors, with the main liquid-fueled rocket engine acting as the sustainer motor. The missile was visually guided, with corrections being given by radio. The winged, 4-meter-long missile was to be fired from an inclined launcher. Tests were promising enough to designate the Schmetterling as the "standard" Luftwaffe surface-to-air missile.

Wasserfall ("Waterfall") was a liquid-fueled design proposed by von Braun's team at Peenemunde. The missile was over 8 meters long, with a stubby cruciform shape. The guidance was visual, with corrections being given by radio signals. Wasserfall was a promising adaptation of the German Army's A-4 rocket, the weapon that would eventually become known as the V-2. The first Wasserfall was launched in March 1944. The Wasserfall had a potential speed of 3200kph, making it a supersonic design. On the other hand, Schmetterling's speed was 940kph, below the speed of high performance interceptors then being fielded by the Allies.

Rheintochter (Rhine Daughter) was a two-stage design that reached the prototype stage after its initial development in 1942. It showed little promise and was canceled by 1944, the few remaining models being used as test beds for different guidance systems. The missile had a projected range of 40km and up to 6000m altitude. A three-stage version of Rheintochter named Fire Lily was also designed.

Enzian was a design based on the Me163 manned rocket interceptor, in effect a pilotless version. It utilized a volatile mixture of hydrazine hydrate and methyl alcohol to power its rocket engine and utilized the same strap-on boosters as the Schmetterling. Enzian was also canceled after experimental models were built because it was feared that development would take too long. An operational surface-to-air missile was needed quickly.

All of these weapons at least reached prototype stage, but many more anti-aircraft weapons were discussed and studied: *Mowe*, Wind Gun, *Hamburg-B*, Electric Gun, *Hecht*, Vortex Gun, *Kampf*, and *Fliegerschreck*, just to name a few of the more exotic ideas that the Allies were able to find information about. In some cases all that is known for certain about these projects is the name and the fact that upon completion each would be able to destroy enemy aircraft.

In hindsight, it is probable that the simultaneous development of so many competing designs drained resources that could have been used to push through development and production of at least one operational surface-to-air missile system. However, when dealing with totally new technologies it usually does pay to try several different approaches in case one or more design concepts prove to be unworkable. Japan concentrated on a single design approach and never even developed a working SAM prototype.

As German industry came close to setting up production lines for new missile designs, a study was done on their possible deployment by Section 700. This unit outlined two possibilities: using the missiles to provide a "point" defense of strategic targets within the Reich or the organization of an area defense, setting up firing batteries along the border to provide a curtain of flak against aircraft entering Germany. The latter was recommended, probably because of the Luftwaffe's successes with the Kammhuber Line. In fact, the new missiles would work well with the Kammhuber Line, itself scheduled to be improved with jet interceptors and radar-guided antiaircraft guns.

Such a flak curtain would have been an ambitious project for Germany even if it were not locked in a life-or-death struggle: 600 Schmetterling batteries and 900 Wasserfall batteries to initially protect the western frontier, where the greatest threat was projected, and about another 210 Schmetterling and 460 Wasserfall batteries to provide the east roughly the same protection at a later date. The first 70 Schmetterling and three Wasserfall batteries were supposed to be operational by the end of 1945.

With 2,170 surface-to-air missile systems in operation, the Luftwaffe would have required over 330,000 soldiers to man the flak rockets. The antiaircraft artillery would still be in operation as well, along with the Luftwaffe's personnel requirements for its interceptors. The fact that the Germans were looking at such numbers for their air defenses seemed to show a belated hope for salvation through flak.

Hope notwithstanding, the Reich's last secret weapons were not ready in time to make a difference in the air war over Germany, even though a few fired experimentally seemed to show promise. The USAAF even had a photo of one of its bombers being intercepted by an unidentified missile (probably a Schmetterling prototype). However, the radio-guided missiles were potentially vulnerable to jamming; in fact, similar radio-control systems were already in use in some German-controlled bombs. The Allies had successfully thwarted higher success rates by jamming the signals after the bombs were dropped from their control aircraft. British and American air forces would certainly have converted heavy bombers to jamming aircraft had the German missiles been used in significant numbers.

But before the Schmetterling and Wasserfall designs were operational, it was too late to produce them in the numbers needed to stem the tide: The disruption and capture of German industry marked the end of the Reich and its secret weapons. In the meantime, the various antiaircraft services had to make adjustments to the worsening military situation with existing air defense weapons. In 1944 the Luftwaffe's flak and interceptors reached a peak strength of 1,250,000 personnel, with the German Army and Navy air defense units adding perhaps another 300,000.

Heavy antiaircraft artillery was massed for concentrated firepower, and radar was used for fire control. The standard six-gun battery was superseded by the *Grossbatterie*. Three batteries were placed side-by-side, sharing the same data from a single central fire-control radar, with a second radar standing by as a reserve. Normally each battery would have needed its own radar; this reorganization saved a radar and gave the overall system a backup.

The Germans did try to develop some kind of proximity fuze, even looking at possible acoustic or infrared models, but they never perfected one. A new percussion fuze was adopted in March 1945 after a mathematical study proved its theoretical superiority over preset delay types.

Dwindling fuel supplies forced Germany to reserve the number of intercept sorties. With a surplus of planes and a shortage of fuel, the once-mighty Luftwaffe deployed *Sonderkommandos*, special detachments, whose volunteer pilots had a single mission: ram the enemy bombers.

Sonderkommando pilots were politically indoctrinated as well as instructed on the best technique for ramming. While they approached the bomber streams the pilots could hear a female announcer on their headset playing "*Deutschland Uber Alles*" and exhorting them to do their duty, reminding the *Sonderkommandos* of the deaths of women and children in the ruins below.

Sonderkommando aircraft, mostly late-model Me109s and Fw190s, were sent aloft with only half their normal load of ammunition. The pilots were instructed to avoid the escorting fighters and to concentrate on the bombers. They were told to bail out after they made physical contact with the enemy plane, but the pilots knew there was little chance of surviving the encounter. For all their desperation, the *Sonderkommandos* achieved very few kills before their bases were overrun by the Allied armies.

Germany had tried and failed to withstand Allied airpower. It had provided technical and direct military assistance to its Axis allies, including Romania and Italy, arming them with German guns and other antiaircraft equipment, to no avail. With the collapse of the Third Reich only Germany's distant Asian ally was left to face the growing might of Allied airpower: Japan.

_____

7

Japan: Defeat through Airpower

Japan's military leaders realized that the United States would counterattack after the Imperial Navy's attack at Pearl Harbor, but the Japanese were unprepared for the swiftness and the manner in which that counterattack was made. American bombers under the command of Lieutenant Colonel Jimmy Doolittle struck at Tokyo itself from the aircraft carrier Hornet. America had done what no one since the time of the Mongol hordes had been able to do: attack the Japanese Home Islands.

This type of raid would not be repeated, and Japan would enjoy a respite of two years before any other major air attacks took place. It was just as well, for Japan's air defense establishment was not prepared for the task of mounting a national air defense of the Home Islands. Only a handful of air defense regiments were in place in Japan at the beginning of the Pacific War, backed by a few hundred Army and Navy aircraft based on the islands. This amounted to roughly 7,000 Army antiaircraft personnel and a few hundred pilots, many of them in training, to resist Allied airpower. Minor weaknesses in the available defenses would become nearly critical as the war progressed.

Japanese aircraft designs were rapidly becoming inferior to the new designs spurred on by the war in other countries. In prewar planning, the interceptors were meant to be the key to air defense in the Home Islands, with a deemphasis on the importance of antiaircraft weapons. As a result, Japan's ground-based air defenses had never really caught up with those of the other major military powers.

At the inception of the Pacific War, Japan's greatest antiaircraft weakness was in fire control, which would continue to be its Achilles heel until its surrender. Its directors were out of date, and its data transmission inefficient.

Japanese gun batteries did not use wind data obtained from weather balloons. They did not practice trial fire or calibration fire, and target practice was curtailed during the war to the point of nonexistence. Even under ideal conditions, Japanese gunfire was not able to lay an accurate heavy barrage.

This failure was partially due to the manner in which antiaircraft artillery was employed as well. Decentralization characterized antiaircraft operations, regardless of how large the defended area was or how many units were available. Divisional and regimental commanders exercised little operational control; instead they established the fire direction and preplanned volumes of fire. Battalion commanders exercised complete control over their guns once an engagement commenced, following the "game plan" that had already been laid down by their superiors.

To fulfill the need for target acquisition in poor weather or at night the Japanese used searchlights (*shoku*) between 60cm and 150cm in size. Support equipment for the searchlights included a comparator that automatically directed the lights onto a target once it was sighted. Sound locators were used right up to the end of the war to help guide the searchlights, even though most other countries had abandoned their use. The primitive devices were easier to produce than complicated radars.

Searchlights were placed in the vicinity of military installations and population centers. If the target was fairly small, the searchlights might be deployed in a simple circle around the defended area. For larger targets searchlights were placed in depth, with pickup lights at the perimeter, assisted by sound detectors, radars, and carry lights, which would lock on to the targets as they left the range of the pickup lights.

The Japanese were aware of the existence of radar and in fact had captured several American and British models during their conquest of the Philippines and Malaya. Copies were made of the primitive sets, but they were not massproduced. Such production would have given the Japanese at least the basis of an electronic defense network, an interim measure to be sure, but better than nothing. Yet few of these sets were found in use.

Instead, much time and effort seem to have been expanded in developing independent Japanese designs based on the captured technology. Only slight improvements were made in mobility and range. Thus, valuable time was wasted in constructing radars that were only nominally better than the captured Allied designs. By the time the Japanese radars were coming off the assembly lines, Allied technology and already gone well beyond the designs of 1941.

Germany tried to help its Axis partner with technological assistance, and one of the areas in which it provided such assistance was in radar. One of the excellent Wurzburg radars was sent by U-boat to Japan, along with a technician to put it together and operate it. The Wurzburg had great potential in either the ground-controlled interception or fire-control roles, but although they did operate it the Japanese seemed to be disinclined to copy the German radar.

Japanese radars were not mobile, usually equipped with skids. Permanent stations, rather than mobile detachments, were the rule for Japanese radar. As a result of their static nature, Japan's radars often operated on commercial power, using their generators as an auxiliary source.

The few models of radar the Japanese possessed were held in low esteem by the soldiers who operated them, which was not surprising considering that few of them understood the concept of radio ranging; in fact, no radar training took place at the antiaircraft school in Chiba until 1943. Though several sets were designed for gun laying, the Japanese would never use them for that purpose unless there was no other means available. The most common use of the sets was to provide guidance for the searchlights.

Not only was the quality of Japanese radar poor, but the quantity was also wanting. Japanese industry was quickly outstripped by the war's demands for heavy weapons and was never geared towards the large-scale production of sophisticated electronic systems. The limited ability it did possess was even more sharply curtailed as the American bombing campaign began to strike at the vacuum-tube production centers. Radar production depended almost entirely on tubes, and Japanese industry simply couldn't keep up with demand; even the operation of the radar sets that were already available was sometimes limited because of the need for replacement tubes.

By the end of the war Japan had barely been able to distribute radars at an average rate of one per battalion. As a result, bombing raids would often go unchallenged by ground defenses for lack of radar even when the target was well defended by antiaircraft weapons. Lack of radar was crippling for Japanese strategic air defense.

Interestingly enough, Japan had little use for barrage balloons, even though the technology was easily within reach. Offensively minded, Japan's militarists would use balloon bombs to attack America, but they deployed barrage balloons at only four cities in their own defense.

Even with America's entry into the war, Japan did not feel threatened. America's closest air bases to the Home Islands lay in the Philippines, which were not in range of the planes the United States possessed in 1941. The Japanese conquest of the Philippines and all other possible bases not already under Japanese control created a "defensive perimeter" that made the Home Islands secure from attack, at least for the time being.

But for the Imperial soldiers on the many Pacific islands and other possessions occupied by the Japanese, airpower was a constant threat. The United States had invested in a carrier fleet that allowed it to bring naval airpower to bear at almost any single point the ships could safely reach, without the need for permanent land bases.

The United States already possessed many excellent aircraft designs at the beginning of the war. The carrier-based TBD-1 Devastator, SBD-3 Dauntless, and F4F Wildcat were all successful aircraft that could assist the invading Army and Marine forces that had to fight from island to island to reach Japan. But newer and better aircraft—the F6F Hellcat, the F4U Corsair, and the TBM-1 Avenger, among others—soon followed. These aircraft would be used in close support of amphibious landings and ground campaigns.

In addition to the Navy's planes, the Army Air Force could attack with B-17s, B-25s, and B-24s, reaching far and wide from their captured islands. Though the Japanese could counter the American's airpower in 1942 with a few excellent fighter designs of their own, they found themselves increasingly out-numbered and outclassed. The Navy possessed the marvelous A6M *Zero-Sen*, which could reach speeds of 535kph and altitudes of 10,000m. The Army pos-sessed the Ki-43 *Hayabusa*, with a performance of 550kph and 11,400m. The American P-38, already in service when the war began could reach speeds of 666kph and 13,410m. The Japanese would continue work on fighter designs, especially in the search for a high-altitude interceptor; but the technical disparity between Japanese and American designs would continue to grow. Antiaircraft Artillery was called on to take a larger and larger burden of air defense from the Air Corps and the Navy, despite prewar planning.

In the field, air defense could be flexible. This was the advantage of having the division commander or garrison commander in control of all local air de-fenses: he could allocate air defense assets to whatever he felt were the most important targets in his command, whether they be bridges, docks, artillery parks, or any other place of military significance.

Passive air defense measures were stressed. Units in the field would dig in and camouflage themselves from the air. Deceptive positions were built to draw fire from authentic targets.

An antiaircraft battery, or *Koshaho Chutai*, could be heavily dug in with visual observation posts and individual revetments for each gun. A command post would be established in a nearby bunker, with installed fire control equip-ment. Heavy antiaircraft guns would often be augmented by automatic weapons in their own bunkers, providing both high-altitude intermittent fire and low-altitude constant fire at targets.

Little use was made of camouflage, but it was not uncommon to build alter-nate or dummy positions, complete with dummy guns. These battery positions might be triangular, if equipped with three guns, or rectangular, if equipped with four. If more than four guns were deployed, they would be dug into an arc- or crescent-shaped bunker complex.

Target acquisition in the field was rarely provided by radar. There were simply too few sets to go around. Instead, the Japanese relied on visual observation posts linked by radio.

To engage targets, the Japanese would concentrate their fire on the lead air-craft of a formation, shifting fire on other targets if time permitted. If overcast, the Japanese would fire their weapons into breaks among the clouds where aircraft could be expected to appear. Barrage fire was also used.

Instances were reported of lone aircraft that would loiter in the area once an air raid was in progress, yet would not engage Allied aircraft. It is believed that these aircraft acted as "altitude spotters" for antiaircraft artillery on the ground, providing the attacking planes' speed and elevation to the guns by radio. This seemed to be effective, as corrections seemed to be made quickly while the spotters were in the area.

Another Japanese tactic was to build "flak traps," dummy targets that would draw Allied aircraft so that waiting guns could engage them effectively. These targets varied, in one case consisting of a painting of a B-24 on the pavement at an airfield. When Allied planes came to investigate, they would be engaged. This tactic rarely worked; the paintings were not convincing enough.

Effectiveness of Japanese air defenses would sometimes be neutralized by the Allied air forces by sending aircraft on flak-suppression raids. Flak suppression against heavy guns would be flown by the faster fighter models such as the P-51 Mustang. Swift fighters could attack at speeds faster than the guns could engage: before they could react, the fighters dropped their fragmentation bombs on the air defense site and got out of range of small arms.

Japanese strategic planners recognized the threat posed by American heavy bombers once the United States entered the war. Operating from bases in Free China, they could conceivably strike some parts of the Home Islands. Even as Japanese forces fanned out across the Pacific to create a buffer zone from U.S. naval power, the Imperial Army in China marched to seize provinces from which bombers could attack Japan. While the reasoning for the attack was sound, the premise behind it was incorrect. America would soon have a bomber that could strike much farther than the B-17 or B-24: the B-29 Superfortress.

The Superfortress was rushed through from its conception in 1940 to production in 1943 and was the longest-range bomber of its day, with an operational range of 8,400 kilometers, routinely able to reach altitudes of 10,200m. The B-29 was truly the first strategic bomber.

Originally, the B-29 was not meant to be used against Japan. It was conceived as a "Hemispheric Defense Weapon" when the war in Europe was going badly for the Allies. The Army Air Corps wanted the means to attack Nazi Europe from the Americas, without the need for bases in England or Africa. As the situation in Europe improved and that in Asia became more difficult, the Superfortress became the weapon of choice against Japan. It could take on targets in Japan even from the few bases made available in what was left of Free China.

The threat mounted from China was not as great as the Allies would have liked, mainly because of the difficulties involved. The air bases in southwest China were isolated from regular lines of communications, especially after the Japanese closed the Burma Road. After the loss of the only land route from India, supplies had to be flown over the Himalayas, or the "Hump," as it was called by Allied pilots. It took six cargo planes carrying fuel over the hump to fill the tanks of one B-29 for a mission over Japan.

Just as Japanese strategy involved taking territory in China to deny the Allies air bases, Allied strategy turned toward acquiring new bases from which air attacks could be launched regardless of the situation in China. B-29 raids were soon being mounted from Okinawa and the Marianas Islands.

Wherever the threat was based, Japan's Home Island defenses were hard pressed to deal with air raids, even as late as 1944, when the first Superfortresses began to appear over Japan. To say that the raids were devastating would have been an understatement: After the U.S. 20th Air Force switched from high explosives to incendiaries, entire cities came close to disappearing in flames. Japanese homes, usually constructed of wood and paper, were vulnerable to fire.

The defense of the Home Islands had been improving, but it was a case of too little, too late. Seven hundred Model 88s were available at the time of the Doolittle Raid; this number was slowly increased. Civil defense measures might have helped control the damage inflicted by the raids, but extreme measures like destroying residential blocks to create firebreaks didn't come until after the B-29s began their devastating raids.

The number of antiaircraft units was increased by establishing entirely new units or by using the expedient of dividing existing air defense regiments, or *boku rentai*, into new formations and then bringing the new *rentai* up to full strength with new recruits. In this way, the defenses of the Home Islands were brought up to a strength of 36 air defense regiments, 85 separate gun battalions, 51 separate gun batteries, 12 separate automatic weapons battalions, and 206 separate automatic weapons batteries.

These forces were divided among four air defense divisions, or *boku shidan*: three on Honshu and one on Kyushu. Honshu possessed many strategic targets, such as the city of Tokyo, while Kyushu was the likely site of an Allied invasion and as such would be subjected to the massive use of tactical airpower.

Each *boku shidan* was responsible for the defense of the territory defended by an Area Army and controlled most of the antiaircraft artillery available to the area army. The exception was Kyushu, where artillery had been divided among individual commanders in anticipation of invasion. The Kyushu air defense division commander was therefore left with the responsibility for training only.

Procedural air control measures were instituted after the Doolittle Raid. Flight paths in and out of the Home Islands were established, with predetermined times and altitudes for aircraft to follow. Planes entering Japanese airspace but not following established air control measures would be intercepted and destroyed. This may have been in response to the fact that several of the Doolittle Raiders were intercepted but not shot down, apparently because the Japanese fighter pilots assumed the aircraft were theirs, despite their markings.

Procedural controls did not mean coordination between aircraft and guns. At no time were Army interceptors and antiaircraft artillery placed under a single commander at any command level. There were no restrictions on when the guns could fire or on where the interceptors could operate. As a result, guns and planes could find themselves operating in the same area at the same time, the interceptors in danger of friendly fire and the guns unable to use their full potential for fear of hitting their own pilots.

A scattered radar net began to operate across the islands that was absolutely necessary when the B-29s struck at night, otherwise the Superfortresses simply could not have been effectively engaged. The Japanese would have had to rely on sound detectors, and the technology was just not up to the task. See Figure 7.1 for a typical sound detector design.

The sound detector was originally invented by France during World War I. The French employed a paraboloid type that depended upon the operator finding the target through maximum sound quality. Though theoretically capable of attaining a sharp focus on the target's azimuth and elevation, in practice it depended entirely upon the judgment of the operator.

The next device was the telesitemeter, and it was this type that continued in service up to World War II, even though it was considered obsolete well before then. The telesitemeter depended upon the binaural phase effect, in which at least two receiving horns are used. By matching the output of the two separate instruments, which at this point would be functioning similarly to an optical range-finding device, the operator could read off a rough azimuth and elevation reading and transmit these to a searchlight unit or even directly to the guns.

Sharp focusing was impossible with a telesitemeter, even with the addition of more receiving horns. That did not prevent the United States and Great Britain from following France's lead in deploying the devices for night combat. "Anything was better than nothing," as one air defense officer put it.

Japan also deployed the detectors. Though inefficient, they were relatively easy to manufacture and could be produced in quantity. Unfortunately, the Japanese inherited the machines' various weaknesses: lack of long-range capability, lack of pinpoint accuracy, and the "spoofing" causes by the sometimes unpredictable nature of sound waves. Atmospheric conditions could cause inaccurate readings, and even with perfect weather conditions one problem could not be overcome: the time lag caused by the speed of sound as it traveled to the instrument. Even had exact focusing been possible, it would have meant little, as the plane simply would not have been at the same point as its observed sound source.

The Type 90 Sound Detector was widely used in Home Island defense, even though there was no direct means of data transmission; corrections were transmitted over telephone or radio as read by the crew. The Type 95 Sound Detector had the means to transmit acquisition data electrically.

The Japanese analyzed signal intelligence to guess what targets would be hit by future raids. They used this analysis to determine where to mass their meager air defense assets. But one weakness in this strategy was the way in which it

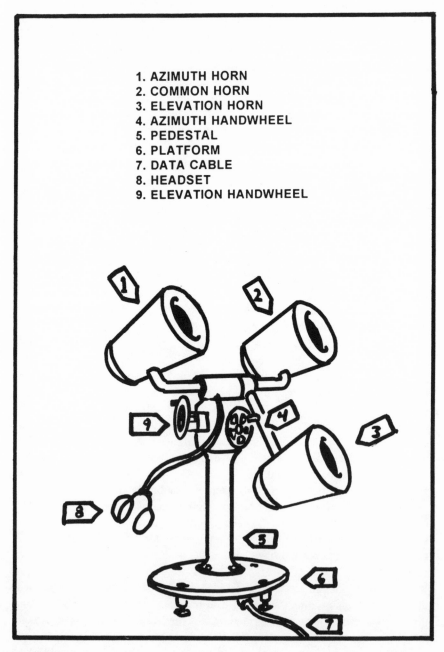

1. AZIMUTH HORN
2. COMMON HORN
3. ELEVATION HORN
4. AZIMUTH HANDWHEEL
5. PEDESTAL
6. PLATFORM
7. DATA CABLE
8. HEADSET
9. ELEVATION HANDWHEEL

Figure 7.1
A Typical Sound Detector

kept many of Japan's antiaircraft guns in transit between potential targets rather than in active air defense operations.

The Japanese had to let many raids go unchallenged. To fire on the high-altitude B-29s without some sort of guidance would have been futile, in that it would not have prevented the raid nor affected the bombing accuracy of the Superfortresses. Japan's industry was becoming hard-pressed to provide enough shells just to keep the guns firing: resource-poor Japan depended upon its Asian empire for virtually all of its raw materials, which were being cut off by merciless attacks on the Japanese merchant marine fleet.

Japanese interceptors were stationed at airfields all around targets and especially in the vicinity of Tokyo, but they were unable to make a dent in the B-29 raids even though the attacking squadrons rarely had fighter escorts. As the Superforts could operate at over 10,000m; without radar to guide them, Japanese interceptors were limited in what they could do against the bombers.

Late-model Japanese fighters included the Ki-61 *Hien*, which was able to fly at almost 600kph and reach an altitude of 11,600m. This meant that the B-29s could no longer count on a high-altitude haven for protection. But night raids were a different matter; unlike most other major combatants, Japan never managed to build a radar-equipped night fighter.

Interceptors started using phosphorus bombs against Allied bombers late in the war. The interceptor would attempt to arc a bomb in the flight path of a formation, where it would explode and hopefully cause fires among the attacking planes. Allied pilots reported such tactics as "ineffective."

The fighters also began using ramming tactics against the B-29s late in the war, a practice similar to the German *Sonderkommando* tactics. Imperial Headquarters sanctioned the formation of special air units for the purpose of suicide missions. Such ramming attacks only served to further deplete the Japanese Air Service of the pilots and aircraft it was having a harder and harder time replacing.

Troops were canvassed for ideas on new weapons to oppose the relentless Allied attacks. Among some of the more workable plans proposed was the use of explosive kites and cheap remote-controlled airplanes. A "death-ray" project for destroying enemy aircraft got as far as the experimental stage but never reached prototype stage. Apart from using intense radio frequency radiation to kill small animals at close range and to shut down gasoline engines, the Japanese had little more success with the concept than their predecessors.

A lack of electronics doomed another, more practical project, an electronic interrogation system. Preceding the Soviet and American efforts in the field (but not the British), Japanese aircraft would have been provided with devices that could identify them as "friendly" to other Japanese planes and to ground forces without relying on visual identification, which was increasingly difficult to secure. Although some progress was made, experimentation ceased sometime in 1944; the problem was considered too complex by the Japanese.

Proximity fuzes were similarly out of reach. A unique acoustic proximity fuze concept was proposed, but no work was done on it. The concept for a radar-type proximity fuze was also forwarded, but the project was probably doomed from the beginning because of the strain it would have placed on Japan's already limited vacuum-tube production.

Multiple-burst shells were developed and used against aircraft flying over the Home Islands. Constructed with several charges that would burst in sequence, these shells theoretically had a greater chance of a hit, but not as great as an accurately delivered shell with a single large burst area would have had.

Japan's research and development base was fairly extensive; it should have produced better results than it did. The Army alone possessed 21 different military laboratories, with many personnel dedicated to the study of radar, atomic power, fuels, and other items vital to the Japanese war machine. Added to this were the research facilities of the *zaibatsu*, the industrial combines of Japan.

Yet even as Japan needed experienced personnel to fight the technical war raging around them, its army was taking more and more of the available manpower to fight the war from the front lines. This affected war industry as well, as experienced workers found themselves drafted from their factories.

More progress might have been made on weapons research if interservice rivalry between the Army and Navy had not been so great. The Imperial Navy had its own extensive network of research facilities and had developed some good antiaircraft gun designs for its ships and naval facilities. But competition between the services was intense to the point of paranoia; the Army and Navy were as much afraid of their opposite number's spies as they were of Allied intelligence.

Early air defense planning had relied upon cooperation between Army and Navy interceptors stationed on the Home Islands. However, friction between the services precluded effective use of the few available fighters, mostly training aircraft. Advanced interceptor designs were on the drawing boards at the end of the war, including a high-performance pusher plane and a jet design similar to the Me262. Neither made it into combat.

Some installations were defended by antiaircraft artillery of the Imperial Navy, an example of the almost suicidal interservice rivalry. The Navy had some 294 officers and over 41,000 seamen manning guns at ports and other important locations by the end of the war. Naval antiaircraft artillery was based on gun types used aboard Japanese vessels.

As naval antiaircraft artillery was not incorporated in the general defense scheme of the Home Islands, the largest unit in use was the battery. Naval antiaircraft incorporated all air defense elements, including guns, automatic weapons, searchlights, and radar when available, placing them all under a single commander. Although naval air defense was not coordinated with the Army Antiaircraft Artillery or the Air Corps, there was some coordination between the gunners and Navy planes. The Imperial Navy's air defense infrastructure also included five different service schools.

Work on more conventional weapons, such as the Model 3 120mm antiaircraft gun project, was slow. The Japanese had begun work on the heavy antiaircraft gun after the Doolittle Raid, but they were not able to field the weapon before the end of the war even though the need for it became more desperate each day. The Model 3 would have had a ceiling of over 11,000 meters.

An even more ambitious weapon was a 150mm gun that would have had an operational ceiling something on the order of 20,000 meters. Such a "reach" would have been high enough to provide a viable threat against the B-29s, had the gun gone beyond the experimental stage. On the success side, a mobile 88mm antiaircraft gun was produced at the end of the war, in very limited numbers.

The Model 88 75mm continued laying down the infrequent barrages against the American air force right up to the end. An improved version, the Model 4, began running off assembly lines in 1944. Its longer barrel and improved shells increased the effective ceiling to 9,000 meters. In April 1944, the situation was sufficiently critical to bring about a change in production priorities, with anti-aircraft artillery weapons given first priority over all other weapons.

To supplement their own automatic antiaircraft weapons, the Japanese Army deployed small numbers of captured guns and tried to mass-produce copies. The Vickers-type 40mm gun was copied and deployed in Japanese designed single- and double-mounts. Bofors 40mm guns were captured in Dutch and British colonial territories as the Japanese expanded their Co-Prosperity Sphere. The Bofors gun would have made an excellent air defense weapon for the Japanese if they could have successfully mass-produced it. The dwindling resources of Japanese industry also prevented them from copying the German "88" when designs for it were provided during one of the sporadic U-boat missions.

Improvements in air defense organization lagged almost as far behind as the air defense technology. In May 1945 Antiaircraft Artillery was finally made a separate branch of the Japanese Army, but the antiaircraft units of Japan were never consolidated into a single national air defense command with a single air defense commander, even though almost 168,000 soldiers and sailors were manning the antiaircraft artillery. The Antiaircraft Artillery had expanded 1500 percent, but the two top antiaircraft generals were still basically in charge of training. Decentralization remained the order of the day.

Even early warning was decentralized. Each Area Army headquarters operated its own air-raid warning center, the most sophisticated established by the 17th Area Army in Tokyo. Data received by means of civilian and military observers, picket ships, and radar were plotted with electrical lights on a huge map. Information was sent from the center to military units and civilian prefectures, who would then activate air-raid sirens and take other defensive steps.

The air-raid warning centers were not operated by either air service or Anti-aircraft Artillery personnel, yet the system ran remarkably well. Usually, the populace had an hour's warning of an incoming B-29 raid. The air-raid warning service did have a weakness in that telephone was relied upon for communications, and as bombing attacks became more frequent the lines became less and less reliable. Reports from one station on the southern island of Kyushu might take hours to reach the air-raid warning center on the northern island of Hokkaido.

Despite the fact that air raids were becoming a daily occurrence, no Antiaircraft Artillery staff officer was assigned to Imperial Headquarters. No one in the headquarters possessed firsthand experience or training with air defense and could have asked for more resources to defend Japanese skies. Yet Imperial Headquarters often decided where antiaircraft resources would be sent and how they would be used.

Imperial Headquarters established a defense priorities system for the Home Islands. The highest priority was reserved for the Imperial Palace; defense of that structure served no practical military importance, but the preservation of the Emperor was important for morale. In any case, guns that protected the palace also defended other important installations in Tokyo. The two available 150mm antiaircraft prototype guns were installed in a position to protect the palace.

Next in defense priorities came airplane, weapon, and munition factories, along with harbor facilities. These were of course vital to the continuing war effort. Surprisingly though, airfields had a relatively low priority. Not so surprisingly, ground troops and Army bases were given a very low priority, if any at all.

American fire raids continued throughout 1945, supplemented by tactical aircraft from carriers and new island bases. The meager resources and poor planning of the Japanese high command opened up the Home Islands to enormous destruction at little cost to the Allies. In Germany, enemy cities were reduced to rubble and the landscape cratered like the moon. In Japan, cities were replaced by charred bits and pieces of wood, interspersed with an occasionally concrete building that survived the firestorm.

During the last months of the war, automatic weapons were called into action more and more frequently, as tactical aircraft began operating over Japan. These were longer-range fighter bombers from captured island bases and carrier-based planes that were able to operate within range of the Home Islands after the Imperial Navy became too weak to defend its own backyard.

Numbers of automatic weapons were insufficient to deal with the new threat. Also, there were no medium-range flak weapons to deal with the high-speed aircraft flying too low for the heavy guns, except for the captured Bofors, which were available in too few numbers. While the B-29s turned the Japanese cities to ashes, smaller American planes sought out and destroyed targets hidden in the countryside, devastating the national infrastructure and causing transportation to grind to a halt.

In exchange, Japan inflicted an overall loss rate on the enemy of only 00.5 percent, which included both aircraft brought down by interceptors and those shot down by antiaircraft.

In the end, Japan had to make a conscious decision not to defend against each and every enemy raid and to conserve and mass their few air defenses against the big raids when their targets could be determined by intelligence. The antiaircraft guns were under no engagement restrictions, had plenty of targets to fire on, and even enjoyed reliable early warning of incoming attacks. But because of built-in weaknesses, they never took advantage of these potential strengths. The two B-29s that delivered the first (and only) atomic bombs used in combat not only ended the war but also delivered profound proof of the inadequacy of Japan's air defenses.

8

Soviet Union: Strela, Shilka, and Volga

During the existence of the USSR, air defense enjoyed a high-priority status that was unmatched by most other countries. By the time of the collapse of the Soviet Union, air defense was a separate branch of service, on a par with the other four Soviet branches—the Soviet Army, the Air Force, the Navy, and the Strategic Rocket Forces. The evolution and influence of the Troops of National Air Defense is unique, as is its history.

Following the Red Army's poor showing during the Russo-Finnish "Winter War," 1939–40, a massive reorganization saw the Air Defense Directorate redesignated the *GU-PVO* (Main Administration of the Air Defense Force) and relieved of its responsibility for air defense units in the field, which were again placed under the command of the military districts. The GU-PVO was relegated to the task of equipping and training air defense units. Further reorganization took place later, which saw the creation of air defense zones corresponding to the military districts of the Red Army.

Despite this reorganization the Red Army's air defense units seemed to be either unable or unwilling to do anything about numerous violations of Soviet airspace that were becoming more and more common in 1939, 1940, and 1941. The British were conducting overflights in the Caucasus from bases in Iraq, and the Germans were probing the USSR's western frontier from Axis airfields in Eastern Europe. Interception of the high-flying intruders was possible, but it was supposedly prevented by personal order of Stalin himself. Whether or not it is true that Stalin chose to prevent the destruction of these reconnaissance flights is academic; the fact is that the information gained by the Luftwaffe as they flew their spy missions over the USSR would prove costly to the Soviet Union.

After the 1939 invasion of the Baltic states and the Russo-German dismemberment of Poland, the Soviets attempted to consolidate their gains by rapidly moving great numbers of troops and weapons into its new territories. The few airfields available in Estonia, Latvia, Lithuania, and eastern Poland were augmented by newly established military fields. I-153s, I-16s, LaGG-3s, and MiG-3s were crowded together in a manner that made them perfect targets for bombing and strafing attacks.

On 22 June 1941 the German Reich attacked the USSR without a declaration of war. Thanks to a thorough aerial reconnaissance, the Luftwaffe was able to attack and destroy a great deal of the Red Air Force on the ground, including significant numbers of the latest Soviet models. In just a few hours the Soviets lost most of the interceptor aircraft along the frontier. Stalin ordered counterattacks after the initial shock of invasion, making the Red Air Force mount what were effectively suicide attacks. This destroyed much of what was left, leaving a total of 1,811 Soviet planes in flames.

Antiaircraft artillery response was minimal and ineffective during the first few days of what the Soviets came to call the Great Patriotic War. Instead of taking over the entire burden for air defense following the loss of virtually all of the interceptors, the antiaircraft artillery seemed to be reeling with shock from the incredible scale of the attack. Poor communications, lack of initiative, and the confusion caused by the Red Army's retreat from the frontier reduced the GU-PVO's effectiveness.

The PVO employed a number of guns in its antiaircraft artillery arsenal, collectively known as "zenith (*zenitniye*) guns." Automatic weapons fire was provided by the M39 37mm and M1933 40mm, which could engage aircraft at 3,660m and 3,050m, respectively. For heavy antiaircraft the Soviets used weapons of 76mm, 85mm, and 105mm types; the M34 105mm could reach targets up to 11,600m. The Soviets also employed different types of machine guns set in various mounts. But while over 1,800 Soviet planes were destroyed in the initial German attacks, the Luftwaffe lost only 35, many destroyed by their own defective bombs.

Stavka, the Soviet high command, decided to disband the Main Administration of the Air Defense Force and to delegate control of air defense assets to local front commanders. Strategic air defenses literally ceased, with the few guns involved in national defense concentrated at a few key population centers and at tank and aircraft factories. This denied the Soviets a defense in depth and left many cities with no air defenses at all.

This only lasted until November 1941, when increasing German raids on Moscow and Leningrad motivated the Soviets to reestablish the PVO, this time as an independent command. It was designated the *PVO-Strany*, or the National Air Defense Force.

The Moscow bombing attacks represented a serious threat to the Soviet state. The Germans withdrew bomber squadrons from as far away as France to assemble large attack forces. Some bomber attacks reached strengths of 150 bombers.

The Soviets put up a spirited defense, pulling antiaircraft guns from all over the USSR and creating a huge concentration of antiaircraft artillery. The Moscow PVO Zone was established under the command of Major General Gromadin and consisted of the 1st PVO Antiaircraft Artillery Corps and the 4th PVO Fighter Corps. The defenses had 796 heavy guns and almost 600 fighters at its disposal, with more aircraft available from neighboring fronts.

At the very least the barrages fired by the Soviets decreased the accuracy of bombing runs, and the fighters made it difficult to get in and out of the zone without being destroyed; but it was not the antiaircraft artillery that caused the Germans to call off their bomber attacks. Most of the available bombers were redeployed to support ground commanders who were increasingly in need of airpower to offset Soviet numerical superiority.

That superiority was coming by a massive increase in the size of the Red Army. Men were being drafted to carry rifles and machine guns, to operate tanks, to become artillery gunners, and to fly bombers. The PVO was also strengthened with new air defenders, some of which included women volunteers.

Female PVO personnel served in segregated units. At least one all-woman fighter regiment was formed, and several antiaircraft units earned distinction with female gunners. German pilots loathed the women gunners; they felt that their antiaircraft fire was more accurate.

The Soviet air force was virtually rebuilt from scratch, the few surviving aircraft being augmented and replaced by new-model fighters manufactured by relocated factories. Interceptor forces were equipped with the Yak-3, which flew at speeds of 660kph and could outmaneuver the best German fighters at low altitude, and the La-7, which was slightly faster. Improved MiG-3s and LaGG-1s continue to roll off the production lines, while American lend-lease aircraft helped to replace some of the Soviet losses.

One area in which the USSR had major deficiencies was the technology of night fighters. Soviet radar technology was in its infancy, and the PVO had very few sets for early-warning or gun-laying purposes. Lend-lease helped offset such shortages with the excellent British GL2 and American SCR-584 radars. The USSR was unsuccessful in equipping night fighters with on-board radar, instead relying on standard fighters guided by searchlights.

Although by definition PVO fighters existed for the purpose of destroying enemy aircraft on their way to attack targets within the USSR, the fighters were often drafted into ground attack duties. The very ferocity of combat on the Eastern Front meant that every available weapon might be drawn into fighting along a single sector. But there were a few exceptional air defense battles.

At the beginning of 1942 a German force near the city of Demyansk was surrounded by the Soviets. A withdrawal was expressly forbidden by Hitler, so the troops has to be resupplied by airlift. The Soviets made the airlift as difficult as possible, sending in their fighters at an extremely low level to intercept Ju52 transports. Antiaircraft artillery and small-arms fire eventually forced the supply planes to fly higher, over 1,800m, and to enter the Demyansk Pocket only with a strong escort of fighters. But Soviet pilots learned to wait until the German fighters began to run out of fuel and attacked the Ju52 when they were left on their own. By May the Germans had lost 265 aircraft in the airlift.

Despite the heavy losses, the airlift was a success. The pocket was kept supplied until it could break out, and the Germans became confident that airlifts could be a viable strategic option. The Soviets learned valuable lessons that would be applied to another air defense battle, at Stalingrad.

The Russian city of Stalingrad became a symbol for both sides in the Great Patriotic War. For the Germans it would represent a struggle of Fascism over Communism; for the Soviets it represented a struggle of resistance over aggression. In practical terms the Wehrmacht's southern offensive threatened to cut the Caucasus and its valuable oilfields off from the rest of the USSR.

The German 6th Army was responsible for taking Stalingrad. Instead, Soviet resistance became too intense. German troops reached the city but became ensnared in urban warfare, fighting from building to building and sometimes room to room. Once the Germans were totally committed to fighting for the city, the Soviets launched a massive counteroffensive, cutting off the 6th Army.

Rather than withdraw, the Germans decided to try to establish an airlift to supply the 250,000 soldiers at Stalingrad. The marginal success at Demyansk was to be retried, but on a much larger scale.

The Soviets also remembered Demyansk, and prepared deliberate air defenses to cut off the 6th Army's supplies. The Red Air Force was augmented along the front in order to gain local air supremacy. Antiaircraft artillery was rushed in to ring the Stalingrad Pocket with guns.

The Soviet defenses consisted of four operational zones. The first zone covered the airfields from which Luftwaffe transports would have to fly. Soviet bombers would attack the enemy air bases, destroying what aircraft they could on the sending end and making maintenance and operations difficult.

The second zone consisted of five sectors; these sectors were patrolled by the fighters of two entire air armies and covered by the ground weapons of a PVO division. Transports had to fly through corridors in the second zone to reach airfields in the Stalingrad Pocket.

A gun-defended area provided a third zone, a ring of antiaircraft artillery that could engage enemy aircraft before they reached the relative safety of the pocket's airspace. The fourth and final zone was within the pocket itself, covering the airfields that the Germans needed for survival. These would be attacked around the clock by whatever means were available: artillery, bombers, ground-attack aircraft, or fighter-bombers.

The defense play meant that the transports were placed in danger throughout their mission. Losses were considerable among the Ju52s and the Luftwaffe bombers pressed into service as cargo carriers.

Soviet air defenses ensured that the Germans would never be able to supply the 6th Army as planned. Three hundred tons of food were supposed to be delivered every day, but the besieged Germans were lucky if even a fraction of that got through. In a monumental effort, supplies reached a peak of 280 tons in December, but often nothing at all got through. Winter weather prevented many flights from even attempting to reach the pocket. When Soviet ground offensives secured two important forward transport bases by the beginning of January, the 6th Army's fate was sealed. Thanks in part to the active antiaircraft measures used by the Soviets, the Stalingrad Pocket surrendered on 2 February 1943.

There was only one last attempt by the Germans to bring the USSR to its knees through strategic bombing. Beginning in January 1943 the Germans attempted to knock out vital industrial targets as part of a concerted bomber campaign.

It was a case of too little too late. The Soviets had moved much of their industrial base eastward during the first months of the war, placing many of their factories beyond the Urals where they would be out of reach of the German Army. With German reverses all along the front in 1942, most of them were out of reach of the German air force as well. But some factories could still be reached, and the bombers returned to attack.

The danger posed by these attacks was never critical, but the Soviets responded by organizing the air defenses into two PVO fronts while local PVO defenses at potential targets were strengthened. As in the earlier blitz against Moscow, the Germans were forced to divert their bombers elsewhere, to support the Battle of Kursk.

The initiative was primarily to the USSR after Kursk. Although German bombers could and did mount attacks on the Soviet homeland, the German forces on the Eastern Front had survival as a growing preoccupation. Eventually, the Luftwaffe would lose its bases in the USSR, and then in Eastern Europe, until finally the Red Army was fighting within the borders of Germany itself. With the unconditional surrender of Germany in May 1945, a whole new era of air defense began, motivated by new political and technical developments.

The Soviets got a respectable boost to several of their research programs as a result of the capture of many German scientists at the end of World War II. The Soviet jet fighter program made progress at a much greater rate than the West had expected, much to the surprise of United Nations forces in Korea. The Wasserfall, Schmetterling, and Rheintochter programs provided the seed for the Soviets' surface-to-air missile program, although considerable rocket research had been taking place in the USSR prior to and during the Great Patriotic War. Captured electronics aided the Soviets in the area of radar technology.

The United States had ended World War II spectacularly, dropping two atomic bombs on Japan. The implication to the paranoid totalitarian state that was the USSR was clear: If the Americans could do it to Hiroshima and Nagasaki, they could do it to Moscow and Leningrad as well.

The Soviets rapidly attempted to create a nuclear offensive capability of their own. In the meantime, the defensive technology needed by the PVO to deny Soviet airspace totally to outsiders seemed to be much more practical and within reach, especially with the few bases available from which the United States could attack the USSR. PVO-Strany was made an independent branch of the Soviet armed forces in 1948, coequal with the Army, Air Force, and Navy.

Aggressive Communist foreign policies led to conflict in several areas around the world. Soviet air defense saw action by proxy during the Korean War in 1950, shipping many new weapons to North Korea. Several different types of Soviet-made antiaircraft guns were sent, aided by new fire-control radars. Some of the new radars weren't actually that new; the Soviets were employing copies of American radars against American bombers.

The MiG-15 jet fighter saw combat for the first time over Korea; its 1,074kph speed and maneuverability was a shock to American aviation specialists, who had doubted the Soviets' ability to build such a sophisticated aircraft. The American F-86 Sabre then entering service was the nearest equivalent in UN service, capable of flying 1,115kph.

The USSR attempted to establish a national air defense for North Korea, to defend the country from American B-29 bombing raids. But the Soviets were not yet capable of establishing a defense that could stop such attacks; North Korean MiG-15s could successfully take a toll on American bombers if they attacked during the day; but after the USAF switched to night attacks, the MiGs could not find the enemy. The Communist forces could not even maintain air superiority over their main operations zone along the Chinese border, known to UN pilots as ''MiG Alley.''

This left Chinese and North Korean antiaircraft units to stop the American raiders, but their fire-control radars were never available in large quantities and were not accurate enough to engage the B-29s effectively. Proximity fuzes were not yet available for the antiaircraft artillery, which also limited their usefulness. Yet, Soviet-built guns claimed the majority of enemy losses, having inflicted 87 percent of them.

The Korean War ended in 1953 with the Soviets more convinced than ever that a national air defense network was needed. The PVO recognized the need for better tactical air defense weapons, employing the first of a long series of self-propelled automatic weapons, the ZSU-57-2. The 1950s also saw the last of the PVO's heavy antiaircraft artillery, with S-60 57mm, KS-18 85mm, and KS-19 guns entering service, and an increase of PVO antiaircraft units to a maximum strength of perhaps 80 antiaircraft divisions and 120 separate antiaircraft brigades. But the gun branch was on its way to obsolescence, and the fighter branch of the PVO would be competing against a new type of weapon for resources and personnel: surface-to-air missiles.

Soviet work on German SAM designs had borne fruit, producing several possible weapons, including a Soviet version of Wasserfall known as the R-101. It may even be possible that several primitive SAMs based on German designs were used by communist forces, as there were reports by American bombers that ineffective rockets of some sort had been fired at them over Korea.

The first Soviet surface-to-air missile recognized by the West was the R-113, given the NATO designation SA-1 Guild. The R-113 was more sophisticated derivative of the R-101, a single-stage missile guided by radio link. The R-113 system employed up to four radars for early acquisition, local acquisition, fire control, and altitude data.

The R-113 was deployed around Moscow in large numbers beginning in 1954, an extensive ring road having been built to service the missile fire and radar units. Some 3,200 launchers were assembled and manned, and the Moscow PVO Region was upgraded to a PVO District.

Despite the fact that the missile system was being deployed in large numbers, it was evident to PVO planners that its usefulness against newer American bombers was limited. Its maximum altitude of 20,000m meant that it could engage B-52s flying at 16,750m, their operational ceiling, but the maneuverability of the missile in the upper atmosphere was poor. It was likely that future American bombers would have even greater performance and be able to fly even higher. The R-113 was never deployed outside of Moscow. In the meantime, another PVO missile system made a spectacular debut.

The Soviets saw U-2 flights over their territory as a threat to the "Socialist Motherland." The U-2 was a special reconnaissance aircraft flown by the CIA to find out what was going on in the interior of the Soviet Union and other parts of the world where it was impractical to get information by other means. But the Soviets, perhaps remembering the Luftwaffe overflights prior to the German invasion, saw them in a much more sinister light.

To stop the U-2s, the PVO's most promising weapon was the *Dvina* system, known in the West as the SA-2. The Dvina was a two-stage, liquid-fueled rocket that was command-guided to its target. In other words, the controller would send radio signals to the missile, instructing it on what course to take in order to intercept the target. It was a strategic missile system intended for use against high-altitude bombers penetrating the USSR's airspace.

A Soviet-style SA-2 battalion (the basic fire unit) consisted of six launchers, each able to fire one missile. A P-12 radar acquired the target, and a single "Fan-Song"-type radar tracked it (NATO code name for the SA-2's fire control radar). Transloader trucks, each with a single missile on a rotating rail, could rapidly reload a launcher without the use of a crane. Transloaders were almost always a key part of larger Soviet missile systems. Three battalions made up a regiment, the basic organizational unit of the V-75.

The original missile system was capable of shooting down aircraft up to a range of 30km and had a maximum effective altitude of 27,400km. At the higher altitude limits of the missile it was possible to outmaneuver the rocket because the small control surfaces had little effect in the thin upper atmosphere, a defect shared by the R-113.

Yet it was Dvina which brought down Gary Powers' high-flying U-2 over the USSR on 1 May 1960. There are conflicting accounts of exactly how Powers was shot down, but almost certainly a Dvina battalion had been repositioned along the known flight path of the intelligence-gathering aircraft and "ambushed" the U-2, firing a full salvo of missiles to make up for the Dvina's guidance problems.

The successful downing of the U-2 came none too soon for the PVO, as they were under pressure to put a halt to the "spy" flights of the United States and to justify the enormous expense of defending the entire country with a ring of missile sites when some Soviet experts thought it could be done by other, cheaper means. The success of Dvina not only resulted in the expansion of V-75 deployment across the USSR and the export of the missile system to Soviet allies but also spurred the development of Dvina modifications and a whole new generation of missile systems that are still in use today.

One apparent development of Soviet air defense was the realization that the missile systems available might not be capable of stopping a determined, multiple-bomber attack force. A V-75 variant appeared with a bulbous nosecone; almost certainly it was armed with a nuclear warhead. The Soviets had probably determined that the atomic bomb had defensive uses as well as offensive, a conclusion the United States would also come to and incorporate into early American SAMs.

The USSR probably made nuclear capability a requirement of subsequent strategic systems. These were of two types, strategic and tactical. Strategic missile systems, such as the Dvina and the R-113, were primarily static weapon systems. They could be moved with difficulty. Tactical systems were meant for defense of the Soviet Army in the field and included wheeled, tracked, and handheld missile and gun systems.

The S-125 *Neva* (known in the West as the SA-3 Goa) missile system was designed to supplement the V-75, providing a HIMAD (High-to-Medium Air Defense) capability. Technologically, the missile system was only slightly more advanced than the V-75, utilizing built-in Electronic Counter-Countermeasures (ECCM) and a two-stage solid-fueled rocket.

The basic fire unit of the Neva was the missile battalion, four of which made up a regiment. The system was capable of reaching targets between 18,300m and 4.5m in altitude, at ranges out to 29km.

The next strategic SAM was the S-200, known in the West as the SA-5 Gammon. The S-200 had a terminal guidance system and was propelled by a single solid-fuel engine and four strap-on boosters. The missile was truly strategic, capable of reaching targets up to 29,000m in altitude and out to 300km in range. The system became available in the mid-1960s, but few S-200s were ever exported, only beginning in the 1980s. The S-200 may have been meant for an Anti-Ballistic Missile (ABM) role.

The follow-on system was similar in configuration to the U.S. Army Patriot, with phased array radar and large service-free missile cannisters. Known as the S-300 (and SA-10 Grumble in the West), the system is highly mobile despite the size of its components, as everything is mounted on wheeled vehicles. The S-300 is capable of engaging cruise missiles and tactical ballistic missiles in addition to air-breathing aircraft. A tracked version known as S-300V (SA-12 Gladiator/Giant) was designed for tactical air defense.

Meanwhile, tactical air defense was not neglected; the *PVO SV* was established as a separate branch of the Soviet Army in 1958. PVO SV was the progeny of the antiaircraft gunners who manned automatic weapons during World War II, but they also benefited from new military technologies.

Automatic weapons were firmly established in Soviet battlefield air defense. The ZU-23 *Sergei* 14.5mm antiaircraft gun was available in towed mounts. The twin-barreled weapons could put up a respectable amount of ammunition, 400 rounds per minute for the piece at normal firing rate. The ZPU series of weapons also used 14.5mm ammunition, designed in single, double, and quad towed weapon systems.

While other major powers were ridding themselves of smaller caliber automatic weapons, the PVO SV was actually developing more sophisticated weapons of this type. The first result was the ZSU-23-4 *Shilka*, a self-propelled 23mm weapon system with its own built-in fire control system. The ZSU-23-4's radar performed search, detection, ranging, angle of fire, and automatic tracking functions. The ZSU-23-4 would vindicate the need for battlefield automatic air defense weapons in combat in the Middle East.

The PVO SV's missiles were a mixed lot. The *Krug* ("Circle") missile system was known in the West as the SA-4 Ganef. The missiles were mounted on self-propelled tracked launchers that could handle two missiles. Like the S-200, the missile utilized strap-on boosters but was of a ramjet design. The battlefield system used a continuous-wave radar with an optical tracking capability on its own tracked vehicle. The system could engage targets up to 27,000m and out to 100km. The basic fire unit of the Krug was the missile battery, equipped with three launchers. Three batteries comprised a battalion, and three battalions an air defense brigade.

Kub, or Cube, was known in the West as the SA-6 Gainful. Kub was self-propelled on tracked vehicles, similar to Krug but with three-missile launchers. A Kub missile battery, the basic fire unit, was set up in a square or diamond with a single launcher at each point and the radar and command vehicles in the center. Five batteries and support units formed a missile regiment.

The Kub missile itself was distinctly different from other PVO designs, utilizing a sophisticated rocket/ramjet propulsion system with multiple air intakes. The Kub is generally assessed as equivalent to the U.S. HAWK system, with a 12,000m altitude and a 24km range. It began entering Soviet service in large numbers in 1970.

The SA-13 Gopher (possible Soviet designation: SA-10) used an Infra-Red

(IR) homing missile capable of homing in on and damaging jet aircraft. The missiles were mounted in cannisters, two on each side of a central pedestal. The missile gunner sat in a "cockpit" set inside the pedestal. "Gopher" also had a unique feature for an IR system, a range-only radar. The Gopher is clearly a follow-on replacement for the Strela 1, and like the Strela 1 is meant to operate in mixed batteries with the *Tunguska*.

Soviet tactical air defense continued to ride the leading edge of technology with the 2S6M Tunguska. The Tunguska was a natural result of the evolution of Soviet self-propelled antiaircraft guns. The ZSU-57-2 was a relatively simple twin-barreled automatic weapon, followed by the ZSU-23-2 Shilka, which would see widespread use in the Middle East and Asia. The Tunguska was the first self-propelled gun/missile system.

The system incorporated two mechanically connected, alternately firing 30mm guns and eight self-contained 9M311 missile tubes per vehicle, with a gun and four tubes mounted on either side of the turret. The turret also housed the complete radar system, which included a surveillance radar, a tracking (fire-control) radar, and an IFF unit.

A target was picked up by the rotating surveillance antenna, and the turret turned to engage the target. Once the tracking radar had a lock, the gunner had the option of firing the 30mm cannons or of destroying the target with a missile. If the gun option was selected, the guns would be given commands through the tracking radar. If the missile option was selected, a pair of the missiles would elevate to the command of the fire control radar. Once in flight, the missile would be optically tracked by a pulsed flare in the rear, with corrections given through a signal transmitted by the fire-control radar.

The Tunguska represented the most sophisticated tactical air defense weapon to see service in the Soviet Army. By combining missiles, guns, and support radar all on one vehicle, the Soviets ensured that accurate and heavy antiaircraft fire could be provided against a wide range of aircraft, even if only one Tunguska was available. The guns could engage targets up to 4000m, the missiles up to 8000m, with both being limited to less than 3000m in altitude. Thus, both on-board systems were mutually supporting, while the system itself filled the gap between the Soviet MANPADS (Man-Portable Air Defense Systems) and static air defense systems, making it possible to hit enemy helicopters beyond the range of the air-to-surface missiles.

Wheeled SAM vehicles also entered tactical service, beginning with the *Romb*, or diamond, missile system. Known in the West as SA-8 Gecko, the Romb combined all air defense functions in a single large six-wheeled vehicle. The original design included a large radar array in the center of the Romb vehicle, flanked by two open missiles on each side. An improved version had a total of six missile cannisters available per vehicle; missile cannisters eased maintenance and handling.

The small radar-guided missile was capable of reaching 12km and 12,200m altitude. As with the Kub, the Romb missile system was organized five fire batteries to a regiment, with four Romb vehicles per battery. Romb began entering Soviet service in the mid-1970s, and the export version would see combat in Syrian service in the Bekaa Valley.

The *Strela 1* missile system, code-named SA-9 Gaskin, utilized a four-missile launch pedestal mounted on a modified BRDM armored car. The Strela 1 used an IR-guided missile, which homed in on the heat generated by aircraft engines. The Strela 1 provided a highly mobile point defense weapon, especially as it was deployed in mixed gun/missile batteries: four Strela 1s and four ZSU-23-4s per unit. Such batteries were also capable of defending armored columns on the move.

The Soviets did not neglect the need for air defense down to the company level. They began work on MANPADS after the United States developed their Redeye system and proved the concept's viability. (Redeye is the idea of an individual soldier as the basic firing unit.) The *Strela 2* was manufactured for use with the ground forces, giving the Soviet soldier the ability to engage enemy aircraft 3-5km away (depending on the model). Like the Redeye, the missile (known as the SA-7 Grail) was limited to a chase engagement; its seeker could only engage a jet aircraft from the rear, making the Strela 2 a "revenge weapon." The Strela 2's infrared tracker was also susceptible to infrared countermeasures (IRCM) such as flares and could be fooled by background thermal sources such as clouds.

The *Strela 3*, codenamed SA-14 Gremlin, was an improvement over the Strela 2, equipped with an improved seeker capable of overcoming simple IRCM. The Strela 3 also used an improved rocket motor, giving it slightly better range. The *Igla* (Needle) MANPADS began appearing in the mid-1980s and is almost certainly capable of all-aspect engagement; in other words, it is able to fire on enemy aircraft, even head-on. The Igla has been code-named SA-16 by the West.

Information is still limited for the next generation of Soviet missile systems, several different models of which had been definitely identified by the late 1980s. One might ask, why so many different systems, particularly as the Soviets rarely withdraw a system completely out of service? The R-113 remained in service even up to the 1980s, when some missile sites began to be dismantled. The V-75 also remained in service up to the 1990s.

One reason the Soviets retained so many air defense weapons in service is the manner in which they deployed them. The key to Soviet air defense is their practice of mixing weapon systems and providing a defense in echelon. Even the national air defense employed some so-called tactical systems as part of the defense in depth.

For Front or Army defense, the Krug was deployed in brigade strength. At the divisional level there would be a Kub or a Romb regiment. At regimental level there would be a Strela 1/Shilka or a Strela 10/Tunguska battery. At company level there would be individual gunners with Strela 2s, Strela 3s, or Iglas. In theory, any aircraft that attacked a particular tank company would first have to deal with the Krug, then the Kub or Romb, or perhaps even both, then Strela

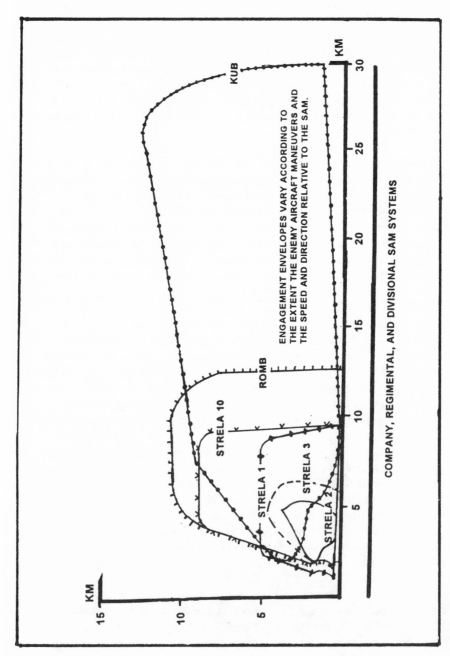

KM
KM

KUB

ENGAGEMENT ENVELOPES VARY ACCORDING TO
THE EXTENT THE ENEMY AIRCRAFT MANEUVERS AND
THE SPEED AND DIRECTION RELATIVE TO THE SAM.

ROMB

STRELA 10

STRELA 1

STRELA 3

STRELA 2

COMPANY, REGIMENTAL, AND DIVISIONAL SAM SYSTEMS

Figure 8.1
Soviet Air Defense in Echelon

1 missiles or Shilka guns, and finally the MANPADS systems available to the company. This was a formidable defense, as illustrated in Figure 8.1. The variety of weapons made it unlikely that an aircraft could carry countermeasures for all of them.

With the advent of the missile age, the PVO Strany was divided into three main components: Fighter Aviation, Zenith Rockets, and Radio-Technical. Both Fighter Aviation and Zenith Rockets fulfilled active, but separate, roles in the air defense of the USSR, while Radio-Technical troops operated and provided maintenance for the radar systems that stood guard over the Soviet Union and provided guidance for both of the other two components.

Radio-Technical Troops, or RTV, operated a host of radars whose coverage always seemed to be increasing. Whenever a Western country develops a new radar system that is easier to maintain, or has greater range or is more compact than an older system in service, the new system replaces the older one. This was not the case with the RTV, which developed new radars with increasing capabilities but did not always take older radars off-line. The obsolecent early-warning systems remained to supplement coverage and to back up the more advanced models. An attack on such a system would be difficult, because to reach a single target an aircraft would have to jam not just one radar but several, which would probably operate at different wavebands, making electronic deception difficult.

The RTV provided early warning for the National Air Defense Forces, as well as surveillance radars used to guide interceptors to their targets. Ground-based radar made up for early deficiencies in Soviet airborne radar, but as a result the pilots of the PVO became overly dependent upon their ground controllers. RTV also provided the acquisition and guidance systems used by the Zenith Rockets.

The Zenith Rocket Troops, known by its Soviet acronym *ZRV*, were the missile branch of the PVO and provided the "defensive" air defense capability. Zenith rocket systems stood guard over the border against incursion and provided defense in depth for the interior regions as well. The USSR was divided into regions and districts for engagement purposes.

PVO aircraft of Fighter Aviation steadily improved first with the MiG-17, similar in design to the MiG-15, and the supersonic MiG-19, MiG-21, and MiG-25. GCI technology steadily improved, with the ability to transmit vectoring data directly to the aircraft from the ground controller, in effect bypassing the pilot. One of the most advanced PVO fighters to see service was the Su-27, which operated a look-down shoot-down radar system and built-in electronic countermeasures (ECM). Several IFF systems were tried and adopted.

Throughout the USSR's postwar existence it never had to go to war directly, but its air defense arsenal did see combat throughout the world through proxies, most notably in the Middle East, in Cuba, and in North Vietnam. Soviet air defense technology would shape several foreign conflicts between 1963 and 1991.

Meanwhile, the PVO was hard at work to defend the USSR from a new threat, that of ICBMs. At the height of the Cold War the Soviet's own "Star Wars" program seemed to have been based on two new components of the PVO, the PKO and PRO.

PKO, or Antispace Defense, was described as being capable of destroying "the enemy's cosmic means of fighting." This would include orbiting nuclear weapons (of which none are known to have been deployed), reconnaissance satellites, and possibly manned spacecraft. PKO was the USSR's means of securing the "High Ground."

The USSR conducted several tests with antisatellite lasers and may have also made comparable progress with particle-beam weapons. These would undoubtably have come under the authority of the PKO.

The Antirocket Defense, PRO, was the component of the PVO responsible for antiballistic missile defense. In contrast to the United States, defense from missile attack has been an ongoing concern. Several ABMs have been developed and set up to supplement each other in great numbers around such important cities as Moscow and Leningrad (St. Petersburg).

Critics of ABM defense have always taken pains to say that missile defense is "pointless" because any ABM system, indeed any weapon system at all, has finite capabilities and can be saturated. In the era of the Cold War, both the United States and the Soviet Union had more than enough ICBMs to send one, or five, or twenty, or a hundred to hit a single ABM-defended target, whatever it took to destroy it.

The Soviet Union officially disbanded in early 1992, and the Commonwealth of Independent States (CIS) was created in its place. Russia, the largest of the former republics and the dominant military and political power, retained the five branch military structure of the USSR, including the PVO, and its various units. In the post-Cold War world it is Russia, the inheritor of the USSR's ABM research, that has defense against a limited nuclear strike, which has become the primary atomic threat in the 1990s.

An early wagon-mounted searchlight.

World War I German field piece mounted for antiaircraft fire.

7.1cm antiaircraft gun mounted on a Krupp Armored Motor Car.

World War I German antiaircraft gun protecting an observation balloon.

American "doughboys" man a machine gun
mounted for antiaircraft defense.

World War I allied
tripod-mounted anti-
aircraft machine gun.

Allied multi-horned sound detector with operator.

Interwar Period American antiaircraft director.

American searchlight and sound detector.

British gunners in North Africa manning a 40mm Bofors antiaircraft gun.

British gunners in North Africa manning an antiaircraft rocket projector.

British automatic tracking radar, No. 3.

A Royal Air Force Bloodhound surface-to-air missile.

German long-range acquisition radar antenna.

Japanese antiaircraft guns captured by American forces.

Japanese fire control radar at the Chiba Antiaircraft School.

ZSU-23-4 "Shilka" protecting Soviet tanks during maneuvers.

Kub (SA-6) target acquisition radar and missile launchers.

World War II barrage balloon training at Camp Davis, N.C.

American antiaircraft
gunners at Remagen
Bridge, 1945.

American antiaircraft tracer fire over Remagen, 1945.

75mm Skysweeper radar-guided antiaircraft gun.

120mm Stratosphere Gun defending Chicago-Gary area.

SAGE display console.

From rear to front: Nike-Ajax, Nike-Hercules, Nike-Zeus.

Royal Canadian Air Force Bomarc missile in launch position.

Dvina missile in the Sinai.

Patriot surface-to-air missile system.

United States: Nike, Hawk, and Patriot

The air defense of the continental United States evolved because of the stimulus of the threat in the 1950s of a Soviet nuclear bomber offensive. It grew from a combination of tactical experience and what was largely strategic theory during World War II.

The gunners of the Coast Artillery Corps' antiaircraft branch had compiled a respectable combat record during World War II, though mostly in the defense of the U.S. field armies or in protecting overseas possessions.

U.S. antiaircraft weapons deployed during World War II included weapons developed during the interwar period, as well the M55 12.7mm quad machine gun developed in 1942 and the Bofors, adopted as the 40mm Automatic Gun M1 to replace the 37mm. If not the most successful, the M118 90mm gun was probably the most famous air defense weapon in America's World War II arsenal. The weapon became known as the "Triple Threat" because of its versatility: It could be used as field artillery piece or an antitank weapon, as well as an antiaircraft gun.

The Coast Artillery earned the motto "First to Fire" for its successes during the first hours of the Pacific War. On 8 December (7 December in the United States) 1941, forces of Japan struck at the American Pacific Fleet in Pearl Harbor and Army Air Corps aircraft at Hickam Field. The raiders had been detected by one of the five radars deployed with the Army Aircraft Warning Service, but the report of the imminent attack was discounted until it was too late. Ten hours after the Imperial Navy attack on Hawaii, planes of the Imperial Army struck Clark Field in the Philippines.

The Japanese attack on the Philippines was mounted from the occupied island of Formosa. Originally, the Army bomber attack was supposed to hit the Philippines at the same time as the raid on Pearl Harbor, but bad weather delayed the planes. By the time the attack was launched, the Japanese were sure that the U.S. Far Eastern Air Force would be ready for them.

But somehow the warning was never transmitted to the Philippines. The attack was opposed primarily by the 200th Coast Artillery Corps Regiment (AA), a unit of the New Mexico National Guard that had recently been called into active service and sent to bolster the islands' defenses. Armed with 3-inch guns, 37mm guns, .50 cals, searchlights, and a few SCR 268 gun-laying radars, the men of the 200th CAC punished the Japanese air force during the first attack; but, ultimately, the enemy forces achieved their goal of destroying American air power in the Far East.

The 60th CAC on Corregidor, the 200th CAC, and the newly formed 515th CAC provided air defense for the Philippines even as the Japanese landed ground troops on the islands. The antiaircraft troops put up a heroic but futile fight as they were forced back to the Bataan Peninsula. The antiaircraft gunners found themselves on the front lines, taking out Japanese planes in the air even as they struggled to survive on the ground. And their suffering was only worsened after the inevitable surrender and the Bataan Death March. Japanese losses to antiaircraft were so high that they did not believe that the three understrength Coast Artillery regiments that surrendered were the only ones on the islands.

Even as the air defenders of Bataan and Corregidor were being herded into captivity, other forces were being prepared for Operation Torch, the Allied invasion of North Africa. The War Department created the Antiaircraft Command in March 1942, as part of Army Ground Forces. Ten independent Automatic Weapons battalions were deployed, along with five antiaircraft artillery regiments. Despite poor training and doctrinal weaknesses in their deployment, the CAC had several local successes in defending ground forces and key assets during Field Marshal Rommel's western offensive.

As the Luftwaffe and the Japanese Air Service got weaker, the air defenses deployed with American field armies simply got stronger. They enjoyed many successes against the Axis forces, in England, during the Italian Campaign, while island-hopping in the Pacific, and on the beaches of Normandy. One of the few black marks on an otherwise admirable combat record occurred during the Allied invasion of Sicily in 1943. Antiaircraft gunners opened fire on friendly aircraft as they attempted to land in the nighttime darkness, killing several soldiers. The friendly-fire incident pointed more to the need for an IFF signal system than to failure of the air defenses.

The Luftwaffe remained a potent enemy right up to the end. The Germans even managed to launch a surprise attack on New Year's Day 1945 on the

Western Front that destroyed 156 Allied planes on the ground. The attack had been a surprise because the Allies had prematurely assumed the Luftwaffe was defeated. There would be yet one more chapter in the annals of the Luftwaffe before it could be considered "down for the count."

The Battle of Remagen Bridge was the high point of the Antiaircraft Artillery. On 7 March 1945, advance elements of the U.S. First Army reached the Ludendorff Bridge at the town of Remagen, the last span still intact over the Rhine River and a gateway into the heart of Germany.

Even though German demolition charges had been detonated on it, the Remagen Bridge was still usable and was quickly captured. The decision was made to reinforce the success there, taking the town of Remagen and establishing a bridgehead. Antiaircraft Artillery was quickly mobilized: three AAA groups quickly dispatched units to oppose the inevitable counterattack from the air.

The AAA did not have long to wait. Ju87s and Me109s appeared over the Ludendorff Bridge on 8 March, attempting to destroy the span before a large force could cross. But antiaircraft automatic weapons and heavy guns were already deployed on both sides of the bridge: All four aircraft in the first attack were shot down. It was by no means the last Luftwaffe attack against the bridge defenses.

As more antiaircraft artillery units arrived at Remagen, they were deployed so that heavy guns provided high-altitude coverage and automatic weapons supplemented them, preventing enemy planes from "sneaking in" under the coverage. SCR 584 radars were deployed for gun-laying in darkness or in inclement weather. The ring of flak around Remagen continued to grow as more units were fed into the defenses and as the bridgehead on the eastern side was expanded.

During night attacks a barrage was set up. On command, every antiaircraft gun opened fire in its sector for exactly ten seconds. The very sight of such a massive, and yet controlled, barrage had to have been enough to unnerve the German pilots.

The Luftwaffe even used its new combat jets, the Me262 fighter and Ar234 "Blitz" bomber, in an attempt to knock out the bridge. Despite their superior speed, the jets were still vulnerable to ground fire. By traveling at high speed they could evade much of the flak, but in doing so their accuracy and effectiveness were diminished.

The Germans never landed a single bomb on the bridge. It collapsed on its own accord on 17 March, but by then the antiaircraft artillery umbrella was defending nearby pontoon bridges across the Rhine. The defense had held against the Luftwaffe's last gasp.

While American antiaircraft artillery was enjoying successes in the Pacific and European theaters, the air defenses of the home front were built up to oppose a possible attack by long-range aircraft. But when the United States was finally bombed, the raids were largely ineffective and the source unexpected.

Antiaircraft units in the United States were under the operational control of the interceptor commands. The Army Air Force had four numbered air forces in the United States, each with its own interceptor command. As in Great Britain, the air defenses were primarily under the control of the pilots, with emphasis given to fighters.

The United States and Canada remained alert against an Axis attack, primarily perceived to be from German long-range bombers. And in fact, the development of an "Amerika bomber" was in progress in Germany, with several companies working on designs. The bomber would have been a multiengine aircraft capable of bombing the United States from bases in western Europe or of using bases in Norway to fly a transpolar route to reach American targets.

Such designs never reached production, but a prototype of the Ju390 extreme-range bomber supposedly once flew within 12 miles of New York City during a 1943 mission without being detected or even challenged. A German air attack on America might have been a remote possibility, but it was still a possibility.

Aside from the obvious targets for an air attack, the Sault Ste. Marie Canal on the Canadian border was recognized as a vital installation for the Allied war effort even prior to American involvement in the war. Nine-tenths of American iron ore moved through the canal, iron ore that was vital to the Allied war machine.

In January 1941 the Permanent Joint Board of Defense was established to coordinate U.S. and Canadian efforts. The board recognized that the Sault Ste. Marie Canal was vital to the interests of both countries, and a tradition of co-operation was begun to defend the important installation and would eventually grow into the present-day defense of the continent. On the U.S. side, the Military District of Sault Ste. Marie was established.

Prior to Pearl Harbor, few troops were allocated to the defense of the canal or its Army installation, Fort Brady, and none of them was antiaircraft artillery. By April 1942 defenses included the 100th Coast Artillery Regiment (AA) and the 39th Barrage Balloon Battalion, as well as the 131st Infantry Regiment for ground security, a total of 7,000 men. A Vital Defense Area was established around the canal, which comprised most of Chippewa County, Michigan. In September this was expanded into the Central Air Defense Zone, reaching up to 150 miles south of the border.

On the Canadian side, an antiaircraft artillery battalion was provided for defense of the canal, equipped with U.S. guns. Canadian authorities established 266 observation posts between the border and Lake Hudson and allowed the U.S. Army to set up five radar stations in northern Ontario to provide early warning of any plane attempting to attack via the polar route. At the canal, facilities and sites were provided for up to 2,000 U.S. soldiers stationed on the Canadian side. In early 1943 Canada established a defense zone similar to the Central Air Defense Zone belonging to the United States.

Air traffic entering and leaving the Central Air Defense Zone (or its Canadian counterpart) was strictly regulated. Flights were coordinated in advance, and defense of the canal was for all practical purposes an antiaircraft artillery show.

No interceptor aircraft were ever assigned to the defense zone on a permanent basis, even though some emergency airstrips were established in the vicinity.

As the threat from German-occupied Europe dwindled, the need for an elaborate defense of the canal seemed to be less urgent. In January 1944 most of the special air defenses at the canal were withdrawn entirely, but they would be remembered later when a different enemy threatened North America.

Germany never mounted an air attack on the United States. On the other hand, the Japanese managed to mount a threat that would evolve into a real, if ineffective, attack.

Early in the Pacific War, Japan seemed capable of launching an air attack on the west coast using carrier-based planes. After operations in the South Pacific up to three carriers might have been available for such an attack, but the Japanese never exploited this window of opportunity. It was fortunate for America; there were few interceptors to deal with such an attack, although enough antiaircraft artillery was deployed to protect vital targets. One such target was Los Angeles.

On the night of 24/25 February 1942 the air defenses of Los Angeles were alerted because of suspicious activities, including reports of unidentified aircraft. A blackout was ordered and gun crews readied.

At around 3 A.M. gun crews began to fire at phantom air targets. More guns followed suit, until 1,400 rounds of 3-inch gun ammunition were expended in the resulting barrage. No enemy aircraft were ever positively identified following the ''Battle of Los Angeles,'' the only full-scale air defense action to take place in North America during the war.

At least one incendiary attack on the United States took place using a submarine-launched seaplane. The attack was not detected by radar, and the huge forest fire it started in Washington State was assumed to have occurred naturally.

Slightly more effective was the threat posed by Japan's balloon bombs. The paper balloons were launched from northern Japan and rode the stratospheric air currents until they were over the continental United States. An ingenious timing device would release several bombs once the balloon was supposed to be over the general target area. Between late 1944 and early 1945 several thousand balloons were launched, but only 300 of them managed to reach the United States and Canada. Most of those failed to drop their bombs.

The United States kept the existence of the balloon bombs a wartime secret, even as Royal Canadian Air Force (RCAF) and Army Air Force interceptors brought several of them down and antiaircraft gunners took a toll. The bombs might have posed a very real threat had Japan's secret experiments in biological warfare created usable weapons for them. The Sunset Project was initiated by the 4th Air Force in northwest Washington State; it established a prototype defense network that would use early-warning radars to detect the approach of balloons from the sea and ground-control radars to guide interceptors to the target.

The most effective defense against the balloons turned out to be censorship:

The Japanese believed that few or none of the balloons were reaching the United States because there were no radio reports of the attacks and no attempts to destroy the launching bases. The Japanese launched the last balloon in mid-1945, before any Sunset Project units became operational.

Interestingly enough, the balloon attacks had a very small success against the war-making capability of the United States, although the Japanese never knew it and few American military leaders would learn of it until after the war. One bomb momentarily knocked out power in an area of Washington State. The resulting outage at the top-secret Hanford plant caused a delay on the atomic bomb project for three days.

In August 1944 American air defense was forever changed when Lieutenant Jacob Schaefer of the U.S. Army submitted a memorandum that proposed a surface-to-air missile (SAM) system, one that would use two radars, one to track the target and the other to track the missile, and a computer that would radio to the missile the direction of intercept. Though relatively simple on paper, the project required staggering improvements in the American radar and computer technology and the construction of a high-altitude missile when U.S. rocket technology was still in its infancy. Nevertheless, the Ordnance Department ordered work to begin in June 1945 on what would become Project Nike, giving Bell Telephone and Western Electric responsibility for its development.

Nike rapidly became the most promising U.S. air defense weapon. Captured German missile research and, more important, the scientists who had accumulated it came to America and helped the U.S. Army gain the high ground in what would become an interservice rivalry over who would control air defense: the Army or the new service, the U.S. Air Force.

When the Air Force was separated from the Army by the National Security Act of 1947, the struggle over which service would have control of air defense weapons, especially missiles, intensified. As one expatriate German scientist put it, "The competition was still against the Russians . . . and the Luftwaffe."

The defeat of Germany had left the Soviet Union a world power in every sense of the term. The USSR wasted no time in developing a nuclear weapons capability, although they initially had no way of delivering their bombs to the primary target: the United States. This changed rapidly.

The Soviets copied outright the B-29 bomber from three planes that had made emergency landings in the Soviet Union during the war against Japan. Redesignated the Tu-4, the piston-engined Superfort was capable of reaching American targets 7,000 miles from its bases in the Soviet Far East, but only if the crews went on one-way missions. Yet, this was conceivable, as the Soviets had proven themselves willing to sacrifice men callously for important missions. Moreover, they would be able to reach the atomic production facilities located in Washington State.

In 1944 work began on the M51 Skysweeper, a towed, self-contained, automatic 75mm radar-guided gun with a 9,000m ceiling. Developed too late for World War II, Skysweeper would be deployed with U.S. Ground Forces around the world and sold to several Allied countries. The Tu-4 could fly above its range only by flying to its maximum altitude of 10,000m.

A 120mm gun was also developed. The appropriately named M1 Stratosphere Gun could reach 19,000m into the sky, the highest altitude ever reached by an American antiaircraft gun. The Tu-4 would be unable to safely fly above the Stratosphere Gun's range, even at maximum altitude.

Antiaircraft artillery would provide point defense in the United States until Nike was available and while the Air Force developed its own air defense weapon: BOMARC. Originally begun as the GAPA (Ground to Air Pilotless Aircraft) Project, BOMARC took its name from the Boeing aircraft company and the Michigan Aeronautical Research Center with which it cooperated. Interest in BOMARC waned until Nike showed considerable progress in 1950.

The BOMARC was an air-breathing, winged interceptor, guided by ground radar and using a ramjet engine to propel it to the target. It required a rocket motor to boost it to the high speed required for the ramjet to work (a ramjet engine has no moving parts; it uses compressed air created from the aircraft's forward motion to provide oxydizer). The BOMARC would have much greater range than the Nike but would fly at slower speeds.

BOMARC and Nike reflected the U.S. War Department's decision that anything with wings, whether it was mannned or not, belonged to the Air Force and that rockets were simply an advanced kind of artillery shell and therefore belonged to the Army. Later, when dealing with air defense, the Air Force was given responsibility for ''area'' weapons while the Army got control of ''point'' weapons. But the line between the two was never clearly defined, and interservice rivalry would continue as new technologies were developed.

In the meantime, air defense was being organized in both the USAF and the Army to meet the threat posed by the Soviets. In 1948 Continental Air Command (ConAC) was created by presidential order. The 1st, 4th, 9th, 10th, 12th, and 14th Air Forces stationed in the United States were subordinated to ConAC, as well as the Air Defense Command. ADC was responsible for planning and operations in the two air defense sectors in the United States, the Eastern and Western.

Each of the numbered air forces corresponded to a U.S. Army, and the antiaircraft artillery of each were supposed to be placed in support of the Air Force, when available. Even though the USAF preferred the use of fighters for air defense, it had difficulty developing a true all-weather interceptor. Radar-guided antiaircraft artillery would have to continue providing point defense for cities and other potential targets. In 1950 the Army Antiaircraft Command (ARAA-COM) was formed to perform a similar function as ConAC.

ARAACOM was initially divided into two subordinate commands, EASTA-RAACOM and WESTARAACOM. These corresponded in geographical area to the USAF's Eastern Air Defense Force and Western Air Defense Force. In effect, the antiaircraft organization paralleled and shadowed the USAF's interceptor structure.

ARAACOM had precious little to command at first. Just the year prior there was only one Regular Army antiaircraft battalion, the one stationed at Fort Bliss. The Korean War added impetus to the build-up of a national air defense, and by July 1950 there were 15 Regular Army battalions equipped with 75mm, 90mm, and 120mm guns available to ARAACOM. Eleven more National Guard heavy antiaircraft battalions were available as well. The remaining antiaircraft artillery units were equipped with light automatic weapons that were tactical in nature and unable to contribute to the strategic defense in a meaningful way.

F-84 Thunderjets and F-86 Sabres entered service, replacing for the most part the World War II propeller-driven fighters. The "Century Series" of aircraft began entering service in the 1950s, providing the USAF with supersonic F-100 Super Sabres and F-104 Starfighters and the RCAF with F-101 VooDoos, among other designs. Air-to-air missiles made their appearance.

In 1950 the decision was made for the USAF's Air Defense Command to supersede ConAC and take over its functions. ARAACOM and ADC co-located their headquarters at Ent Air Force Base in Colorado Springs, Colorado. Meanwhile, the Coast Artillery Corps became the Antiaircraft Artillery and was merged with the Field Artillery, becoming the Artillery Branch of the U.S. Army.

ARAACOM published a plan to integrate the National Guard into the new air defenses. National Guard Antiaircraft battalions, after achieving the designation of "special security forces," when notified of alert would deploy to on-site positions. In this way the National Guard would remain a cornerstone of Army air defense, even as its guns were replaced by missiles.

The Army and the Air Force each made studies of where the scarce air defense artillery assets should be deployed; the resulting plan established 44 Regular Army battalions and 22 National Guard battalions around critical targets that included nuclear facilities, industrial targets, population centers, and strategic air force bases. In addition to those 66 battalions, Canada had pledged the equivalent of two more antiaircraft battalions for the joint defense of the Sault Ste. Marie Canal, still of strategic importance to both countries. Most of these deployments were in the northeast United States or in Pacific states.

ARAACOM projected a command structure consisting of seven brigades and 20 antiaircraft artillery groups. A third command, Central ARAACOM, was established to control the few air defenses deployed in the central United States.

To provide a minimal early-warning capability to the air defense elements in the United States, the "Lashup" radar project was put into place. Using AN/CPS-5 radars, temporary Lashup sites were concentrated in the same zones as the few available antiaircraft gun battalions, the Pacific coast and the northeast United States. Lashup was to provide coverage of some parts of the United States until a permanent radar fence could be established.

Even as Lashup took shape, the air defenses of the United States would have to rely on the old-fashioned expedient of using civilian volunteers to provide reports of enemy aircraft. The Ground Observer Corps (GOC) consisted of volunteers who manned observation posts and filter centers. The GOC would remain organized until 1959, long after electronics had rendered it obsolete.

Upon the detection of an enemy attack, the antiaircraft defense of the United States was was to be divided into Gun Defended Areas (GDAs), in which the Air Force would place minimal engagement restrictions on the ground weapons, and Inner Artillery Zones (IAZs), on which the USAF could place no firing restrictions. The larger mass of the United States would be a de facto Fighter Engagement Zone (FEZ), in which enemy aircraft would be whittled down by interceptors before delivering their nuclear payloads.

Antiaircraft batteries would be positioned around a target as part of their parent battalion. These in turn were part of brigades, some of which were changed to commands, their numbers changing to correspond to the armies they would defend. Thus, the 56th Brigade became the 1st AA Regional Command, defending 1st Army. Upper-echelon divisions of ARAACOM would go through many different incarnations throughout the 1950s.

Doctrinal conflicts flared between the Army and the Air Force about the types of procedural controls that would be in place. The USAF was totally opposed to the establishment of GDAs. But although the GDAs would not be established in peacetime, air defense commanders could in theory establish them in wartime. Air Defense Identification Zones (ADIZs) would be established along the national perimeter; if an aircraft flying within such a zone could not be identified, it would be designated as a hostile.

Initially, the antiaircraft units were required to be capable of positioning themselves within range of the target they were assigned to defend. Few of the potential targets possessed any sort of military facility on site. The 6-hour readiness requirement then standard for antiaircraft units was deemed unrealistic, and funds were provided to build permanent sites that could be brought to instant readiness in the event of an air defense alert.

In 1951 the first tests of Nike were conducted at White Sands Proving Grounds in New Mexico. The weapon was a spectacular success: In some cases the missile did not require a proximity burst to destroy its target; instead, it made a contact hit. The surface-to-air missile system, as seen in Figure 9.1, had come of age.

Meanwhile, time seemed to be running out for the United States. By 1953 the USSR had three air armies of 1,000 Tu-4 bombers. The threat was growing, and the United States slowly began to react to it.

If defense against the bombers was going to be provided for the entire country, a better system than Lashup would have to be in place to provide early warning. The more warning the interceptors and guns had, the better chance they would have of destroying incoming aircraft.

The Pinetree Line and the Mid-Canada Line were constructed first, with completion in 1954. The Pinetree Line consisted of radar stations along the U.S.–Canadian border, providing both detection and intercept instructions for fighters. Pinetree formed the first true radar fence in the United States.

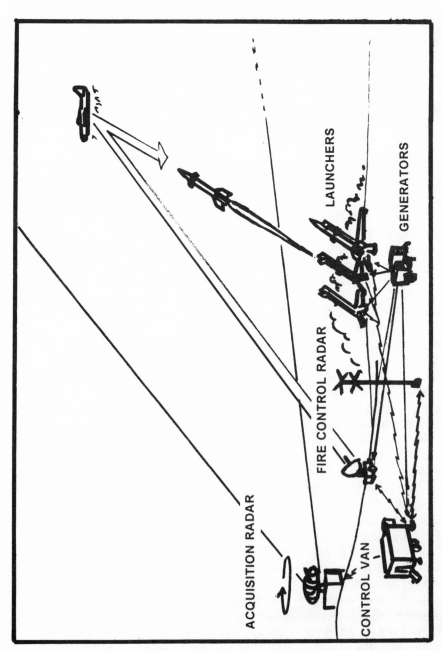

Figure 9.1
Typical Surface-to-Air Missile System

The Mid-Canada Line was much more modest. Instead of radar, Mid-Canada was more of an unmanned microwave "fence" constructed at about the same time as the Pinetree Line. It detected flying objects that crossed the line, but it could not give a bearing, altitude, or speed. Despite these drawbacks and its tendency towards false alarms, the Mid-Canada Line was an important asset in alerting the Pinetree Line. It served as a "tripwire" to snag enemy aircraft.

The furthest line of detection was the Distant Early Warning (DEW) Line, begun in 1955. The network of radars were stationed north of the Arctic Circle, forming a solid line of coverage that any Soviet aircraft would have to cross in order to reach North American targets via the great circle route.

The DEW Line represented enormous technical and engineering difficulties. Canadian cooperation was vital, even though the system was constructed mainly with U.S. funds and personnel. Harsh Arctic conditions made it hard to build the system, but by 1957 the DEW Line was operational. In theory, Soviet bombers would be detected by the DEW Line, confirmed by the Mid-Canada Line, and tracked by the Pinetree Line over several hours.

In case of attack from the sea, Navy picket ships and radars mounted on platforms called Texas Towers watched for incoming aircraft. Airborne radar platforms patrolled parts of the Atlantic and Pacific coasts, in some cases extending the coverage of the picket ships and the three Texas Towers off the New England coast.

To provide command and control, SAGE was created. The SemiAutomatic Ground Environment grew out of the United States' early Whirlwind computer research. Air Defense Command SAGE direction centers would process data received from different radars in its sector, as well as from Texas Tower stations or airborne aircraft. Datalinks were by telephone or UHF.

Inside the SAGE's concrete, above-ground structure (it had to be above ground to provide cooling for the primitive computers), information was provided on screens. Controllers then determined what measures to use to destroy enemy aircraft, ordering out interceptors, alerting gun crews, or even firing a BOMARC missile from the center itself.

The New York sector was the first to become operational, in 1958. Others also took their place, even as funds were being cut for antibomber defense. SAGE was the first of what would become known as "force multipliers."

Force multipliers were necessary, as it became obvious that the services were never going to get the kind of forces it would take to thoroughly defend North America, at least not in peacetime. But SAGE allowed American air defenders to maximize what resources were available.

Finally, those resources included Nike-Ajax missile units. Deployment began in 1953, with whole new battalions created for the surface-to-air missiles (SAMs) while some existing heavy-gun units were armed with missiles. By the end of 1954 almost all 120mm gun units had converted to Nike. National Guard units were integrated into the defense, with full-time crews on duty at the fire batteries.

Nike-Ajax battalions required a site network for support. The original requirements called for a battalion missile assembly area and four firing battery sites, each consisting of a battery control area and a battery launch area. The battalion headquarters would be located at one of the battery control areas. Some sites had above-ground launchers; others were underground, waiting for the signal of the alert siren to bring their missiles to the surface to fire. By the end of 1955 there were 38 operational Nike-Ajax battalions.

The creation of Nike sites established an ARAACOM presence throughout the country. Ringing major urban centers, the missile sites were miniature Army posts, providing visible reassurance that a credible defense was being mounted.

Nike-Ajax units were placed on a rotating alert system. Twenty-five percent of all missile batteries would be capable of launching at least one missile within 15 minutes of warning. These would form the first line of defense. Another 50 percent would be capable of launch within 30 minutes. These units would provide the firepower to sustain the air defense battle. And the remaining 25 percent would be on a training and maintenance cycle, yet required to be fully operational within two hours. These batteries would form a sort of reserve.

ARAACOM maintained this rotation schedule 24 hours a day, seven days a week. Nike crews maintained a high level of combat readiness, running exercises and alerts at a moment's notice. As the missile battalions reached their defense sectors they became a credible threat to enemy aircraft, always ready at a moment's notice despite weather conditions that might interfere with interceptor operations. Nike-Ajax was ready, test-proven, and in place. ARAACOM superseded ADC as the nation's major air defense element.

Yet another reorganization, in 1954, created CONAD, the Continental Air Defense Command, from the USAF's old ADC. Technically part of a joint command, the air force retained key staff positions in CONAD, keeping ARAACOM under tight control.

Even as Nike-Ajax was being deployed, an improved Nike was also becoming available. Nike-Hercules was based on the same technology as the Nike-Ajax, but the missile itself utilized a four-cluster booster that gave it increased range, 155km to the Nike-Ajax's 49km. The increased lifting power of the Nike-Hercules also made it possible to utilize nuclear warheads for the destruction of airplane formations.

ARAACOM made plans to integrate the new missile system into the air defense network, first supplementing and later replacing Nike-Ajax. The AN/FSG-1 Missile Master fire-control system would also enter service to provide greater system integration. The Missile Master was designed to operate with SAGE.

The HAWK missile system was also reaching the end of its development phase. Unlike the Nike system, it did not rely on command guidance: HAWK employed a semi-active guidance system, using a high-powered radar illuminator to "paint" the target, making it visible to the HAWK missile. HAWK had the advantages of a low-level engagement capability and of not requiring a radio link for guidance.

A ground-based version of the Navy's Terrier missile system was also supposed to enter the Army inventory, with two battalions already slated to receive it. Terrier would never see Army use because testing found the ground-based version unreliable.

In 1958 the last of the heavy-gun batteries were deactivated at the Sault Ste. Marie Canal, while the first of the Nike-Hercules battalions took their place around American cities. ARAACOM had become Army Air Defense Command, ARADCOM, a missile-based force. Nuclear warheads were made available to Nike-Hercules batteries, and even USAF interceptors carried Genie rockets, unguided missiles that could destroy an entire enemy bomber formation in a single blow.

North American Air Defense Command, known as NORADCOM or NORAD for short, came into existence in 1957, formalizing American and Canadian cooperation in air defense. Elements of ARADCOM, ADC, and the RCAF (later, the Canadian Defense Forces) all answered directly to NORAD. The command structure was set up so that an American general commanded while a Canadian served as deputy commander; the organization itself was responsible to the joint chiefs of staffs of both countries. See Map 9.1 for NORAD early warning and defense.

BOMARC entered service with the USAF in 1959 and the RCAF in 1961. BOMARC sites consisted of rows of above-ground shelters, each protecting a single BOMARC missile in concrete and steel. Upon launch, the steel roof of the shelter would be opened by hydraulics and the missile raised to a vertical launch position. SAGE control would guide the BOMARC to the vicinity of the target; once there, its on-board radar would provide terminal guidance.

Improved BOMARCs were soon made available, the IM-99Bs, which used solid-fuel boosters and improved ramjets. Nuclear weapons were provided for the air defense squadrons of both countries, although RCAF squadron nuclear devices were kept under the control of U.S. personnel. Canadian BOMARC would provide supplementary firepower for the RCAF interceptor squadrons.

The improved BOMARC's superior range (780km) gave greater flexibility in deployment. The IM-99B units were routinely kept on two-minute alert status. In the event of war, BOMARCs would be launched on command from SAGE to destroy enemy aircraft over the oceans or above the vast emptiness of northern Canada, leaving fewer targets for interceptors and missiles to deal with in the Zone of the Interior.

North American air defense was rapidly resembling the "thin defense" envisioned in the early 1950s, a perimeter defense that, once complete, would be augmented and improved until it was impossible for enemy aircraft to fly at will over the continent. As envisioned, early warning would alert the interceptors and ground-base weapon systems long before the enemy was picked up on their radars. BOMARCs could strike at the enemy formations long before they reached the borders of the United States. Nike systems would hit at them as they began their bombing run, and HAWK would prevent the enemy from flying

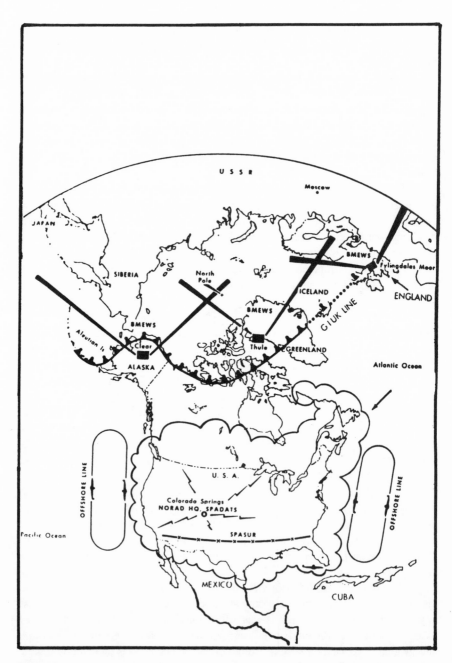

Map 9.1
NORAD Early Warning and Defense

below the reach of the high-flying Hercules and Ajax batteries. USAF and RCAF interceptors would harass them the entire way.

Just as ARADCOM utilized National Guard Nike-Hercules battalions as part of the national defense, ADC (which was now Aerospace Defense Command) increasingly placed the burden of maintaining continental interceptor strength on the Air National Guard.

Following Cuba's entry into the Soviet sphere of influence, the air defenses of Florida were given priority, both Nike and HAWK sites being established on the peninsula. Alaska's ground-based air defenses were also augmented, protecting America's northernmost state from the proximity of the Soviet threat.

Having developed the weapons for defending against low-level and high-level air attacks, the U.S. Army next looked at the danger presented by ballistic missiles. The 1957 launch of Sputnik into space proved that the USSR could place objects into orbit; military logic dictated that these same missiles could place a nuclear warhead anywhere in the world. The ICBM had been born and would come to dominate strategic defense planning.

The answer to the new threat seemed to be to develop further the already successful Nike family. Nike-Zeus was the first project to be studied, improved into the Nike-X. Neither of these systems were adopted for service, but experience with Nike-X led to the Sentinel Anti-Ballistic Missile System.

Sentinel utilized two missiles, Sprint and Spartan. Spartan was a long-range ABM missile that could intercept enemy missiles at the edge of space, while Sprint would serve as a point defense weapon. American technology was not yet efficient enough to achieve a contact kill on incoming missiles, so Sprint and Spartan would carry nuclear warheads to ensure destruction.

Planned deployment was extensive, providing Spartan coverage over most of the United States, including Alaska and Hawaii. Sprints would provide supplementary coverage for the largest metropolitan areas. Combined with ARADCOM's other air defense assets and the USAF's interceptor forces, Sentinel would protect the United States, in theory, from all but the most determined nuclear attack.

With the Antiaircraft Artillery taking on more and more responsibilities distinct from the traditional Artillery Branch missions, a new branch was established in 1968: Air Defense Artillery. ADA officers manned ARADCOM and the air defense units protecting the Army in the field. Nike-Hercules, HAWK, and BOMARC were already in place; Sentinel seemed certain to become operational in the next decade, manned by both Regular Army and National Guard soldiers. This was American air defense at its height.

But defense planners were moving away from the concept of organized national air defense. Civilian theorists adopted the idea of MAD: Mutually Assured Destruction. This theory was based on deterrence by immediate and total retaliation against an enemy attack. MAD required far less determination and technological ingenuity than would ABM.

The ABM system that was adopted for use was Safeguard. This ABM was merely Sentinel scaled down to meet the needs of the civilian theorists, in other words, to defend the USAF's ICBMs. Safeguard would be based on a fixed phased array radar complex, with Sprints and Spartans standing by in missile cells. Funding even for this was slow in coming, and in the end ABM was canceled altogether after having been used as a pawn in defense talks with the Soviets.

Meanwhile, the Air Force was getting out of the field of ground-based air defense. Its BOMARC was never deployed as extensively as planned; except for the two Canadian squadrons the unmanned interceptors were largely limited to use in the upper Atlantic seaboard. Redesignated CIM-10 (Coffin-launched Interceptor Missile-10), the unmanned interceptors did enjoy a high operational-readiness rate. However, Canada made the decision to rid itself of its two BOM-ARC squadrons in 1971, leaving only three CF-101 VooDoo squadrons to provide air defense. The USAF followed suit in 1972.

ARADCOM found itself shut down, the logic being that if the United States was not going to defend itself against missiles, why should it defend itself against bombers? Nike-Hercules units were phased out, with a few remaining in service in Europe. HAWK continued to be modified and improved, but its deployment was mostly in support of U.S. Army corps and divisions; few were ever deployed to supplement Nike and provide the national air defense with depth.

The Air Defense Artillery would continue to guard the skies of Florida against a Cuban-based threat, but in the end even that was shut down. ADA's primary concern would turn to tactical, or field, air defense, although a promising missile project meant for combined ABM and aircraft defense would continue, if fitfully and painfully. Originally named SAM-D, it became known as Patriot in 1976.

The USAF's ADC was deactivated as well; the last of the SAGE centers were shut down. NORAD became an air defense command in name only.

10

Vietnam: People's Air Defense

One of the first combat tests of Soviet air defense technology was also the longest-running air defense struggle since the inception of airpower: the Vietnam War. It pitted the tremendous airpower of the United States against the Soviet-built (and sometimes Soviet-run) air defense of the small country of North Vietnam.

Air defense played an important role in an episode of Vietnamese history that made the very existence of the Democratic Republic of Vietnam (and incidentally the Republic of South Vietnam) possible: the Battle of Dien Bien Phu.

Following the end of Japanese occupation during World War II, the French returned to reclaim their colony of Indochina. Guerrilla warfare ensued; some of the freedom fighters trained by the Allies to fight the Japanese now turned against the French. Rebellion was virtually a part of Vietnamese culture.

The Vietnamese nationalists fought the French under a Communist-inspired front organization, the Viet Minh. The Viet Minh began a guerrilla war in 1946 that would last for almost a decade and demand the commitment of large numbers of French troops.

The French decided to lure the Viet Minh guerrillas into a set-piece battle that would favor the French Army by enticing them to attack Dien Bien Phu. By placing 13,000 troops at the isolated post, it was hoped that the Viet Minh would commit themselves to a conventional attack; the French would supply and reinforce their garrison from the air while bringing superior firepower to bear on the Viet Minh to destroy them.

The operation did not work out as planned. The Viet Minh committed 50,000 troops to surround Dien Bien Phu and place it under siege in January 1954. They were able to bring up field artillery and initiate a barrage that knocked out the post's airstrip in March 1954. Afterward, supply would be by parachute drop.

The guerrillas brought up antiaircraft guns of their Air Defense Corps and placed them in the hills surrounding the French post. The AD Corps had been established on 1 April 1953 to man the light weapons available to the Viet Minh, and already they were showing a true skill for air defense. Supply planes came under increasing fire as they approached the target; pilots became more concerned for preserving their lives than for dropping their supplies, and more and more often the supplies ended up in Viet Minh hands.

America's decision not to intervene to save Dien Bien Phu left the French in a position similar to that of the Germans in Stalingrad: Air transport could not supply the troops in the face of air defenses that daily became more effective. The garrison surrendered on 6 May, and with it French hopes to retain their colonial empire in Asia disappeared.

In the ensuing peace conference and the resulting political machinations, Vietnam was broken into two states: North Vietnam, or the Democratic Republic of Vietnam (DRV), and South Vietnam, known simply as the Republic of Vietnam (RVN). With North Vietnam intent on uniting the country under its communist leadership, conflict was inevitable.

The conflict evolved into two different wars: a guerrilla war in the South, conducted by the DRV and increasingly becoming conventional in nature, and the air war in the North, carried out by the RVN and its American ally and meant to bring the DRV to its knees and stop its support of guerrillas in the South.

As North Vietnam committed more arms and men to the fight in the south, American strategic planners logically deduced that one way of cutting off the flow would be to destroy it as it traveled down the Ho Chi Minh Trail and to eliminate its supporting infrastructure. The infrastructure consisted of the highways, railroads, ports, depots, and other facilities of military value belonging to the DRV.

American raids began as retaliatory strikes, such as the 1964 Pierce Arrow attack on PT bases after a PT boat attack against the USS Maddox or the 1965 Flaming Dart I attacks on Dong Hoi following a guerrilla attack against the U.S. Army's Camp Holloway. These were initially conducted with VNAF (Vietnamese Air Force), USAF, and USN aircraft operating from bases in North Vietnam and from carrier stations in the Gulf of Tonkin. The VNAF suffered particularly hard in raids against the North, as their tactics, training, and aircraft were largely inferior to that of their American allies.

Vietnam was a jet war as well as a helicopter war. The USAF and USN aircraft were designed under a philosophy that the next major war would be fought with nuclear weapons, that minor wars would not be fought for fear of nuclear weapons. Newer aircraft were all originally designed for carrying atomic bombs, and little training was done involving close support.

Similarly, the advent of long-range air-to-air missiles seemed to make aircraft cannons and machine guns obsolete. The F-4 fighter, in use in both the USAF and USN, had no guns at all, relying entirely on missiles. Combat over Vietnam would show that "dog-fighting" was still a necessary skill, as maneuverable MiGs took on America's best fighters, pitting guns against missiles.

As the United States committed itself more and more to the war, the conflict drew on wider resources. Bases in Thailand were secured for operations; and when B-52s were added to the attack force in 1966 for the sheer tonnage of bombs they could carry, they operated from U.S. bases as far away as Guam.

Passive measures were employed to limit the effect of American bombing. Nonessential personnel were evacuated from urban centers to the rural areas following an order given on 28 February 1965. More important, North Vietnam's modest industrial capability was broken up into smaller production units, camouflaged, and dispersed into the countryside.

Those people who remained were put to work installing one-man bomb shelters. The concrete cylinders could be seen along roads and avenues in cities, providing protection for individuals once their concrete or bamboo lids were put in place. More elaborate shelters were built where practical, usually at factories that were not dispersed. The DRV's 1965 Civil Defense Program had the ambitious goal of providing a shelter for each of North Vietnam's 18,000,000 people, a goal the DRV claimed to have surpassed by the following year.

Industrial dispersion resulted in lower efficiency and decreased production, despite whatever measures the Communists used as incentives. It did, however, prevent the destruction of the industrial base by American airpower. DRV industry was light and could contribute little to the war effort, but was important to the Communist party for ideological reasons as well: A Communist state building socialism on the Soviet model required an industrial base as a matter of doctrine.

Some of the DRV's industrial strength, its machine shops, assembly lines, and storage sites, were literally moved underground. They continued to operate in caves and deep bunkers, beyond the reach of the bombs. Others were hidden, camouflaged to look like peaceful villages. But there were still many targets, such as bridges and port facilities, that could not be moved. These would be protected by the "People's Air Defense."

North Vietnam's air defenses evolved in organization over time to meet the changing threat posed by the USAF. In 1957 the Air Defense Corps was upgraded into the Air Defense Force but remained under the control of the Field Artillery Command until 1962, when it was detached and placed under the control of the PAVN (People's Army of Vietnam) Air Force.

As a part of its active defenses, the PAVN's Air Force employed interceptors.

These aircraft were few in number until USAF intervention and consisted of older Soviet models such as the MiG-15 and MiG-17. Vietnamese pilots were of poor quality, and Soviet (and possibly People's Republic of China) pilots flew some combat missions.

Although North Vietnam's air force improved in quality as the war dragged on and as supersonic MiG-21 fighters were provided by the USSR, they usually restricted themselves to hit-and-run tactics. DRV jets would suddenly attack and just as suddenly disappear during missions; other times they would simply shadow USAF aircraft on their way to Vietnam, and on yet others they would never appear at all.

Communist pilots managed to bring down a few American aircraft, and the attack formations started to include a few escort planes flying MIGCAP (MiG Combat Air Patrol). MIGCAPs would position themselves between the mission target and the MiG airfields. The interceptors flew under Soviet-style GCI, a capability that improved as the radar net over North Vietnam improved.

There were some twenty older-model radars in use in PAVN's Radar Force, which was established on 1 March 1959, but no integrated air defense network to fully use them. On 26 March 1965, USAF and USN planes began what became known as "Radar-busting Week," one of the few instances in which the political leadership allowed the military to strike at the North's air defense net itself.

Nine radar sites were targeted, but the attacks met resistance in the form of antiaircraft artillery set up to engage the enemy planes. All nine sites were knocked out, but several American planes were hit and some went down in the process.

The USSR would replace Vietnamese losses in short order, expanding the net to 50 radar sites employing standard Soviet radars, and operating through six radar centers. Thanks to the radar network, the DRV could almost always count on early warning of attack.

Radar and civilian observers contributed to the early-warning network and its three-stage alert system. A preliminary warning might be given over state radio and over the public loudspeakers that were all over North Vietnam. A second signal was broadcast if a specific city was approached and public places were evacuated. And finally, air raid sirens would sound and the loudspeakers announced *"Nhan Dan"* when enemy aircraft were 10-15 minutes away. The system worked well for the urban centers, and other systems were improvised for rural areas.

In August 1966 the North Vietnam Army (NVA) arsenal possessed only 700 antiaircraft guns, and few radars. The state of North Vietnam's air defenses would change as the threat escalated and as the NVA defenses evolved, soon doubling and continuing to grow in strength throughout the war. The NVA was equipped with more Soviet and Chinese antiaircraft guns from the small automatic 12.7mm MG to the 100mm high-altitude antiaircraft gun. Guns were placed on rooftops, on street corners, almost any place in fact that could accommodate the weapons. The barrels of antiaircraft artillery became a part of the city skylines of North Vietnam.

The North Vietnamese gunners enjoyed an unprecedented amount of prestige as the war continued. A special decoration was instituted, the "Gallant Destroyer of Aircraft" Medal. The DRV issued stamps to commemorate their air defense "victories." This included the Viet Cong triumph at Ap Bac, the mortar attack on aircraft parked on the Bien Hoa airfield, and of course stamps that marked the number of "air pirates" shot down during the war. Stamps commemorated the 1000th, 1500th and 2500th (these numbers were undoubtably inflated for propaganda purposes) aircraft shot down by the ADF and ADMF by showing American planes going down in flames, thanks to the "valiant efforts of the gunners and fighters of the People's Air Defense."

Graffiti celebrated the air defense war in crude artwork. Soldiers and civilians would draw American planes being shot down by their gunners on the shattered walls of bombed buildings and in work areas. These were supplemented by posters and murals celebrating the small country's defenses against a world superpower. Air defense actually became a part of the DRV's culture.

ADF gunners studied the tactics of enemy pilots. The antiaircraft artillerymen "lay" their weapons to give them the most effective fire with a minimum of ammunition expenditure. The guns remained mobile enough to relocate and concentrate to defend the targets that DRV intelligence organizations warned them were going to be attacked. Important targets like the Paul Doumer Bridge could be protected by as many as 100 guns massed to put up a wall of flak.

North Vietnamese flak could be intense and accurate. Hanoi got its nickname from USAF pilots because of its dense antiaircraft fire: Dodge City. The name came from the inevitable jinking that USAF planes had to do to avoid the dense flak.

American pilots noted the presence of MiG-21s that would shadow but not attack strike forces. It is possible that these planes were used to scout the altitude and speed of enemy aircraft for ADF guns, transmitting the information to the ground.

Selected antiaircraft units were kept on instant alert, to react as soon as enemy aircraft were sighted. Combat Standing Teams, as they were called, were kept ready at targets that were frequently attacked. Gunners could be seen wearing straw "armor," partially for camouflage and as a minimal protection against shrapnel.

ADF gunners experimented with different site configurations, trying various shapes to maximize the effectiveness of their antiaircraft artillery. They found that triangles, diamonds, and pentagons were the best arrangements. Guns were well camouflaged when possible, using local foliage to disguise their locations.

Some antiaircraft units were manned by People's Militia. A significant percentage of the People's Militia were women, some units being entirely made up of females. A large number of lower-level commanders were women as well.

Many members of the People's Militia were armed by the DRV with small arms, including rifles and machine guns, and encouraged to engage the "Yankee Bandits" as they approached their targets. Although it seems unlikely that the thousands of factory workers, school teachers, peasants, and others who took potshots at passing American planes ever hit any American aircraft, much less brought any down, it did serve as a morale booster. It was better to be doing something than to wait helplessly for the bombs to fall.

Barrage balloons were also set up in Hanoi. There were no reports of success against enemy aircraft, but the balloons probably had a morale-building effect similar to the People's Militia small-arms campaign.

The Soviets began delivering Dvina missiles to the DRV in 1965 with Soviet support and even manning as necessary, the first missiles being deployed around Hanoi and Haiphong. In the air defense battles to come, the Dvina was deployed in a manner it was not originally designed for, against low-altitude, high-speed fighter-bombers. But through Vietnamese use of the missile, American forces were denied the high-altitude sanctuary they had enjoyed at the beginning of the war.

With the new weapons, Air Defense Force continued to man the antiaircraft guns while a new organization, the Surface-to-Air Missile Force, fought the enemy with the Dvina. In 1966 the SAM Force was detached from PAVN Air Force, renamed Air Defense Missile Force, and placed under the direct control of the Military General Staff Directorate.

Most of the Dvina sites were manned by North Vietnamese "missile troops," once enough crews were trained and available. Many of the Vietnamese crews were simply infantry drafted into the job; others had no military, or for that matter technical, experience at all. Soviet and East European technicians were vital to maintaining the missile systems, and some Dvina missiles were fired by Russians manning the controls.

Interestingly enough, because of the effects of separating the People's Air Defense into the antiaircraft artillery Air Defense Force and the SAM Air Defense Missile Force and by maintaining the interceptor forces under a separate organization in the air force, coordination would remain a problem throughout the war. The Soviets' reluctance to upgrade the ADMF with newer missile types also limited the air defense net on a strict reliance on the Dvina.

In deploying the missiles, the NVA rejected the construction of hard sites. Although the Soviets believed that the missiles would be better protected against attack by hard sites, the Vietnamese believed mobility to be a better protection and kept the systems moving among 300 predetermined sites. Because of Washington's strict control over bombing, there was no such thing as a "target of opportunity" for the U.S. Air Force in North Vietnam. This meant that missile units would not be attacked where they were most vulnerable: on the road.

Once a U.S. pilot spotted an incoming missile coming at him, the best maneuver would be to dive toward the missile and then break at the last second. The Dvina was not maneuverable enough to follow the aircraft and would detonate harmlessly overhead. Some crews fired the missiles in pairs, knowing that the pilot would be able to avoid only one missile at a time.

Inexperienced ADMF crews would sometimes simply launch all six of a Dvina battalion's missiles, salvoing them in an attack that would rely more on luck than on skill to get a kill. A salvo fire did occasionally serve a purpose in rattling a strike force.

Dvina crews occasionally set up flak traps in areas where they knew U.S. pilots would overfly on approach to targets. Soviet crews reported successes using these types of tactics.

On the other hand, the North Vietnamese purposely allowed some of the missile sites to be detected by raiders flying over the country. Knowing that a low-level strike would shortly be directed against the site, PAVN would move the missile battalion to a new location and replace it with a gun unit. Attacking planes would come in low, right into the waiting barrels of a North Vietnamese flak trap.

PAVN also employed dummy missile units to attract U.S. planes into flak traps. These decoys even employed cardboard missiles that on a fast pass appeared to be the real thing. Some fake sites were equipped with transmitters to simulate the radar transmission characteristic of the Dvina.

F-100 Supersabres flew flak suppression missions, flying ahead of the main strike force and hitting antiaircraft artillery positions with napalm and antipersonnel bombs. Later, flak suppression was turned over to aircraft within the main force as the antiaircraft artillery gunners would merely abandon their positions when they saw the Supersabres and take cover. Once the flak suppression aircraft were gone, the gunners would return to their positions. With the change in tactics the gunners had to remain at their positions during attacks, sometimes to their death.

Hunter-killer units flying what was called "Iron Hand" missions were later authorized to try to take out the missile sites—within "reason"; there were certain off-limits areas and a requirement that the site be confirmed as operational. The first strikes were disorganized and met with no success.

Then Iron Hand flights were handled differently: two or four planes flying formation against the Dvinas. The first plane, or pair of planes, would fly ahead of the second half of the formation to try to spot a missile site or draw its fire. Then the lead "hunters" would hit the radar van with napalm cannisters, the "killers" following with 750-pound bombs to smash the remaining elements of the missile site.

The tactics placed the attackers at a disadvantage, flying low where the antiaircraft guns were in their element. Many of the sites attacked turned out to be flak traps, and Iron Hand was considered by pilots to be a good way to get killed.

The next type of anti-SAM mission "Wild Weasel," was more effective. Wild Weasel aircraft flew escort with the main attack mission, arriving with the lead elements and leaving only after the last of the strike force had turned for home base. The planes were equipped to detect the enemy's radars and had a new weapon to go after them, the Shrike.

Shrike became the first combat-proven antiradiation missile. It was launched from Wild Weasels to home in on the Dvina's radar beam and follow the signal down. Even if it didn't get a direct hit on the radar itself, the resulting explosion would mark the site with smoke, showing the F-105s following the Wild Weasels where to drop bombs and Cluster Bomb Units.

The missile troops responded by shutting down their radars when they recognized the maneuver made by the Wild Weasel prior to Shrike launch; the move was distinctive on the radar's screen. With the radar shut off, the missile could not follow the beam to its site, so the Shrike was further modified with a memory feature that made it possible for the ARM to "remember" the location of the enemy radar.

Shrikes were available only in small numbers, especially at the beginning of the war, and before long the gunners would keep their radars on despite the danger. Wild Weasel pilots had a notoriously short lifespan.

Specialized jamming aircraft were secured for use over Vietnam by taking old B-66 airframes and loading them with ECM equipment. Some EB-66s were used as jammers, while others passively listened for the signal emitted by the radar, known by its codename of "Fan Song." Jamming by the use of chaff was practiced as well.

Chaff is an electronic countermeasure that employs long thin strips of metal that reflect radar energy and deny radar coverage to the enemy temporarily. Chaff was originally developed during World War II, but then it was rarely used by either side.

In Vietnam, fighters and fighter-bombers carried chaff in their air brakes, giving the pilot instant access to it with a push of a button. Chaff dispensers were carried later, lessening the bomb load that could be carried by American planes.

Raids against a single target became a massive undertaking, involving Wild Weasels, tankers, MIGCAPs, electronic surveillance aircraft, airborne radar planes, rescue aircraft, and finally the bomb carriers themselves. Virtual attrition of U.S. forces through specialization meant fewer bombs dropped on North Vietnam. The antiaircraft ammunition and SAMs being hurled upward at the attackers also affected their accuracy. The radio call, "SAMs up!" could result in premature bomb dropping by the attackers in order to gain maneuverability.

Because the Soviets wouldn't supply the ADMF with S-125 Neva or Kub missile systems, the DRV could not build up a missile defense in depth or rely on a mix that would be technically difficult for the USAF to overcome. Even though the Soviets would continue to provide improved models of the Dvina to their client, the fact of the matter was that the Americans were getting more and more familiar with the "flying telephone pole." As a result, the success rate of the missile system would decrease until it became a rare thing for a Dvina to bring down a plane.

Conventional antiaircraft artillery continued to account for well over half of U.S. losses in the North. The Dvinas often forced the USAF and USN planes to fly at a lower altitude, where they were vulnerable to heavy caliber guns and automatic weapons fire. The antiaircraft artillery was aided by American political restrictions as well, using "hospitals" as antiaircraft sites and taking advantage of the strict, target approaches and timing observed by enemy pilots. Informal control measures seemed to have been practiced, with the urban areas over Hanoi and Haiphong being de facto gun zones, off-limits to interceptors. American pilots reported MiGs being engaged by their own antiaircraft artillery as they entered the range of the guns.

To determine future targets, specialized reconnaissance aircraft were sent north. Most of them were recon versions of fighter aircraft, while others were a new innovation: remotely piloted vehicles, or RPVs. These jets were launched and controlled by mother ships that would remain safely out of range of the DRV's air defenses until the RPV completed its mission and was recovered with its valuable data. Though many RPVs racked up a number of successful missions over North Vietnam, there was also the chance that they wouldn't come back. The ADF and ADMF managed to bring down several and put them on display.

But throughout its war in Southeast Asia, the American pilots' greatest adversaries lay not in Hanoi, nor in Peking, nor even in Moscow. The civilian policy makers in Washington, D.C., full of their own theories on how the war should have been fought, laid restriction after restriction on American pilots, as seen in Map 10.1. As the total defeat of the North Vietnamese was not an objective in the war, the USAF was forced to engage limited objectives against an enemy that was willing and able to commit every resource it had available to the war effort.

One example was an incident in which a USAF patrol over North Vietnam spotted a train loaded with Dvina missiles headed toward Hanoi, where they would be immune from attack until they were distributed to missile units. The train was immobile and presented a logical, and extremely lucrative, target. Permission was asked to destroy the train before it escaped. By the time permission was refused it was irrelevant: The train had escaped, and American pilots ended up having to deal with the missiles one at a time.

To meet the political desire to minimize civilian casualties and to prevent the deaths of Soviet and Chinese advisors, the politicians demanded that raids be carried out only in daylight and in good weather. These were also the best conditions for the artillery, as many of the ADF guns were still optically guided.

Starting in June 1966, American forces began a true strategic bombing campaign, one aimed at petroleum products, or POL. The DRV's smashed rail lines left them with a heavy dependence on truck and boat transport. It was hoped that, by destroying the fuel and oil supplies, transport to the South would be strangled. The POL sites presented a vulnerable and concentrated series of targets.

USAF and USN aircraft hit fixed storage sites in Hanoi and Haiphong, bomb-

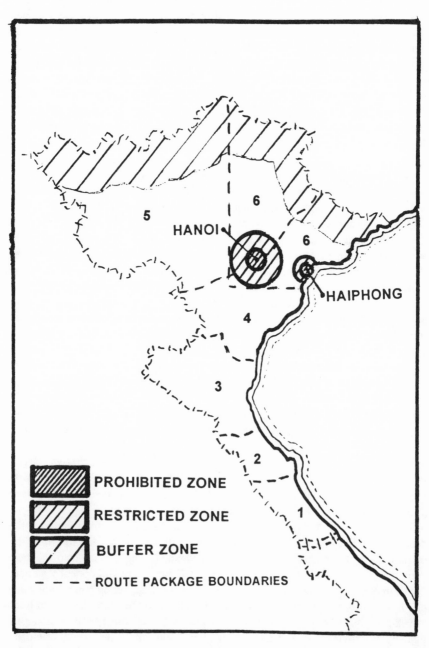

Map 10.1
North Vietnam: U.S. Restrictions

ing Hanoi for the first time in the war. In approaching Hanoi, the raiders followed a set of mountains that would became known as Thud Ridge (named after the F-105 Thunderchiefs that flew most of the missions). The ridge provided protection until reaching the target, as the steep mountains made the mounting of antiaircraft units difficult.

The attacks initially took the ADF and ADMF by surprise, but after an internal shakeup PAVN returned to take its toll. Antiaircraft artillery was relocated around the storage centers, and SAMs began firing in volleys against the raiders despite the danger from Iron Hand and Wild Weasels. Even Thud Ridge would cease to be a safe approach as guns were mounted among its steep crags with the use of Soviet helicopters.

POL supplies in North Vietnam did diminish, but they were never completely cut off. Communist tankers began avoiding Haiphong and instead unloaded at nearby off-limits Chinese ports. The POL could then be shipped by rail or truck to Vietnam. Storage was dispersed into sites all over the countryside, even if it meant siting a few dozen barrels in a village. As such sites would have been prohibitively expensive for the American air forces to hit, the campaign came to an end in September.

American planes were next given permission to go after the MiG interceptors that were becoming a major problem for the attackers. As the air bases were off-limits to U.S. pilots, the only way to inflict a crippling blow on the communist pilots was to lure them into a large air battle. This resulted in Operation Bolo.

Operation Bolo would rely on F-4s of the 8th Tactical Fighter Wing (TFW) to fool the air defenders into believing they were a strike force of unescorted F-105 fighter-bombers. They would achieve this by flying the same profile as a strike mission and using the same type of call signs. On radar and to the signal intelligence experts it would be just another Thud mission. F-4s of the 366th TFW would fly on another course to cut off any interceptors that tried to return to the airfield or fly to China once the ruse was discovered. The fighter mission totaled 56 Phantoms, loaded with air-to-air missiles.

The mission was launched on 2 January 1967. The 366th TFW was forced to turn back because of poor weather but the remaining 28 Phantoms of the 8th TFW were able to hold their own as MiG-21s emerged from the clouds to do battle. In the furious 15-minute air battle that resulted, seven MiGs were brought down, almost half of the 16-plane MiG-21 force that was currently in operation in North Vietnam.

A new emphasis was placed on cutting the DRV's rail link with China, but of course with restrictions. Because of political considerations, only a specific 40km strip of the line was targeted. So many ADF guns were concentrated along the line that American pilots gave the strip the nickname "Slaughter Alley."

A new-model Dvina system that was brought into use at about this time made life more difficult for the attackers. It had an optical tracking feature that made it possible to continue missile tracking in a dense ECM environment. The more effective Standard ARM also entered the fray, carried aboard Intruder aircraft. The Standard ARM had a much wider frequency spectrum with which to seek out enemy radars and also could be programmed for an off-axis approach, making it more difficult for the missile crew to identify the incoming ARM.

In March 1968 a temporary halt was placed on the war in the North, to show the Communists that the United States and the RVN were serious about negotiating. The DRV took advantage of the respite, repairing damage and improving the air defense while continuing to supply the uprising in the South.

In May 1971 President Nixon, frustrated with North Vietnam's stalling at the Paris talks, authorized the mining of Haiphong Harbor, where Soviet arms shipments were arriving. During the ensuing Christmas bombings of 1972, the USSR was unable to resupply North Vietnam with Dvina missiles and the DRV could not maintain the volume of fire after the first week. One mission of nine B-52s had 17 missiles launched at it during a raid, but after North Vietnam fired over 1,200 missiles the reduction in its stockpiles made it necessary for missile sites to cut back on firings.

By cutting off the supply of the "Guidelines," the United States was able to deplete the number available and eventually reduce their effectiveness. The USAF discovered that there was a limit to the number of Dvinas available for the 200 launchers ringing Hanoi and Haiphong after all. This may have been a factor in causing the North Vietnamese leaders to return to the negotiating table.

Even while the war over the north was being waged, streaking the skies of Hanoi and Haiphong with missile contrails and bursts of flak, the war in the south continued. It relied upon the Ho Chi Minh Trail, a supply route running from points inside North Vietnam through Laos and Cambodia, parallel to South Vietnam's border. Infiltration routes led into South Vietnam, where irregular forces were operating. Troops and ammunition ran through this conduit, sustaining the guerrilla war against the Republic of Vietnam.

In the South what air defense the Viet Cong initially enjoyed was either improvised or provided by NVA antiaircraft units sent down the Ho Chi Minh Trail to join the fight. An NVA Infantry regiment had an antiaircraft company assigned to it; Viet Cong regiments were equipped with the same whenever possible.

Part of the specialized training received by NVA cadres infiltrating to the south was devoted to air defense. The troops were trained in passive measures, as well as special tactics such as laying flak traps.

The USAF turned to interdiction on the Ho Chi Minh Trail itself, trying to cut the supply line. The NVA responded by moving in light antiaircraft units at first and then adding heavier and heavier weapons from the defenses in the North.

The Americans deployed gunships, relying on AC-47s equipped with gatling guns at first. Flying at night, the gunships could orbit around a target, their left-mounted armament able to pour fire into the enemy at its leisure.

These gunships would evolve over time, the airframe replaced by AC-130s with a larger cargo capacity than the AC-47s. More gatling guns were installed and supplemented by specially mounted 105mm howitzers. Radar and infrared sensors helped the gunners seek out and destroy the trucks and troops moving along the trail.

The NVA responded by installing a warning network along the trail to let troops moving along it know the gunships were coming. The NVA gunners watched the air action with their radar sets and would keep their guns silent until the gunships' escorts turned back for lack of fuel; then the antiaircraft artillery would open up. If the crew failed to hit the gunship with their first rounds, the gunship would return fire with its own airborne arsenal, destroying or at least suppressing the enemy gunners.

In late 1971 the Ho Chi Minh Trail defenses were upgraded for the first time with Dvina regiments. The USAF lost its first AC-130 to a Dvina in March 1972, and other gunships would find themselves being radiated by the missile system's radar. The relatively slow gunships would require more escorts and ECM to continue operating over the Trail.

Once inside the jungles of South Vietnam, the infiltrating NVA troops would camouflage their positions and harden them against air attacks. American operation planners could never be certain whether enemy troops were present during raids in the South unless they were involved in a conventional type of attack. The bunkers NVA troops built for themselves proved surprisingly sturdy against heavy bomb attacks.

The NVA tried to mount another Dien Bien Phu at Khe Sanh, as part of their 1968 Tet Offensive. U.S. Marines were surrounded, and their only means of resupply became through the air.

NVA troops massed every gun they could bring in. The flight path to the Khe Sanh runway was crisscrossed by gunfire; some guns lay directly under the flight path. Though the NVA/VC mortared the runway every time a plane came in, they never managed to close it. Planes and artillery turned the tables on the ADF and broke the siege.

USAF, VNAF, and USN aircraft frequently came to the rescue of the Army of the Republic of Vietnam (ARVN) and American forces, intervening with the use of rockets, cluster bomb units, and napalm. USN aircraft based on board carriers at Dixie Station, an operations point off the coast of South Vietnam, participated in missions over the South prior to rotation to Yankee Station, off the coast of North Vietnam. Operations over the South gave USN pilots time to familiarize themselves with the combat environment prior to being exposed to the dense flak in the North.

NVA troops could, and did, concentrate their weapons in elaborate flak traps to hit American aircraft. One such flak trap was set up in the A Shau Valley, when NVA regulars attacked a Special Forces post there. The mile-long valley became known as the "tube"; its two ridges were loaded down with hundreds of antiaircraft guns and automatic weapons.

As the American and ARVN forces began utilizing helicopters to give them greater mobility and firepower, the NVA and Viet Cong forces started employing antihelicopter tactics. If an enemy outpost was to be attacked, potential landing zones, or LZs, were identified beforehand. Flak traps were often set up to ambush helicopters trying to bring in relief forces, with antiaircraft guns positioned to cover approaches and mortars zeroed in on such clearings.

The Lam Son 719 offensive in early 1971 showed the perils that NVA and Viet Cong air defenses could inflict on American and South Vietnamese forces. The combined assault into Laos was aimed at cutting the Ho Chi Minh Trail with air assault and ground troops.

U.S. and ARVN planners knew that there were between 170 and 200 antiaircraft guns of various calibers in the area that was to be attacked, but the planned air strikes meant to silence the gun positions were canceled because of poor weather. The antiaircraft artillery in Laos enjoyed overlapping fields of fire to the LZ approaches, and 12.7mm machine guns shredded American helicopters in unprecedented numbers.

The gunners avoided opening fire on Cobra gunship escorts in order to ambush the transports that would soon follow. Cobras represented a new weapon in the war, a helicopter designed especially for the attack role. Previous American helicopter gunships were modified UH-1 Iroquois equipped with heavy-caliber machine guns and rockets. The Cobra was small and fast, and their pilots literally flew right down the barrels of many of the antiaircraft guns to silence them.

The helicopters had to follow the valley that Route 9 ran through, and the ADF crewmen were prepared to give them a warm welcome. Experienced pilots called it the heaviest concentration of flak they had ever seen, possibly even heavier than that of the North. As in the North, Dvinas were repositioned to cover the area, although none were launched.

To evacuate troops and casualties, ARVN troopers had to suppress mortar fire and automatic weapons fire on the LZs. ARVN and American support units withdrew, having accomplished some of their objectives but leaving the Ho Chi Minh Trail operational.

In the 1972 Easter Offensive the sophistication of the NVA fighting in the South rose another notch. Thirty thousand soldiers, supported by armor, drove south through the DMZ to attack ARVN. As part of the offensive self-propelled ADF guns made their appearance in the South for the first time.

The ZSU-57-2, along with towed 100mm and 85mm antiaircraft guns, leapfrogged to provide continual coverage for the logistics bases and other vital battlefield locations against air attack. The air defenses in the South were becoming markedly more conventional in nature. Strela 2 shoulder-fired missiles were carried into battle for the first time by the NVA soldiers to provide protection.

The man-portable heat-seeking Strela 2 was capable of inflicting minor damage on an aircraft under ideal conditions. Like the Dvina, the Strela 2 could be outmanuevered if the pilot spotted it in time. Its smoke trail made it easy to spot and made it easy to find the source of the gunner using it. Because of its heat-seeking mechanism, the Strela 2 was strictly a revenge weapon; in other words, it could get a lock on a jet only after it had already made a pass. The Strela 2 did succeed in forcing the Forward Air Controllers to fly higher and diminish their effectiveness.

Strela 2s, known to American pilots as SA-7s, were so numerous along Highway 1, Hue to Quang Tri, that American pilots nicknamed it "SAM-7 Alley." The sight of the smoky missiles streaking upwards was enough to make pilots drop flares or maneuver. Until the offensive was contained and a counteroffensive mounted, the Strela 2 would be foremost in the minds of VNAF and American pilots.

Following a 1973 ceasefire, the NVA/VC continued to upgrade their air defenses throughout the DMZ, the Ho Chi Minh Trail, and "liberated zones" in the South. American airpower had ceased to be an immediate threat but was still a possibility. Heavier weapons continued to reach NVA forces in Laos, Cambodia, and South Vietnam itself. The NVA/VC forces being built up would resemble a Soviet-type army waiting to go on the offensive.

The NVA began offensive action in late 1974, and when the March offensive met with tremendous success the NVA/VC initiated the final push for victory. Air defenses moved up to protect the NVA/VC forces that were now vulnerable to air attacks because of their conventional tactics.

As South Vietnam's cities fell one by one, the ADF set up radar-controlled antiaircraft artillery. The ADMF began moving Dvinas in to consolidate their gains and prevent a last-minute intervention by American B-52s. Dvina battalions even began setting up to the northwest of Saigon itself. The situation was rapidly becoming untenable for the South, as the amount of air defense firepower being deployed would have called for a serious effort on behalf of the United States to stop the NVA. Such an effort was politically impossible.

By April 130mm antiaircraft guns and Dvinas were on their way to set up outside of Tan Son Nhut airfield and shut it down. Captured A-37 fighter bombers hit the airfield on 28 April in the "Determined to Win" airstrike. American ADA units had been withdrawn, and South Vietnam's remaining air defenses were shattered and unable to deal with the only North Vietnamese air attack of the war.

As the situation worsened, the United States began evacuating military and civilian personnel from Saigon and other locations. As the last American and VNAF pilots left for the fleet waiting off the coast, they could hear tones indicating they were being tracked by fire-control radars. By 30 April virtually all Southern resistance was gone. The war was over.

Air defense became a key factor determining the course of the war. Without the means to fight back against the American pilots, the Democratic Republic of Vietnam would have had to negotiate a peace, or at least a truce. Its achievement was not merely the limitation of damage: Despite their intensity, the air defenses caused only limited interference with raids when American airmen attacked a known target. Rather, the air defenses gave the populace and the military some visible sign that the government was making an effort to protect them.

On the other hand, the People's Air Defense had its limits. The formidable air defenses never once stopped a mission, even though virtual attrition reduced the potential effectiveness of the missions. Losses never approached numbers high enough to make the American military or political leadership consider a cancellation of missions based on that factor alone; loss rates reached a high of .34 percent (by sortie) in 1965. But of those, 60 percent were caused by anti-aircraft artillery, rather than by missiles or interceptors.

The air defense of North Vietnam was a unique, paradoxical phenomenon. Although, of course, no air defense exists without an air threat, the success that is attributed to North Vietnam's air defense system would not have been possible without the political limitations put on American forces.

11 _____

Middle East: Conflict in Holy Skies

The modern history of the Middle East has been dominated by conflict, between the Arab states that gained independence in the postcolonial world, on one hand, and the State of Israel established following the British Mandate of Palestine, on the other. In this conflict, Israel has (mostly) been supplied by the United States and Western Europe; the Arab states have been well supplied for the most part by the Soviet Bloc. Israeli airpower has come to be a dominant factor in the Middle East balance of power, and in response Arab air defense has come to play an important role and in one case came close to deciding the outcome of a war.

Palestine was administered under a British mandate following World War I. Following World War II, anticolonialist sentiment, Arab nationalism, and Jewish immigration all contributed to an explosive situation in the small state.

Preempting the United Nations' plan to create separate Arab and Jewish states from Palestine, Jewish underground organizations began a War of Independence to prevent their people's annihilation by their Arab neighbors. The State of Israel was created in this cauldron on 15 May 1948.

For the first two weeks of the war, Arab air forces had the skies of Palestine to themselves. Iraqi and Syrian pilots mostly flew Harvard fighters, obsolete even by World War II standards, but the Egyptian Air Force possessed Spitfires and pilots with RAF experience. All three of the Arab air forces were small, but Israel possessed no planes at all until they began receiving Me109s from Czechoslovakia.

Until the surplus Me109s were available, Israeli antiaircraft gunners did what they could to defend the skies of their new state, providing the only means of air defense. Antiaircraft brought down one Spitfire during a raid on Tel Aviv, the first Arab plane to be downed by Israel.

On 29 May the nascent Israeli Air Force (IAF) flew its first sortie against an Egyptian column. The Me109s surprised the Egyptians, but not completely. Antiaircraft fire brought down one (the first Israeli plane to be shot down by Arab antiaircraft artillery), and another crashed on landing. Israeli losses on their first air mission was 50 percent, but more Messerschmits would enter service as they arrived in Israel and were made operational. Other planes would enter the IAF inventory before the end of the war, including Spitfires and B-17s.

Antiaircraft weapons consisted largely of French and British guns left behind after the years of colonial rule, along with whatever surplus weapons could be purchased. Bofors 40mm guns continued to prove their worth in the Middle East.

There was little in the way of coordinated air defense or strategic bombing by either side. Operations could largely be characterized as either bombing raids or close support. The number of aircraft involved was too small for much else, and neither side possessed weapons of sophistication. When the war ended in 1949, the technology was still World War II vintage.

Israel rapidly worked to build up a first-rate air force after the War of Independence. Formerly stymied by an arms embargo that made it necessary to access aircraft by subterfuge and guile, the Israelis were later stymied by budget constraints. More surplus aircraft were bought, including P-51 Mustangs and twin-engine Mosquitoes.

In 1954 the IAF got its first jets in the form of Gloster Meteors. Israel's 1955 purchase of Ouragan jet fighter-bombers from France marked the first time the IAF would get a plane that had gone into service after World War II. But finally, in early 1956, the Israelis purchased their first truly first-rate aircraft: the Super Mystere IV. The Super Mystere would prove capable of taking on even first-line Soviet designs.

During the 1956 War the sound of combat jets could be heard for the first time in the skies of the Middle East. IAF Ouragans and Super Mysteres took on Egyptian MiG-15s and Vampires, usually besting them as Israeli armor charged across the Sinai to the strategic Suez Canal. The piston engines of Mustangs and B-17s could still be heard as well, since the Israelis kept them in service despite their age.

Also, a new element was added as British RAF and French aircraft entered the fray to maintain control over the Suez canal. Although the IAF flew mostly close support missions, the Anglo-French air forces attacked targets inside Egypt proper. Much of the Egyptian air force was destroyed in these attacks, leaving Israel free to fly at will over the battlefield.

Israeli aircraft flew close support for the ground troops. They attacked and destroyed Egyptian armor, mostly T-34/85s purchased from the USSR. Such use of airpower was devastating for the Egyptians, leaving as it did entire columns of twisted and burned metal hulks that had once been tanks, trucks, and artillery pieces. The Egyptian air force did occasionally sortie against the Israelis, but they were usually bested in the air-to-air encounters over the sky. The sky over the battlefield belonged to the Israelis.

This air supremacy, both over the battlefield and in Egypt itself, was challenged by the occasional antiaircraft gunner. Unfortunately for the Egyptians, most of their gunners seemed to fire erratically. There was little in the way of good tactical planning to provide mutual fires—and no strategic air defense planning.

The ceasefire called at midnight 6/7 November ended nine days of combat and resulted in a humiliating defeat for the Egyptians. The return of the Suez Canal and the Sinai by a United Nations settlement did little to assuage the Egyptian desire for revenge.

Following the 1956 War, the IAF worked hard to become an all-jet force. Israel put plans in motion that would give it a domestic aircraft production capability while purchasing Super Mystere B-2 and Mirage IIIs. The last of the piston-engine planes were phased out.

The threat posed by Arab airpower was beginning to lag behind the Israelis in technology but threatened to overcome them in sheer numbers. More MiG-15 fighters were sent in to replace 1956 losses while superior MiG-19s also began to arrive in numbers. Mach 2+ MiG-21 interceptors also arrived, threatening to break Israel's slim advantage in air superiority.

The Six Day War of 1967 began with an Israeli preemptive strike against the United Arab Republic, a union of Syria and Egypt. War seemed bound to come sooner or later, so Israel chose sooner—on its own terms. IAF fighter-bombers struck airfields in Syria, Jordan, and Egypt in a daring first strike, blowing up the planes in protective revetments.

By 1967 the Egyptians had at least a rudimentary air warning system based in Cairo and were relying on radar stations to provide information on approaching aircraft. Orders to scramble would then be relayed to airfields where MiGs would wait on the tarmac on air defense alert. But the alert system was circumvented by the expedient of flying under the coverage of the radar screen. The only warning Egyptian fighters received was the sound of IAF jets seconds before their bombs exploded.

By attacking first, the outnumbered IAF was able to destroy the Arab air forces on the ground in less than three hours and soon had air superiority. Israel's control of the air greatly inhibited the Arab armies' freedom to maneuver. Israel had seized and retained the initiative and as a result won a stunning victory over its enemies.

Antiaircraft guns were so surprised that few of them attempted to engage their targets during the first raids. Besides, few of the airfields the IAF attacked had any kind of serious antiaircraft artillery; radar-guided guns were a rarity. But the intensity of the fire increased throughout the war, even if it was largely uncoordinated. During the 1956 War 12.5mm, 14.7mm, 37mm, and 57mm guns were available and in place throughout defense installations and with Egyptian Army units, but in 1967, for the first time, surface-to-air missiles took their place in the Arab arsenal.

The Egyptians had taken the precaution of installing Soviet Dvina missile battalions in the Sinai, housed in concrete "hard sites." The Israelis were apprehensive about facing the new weapons at first, but they found that the missile system was largely ineffective at lower altitudes. Some Dvina sites were captured intact as Israeli armored forces drove across the Sinai, abandoned by the crews before they could come under the fire of tanks.

American intelligence also gave the Israelis some help in dealing with the "Guidelines." The electronic countermeasures provided to Israel did not come cheap; they were battle-tested in the skies over Vietnam.

By the end of the Six Day War, Israel had occupied the Sinai all the way to the Suez Canal in Egypt and had wrested the Golan Heights from Syria. The additional territory gave the Israelis a buffer against Arab attack but left the neighboring states more determined than ever to destroy them.

Egypt and Syria strove to learn from the mistakes that led to the humiliating defeat of 1967. The result would be a marked improvement in the Arab soldier and his arms.

Military professionalism was improved. Soviet instructors instilled their students with a true sense of tactics and strategy in the new weapons being shipped from the USSR, which included new air defense weapons. The Arab states had been purchasing Soviet hardware for over a decade, but it was not until after the 1967 War that Arab soldiers were thoroughly indoctrinated in the effective use of their war material.

The leadership of the soldiers was better. Prior to the 1967 War, Egyptian officers traditionally abandoned their units to spend long weekends in Cairo. They enjoyed all the privileges of their rank, but little of the responsibility. That was changed when Lieutenant-General (LTG) Saad el Shazli became Chief of Staff of the Egyptian Armed Forces following the death of his predecessor during the War of Attrition.

LTG Shazli breathed new life into the officer corps, encouraging officers to show initiative and energy in their profession. He made them learn their craft firsthand by "eating sand" in the desert, fighting exercises alongside the troops. Shazli also developed what he called the calculated risk doctrine, an acceptance that some losses would always occur, even in peacetime. Egyptian officers throughout the armed forces were thus instilled with a bit of daring as well.

The position of O/C (Officer Commanding) Air Defense also got a new general. Hassan Kamal was dismissed by President Nasser after an incident in which two IAF Mirages managed to enter Egyptian airspace undetected and create a sonic boom right over the residence of the president.

Syria and Egypt turned to the Soviets to replace the equipment lost during the Six Day War, but this time striking a better bargain. The weapons given to the Arabs prior to 1967 consisted mainly of discards, good weapons but older models that were being replaced in frontline service with the Soviet armed forces. After the loss of virtually all of their equipment, the Arabs demanded and got top-of-the-line weapons from the USSR. Many of these weapons were just as good as if not better than their Western counterparts.

These changes were made during the period known to the Israelis as the War of Attrition. The period between the end of 1967 and August 1970 was not peace as much as it was an armed truce: Israeli pilots fought Arab pilots and their Soviet mentors, testing each other's defenses in the skies while on the ground there were sporadic commando raids.

At first, the Egyptians attempted to deploy their missiles in a zone west of the Suez Canal. The struggle that resulted became known as the Battle of the Missile Box, as Israeli aircraft conducted air strikes against individual sites to keep the missile box from becoming fully operational. The Soviet-built hard sites were easy to spot by reconnaissance flights, housing as they did the missile launchers and radars in concrete bunkers. Such facilities provided little protection from Israeli anti-SAM strikes.

The Missile Box mainly used Dvina and Neva missile systems. Israeli attacks focused primarily on the Dvina units, probably because of their familiarity with them. Egypt was determined to use ground-based air defense weapons to offset the IAF's qualitative edge in airpower, despite the newer model American jets then coming into service.

The Egyptians deployed the missile battalions in temporary sites that could be constructed overnight by engineering equipment. Sand berms seemed to provide just as much protection for the equipment but did not telegraph to the Israelis the intention of emplacing a missile site perhaps weeks before the site would be operational.

In the meantime Israeli commando raids against conventional-type antiaircraft emplacements, such as the sophisticated one at Green Island, continued to take place on occasion. In at least one daring operation, the Israelis landed troops well within Egypt proper to airlift a new Soviet surveillance radar intact for later study.

When a ceasefire was agreed upon in August 1970, the Missile Box was just beginning to become effective. The Egyptians claimed to have shot down 14 Israeli aircraft during the Battle of the Missile Box. The Egyptian Air Defense Command gained valuable experience during the struggle.

The Israelis also gained experience, but of a different kind. The IAF felt that the Dvina could be "handled" using the Wild Weasel tactics they had developed in battle. But the Egyptians had enough time to make a few local modifications on the equipment and to receive improved models from the Soviets.

After a 1970 trip to Moscow by President Nasser, Egypt began receiving newer air defense weapons. The USSR saw the deployment of its newer anti-aircraft guns and missiles as an opportunity to test the weapons that were taking a larger and larger share of the defense of the Soviet Union, as well as an opportunity to help out one of its client states. Although Dvinas and 1950s-era antiaircraft artillery were deployed to North Vietnam, these weapons did not represent the state-of-the art in Soviet technology.

Egypt received more Dvinas and Nevas, as well as Kubs, ZSU-23-4s, and Strela 2s. In addition to war material, the Soviets sent 15,000 personnel of the PVO, an entire air defense division, to provide the necessary training on how to operate the systems. This was the first step of a four-step program to take over the air defense of Egypt.

By the time President Nasser expelled the Soviets in July 1972, Egypt possessed a formidable air defense force, independent of the other branches of the Egyptian armed forces and probably a better service than many European countries had available. Seventy-five thousand men, or a quarter of the Egyptian armed forces, served in the Air Defense Command under Major General Ali Fahmy. These air defenders were well trained and in many cases combat veterans from the 1967 War or the Battle of the Missile Box.

The 1967 War was never far from the minds of Egyptian and Syrian war planners. Israeli tactical airpower had decimated the Arab field armies, destroying entire armored columns. The Arabs had depended on their air forces to protect them during the Six Day War; their air forces failed. In the new war they were planning, they would rely primarily on ground-based air defense for protection, relegating the air force to a secondary role.

Egypt intended to force a crossing of the Suez Canal. To protect the assault forces, they would have a defensive "umbrella" deployed in echelon, similar to the way the Soviet front defenses would have been set up. Surface-to-air missiles would provide high coverage while radar-guided guns would defend against low-flying aircraft.

As in Soviet air defense, each echelon, from the company up to the army, possessed organic air defense weapons. If a single aircraft were to attack a company it might have to fly against the company's Strela 2 gunner, against the regiment's ZSU-23-4, against the division's Kub missiles, and against the army's Neva and Dvina networks. In theory, an attacker is subjected to denser flak as he bears down on a single target.

Based on the western side of the Suez Canal, the Egyptian Air Defense Barrier extended over the ground troops massing for the crossing on the west side of the canal and at least 30 kilometers over the eastern side.

The Egyptians also used passive air defense measures, building fake targets such as dummy missile sites. While crossing the canal they built dummy bridges, which caused the Israeli Defense Force (IDF) to dilute their air attacks across the front. Concentrating on fewer targets would have made it easier to deal with the air defenses. To protect Arab aircraft from another IDF surprise attack, reinforced concrete hangerettes were constructed for individual planes.

Generally, the Arab air forces would be held back to protect them from destruction, with them rarely venturing forth to do battle. The interceptors might not play a role in the air defense battles, but would take to attacking the enemy en masse. This was done by shutting off the entire barrier, in effect lowering the curtain while the planes passed through it. Following these attacks, the curtain would be raised back into place for pursuing Israeli planes to run into after the Arab planes were safely back in friendly airspace.

Such simple air control measures were necessary, given the poor state of Soviet IFF technology and the difficulty the Arabs were still having with the tactics and operations of air defense. Fratricide would be an unfortunate element throughout Arab missile operations; among other Arab air losses, Iraq lost four MiG-21s on its first day of air operations to the Syrian Air Defense Barrier.

On 6 October 1973, it began. Egyptian commandos started to cross the Suez Canal in rubber boats, seizing positions on the Bar Lev Line. Combat engineers were soon building pontoon bridges over the canal, and beachheads were established.

Israeli aircraft were soon called in. They ran right into the Egyptian Air Defense Barrier, as seen in Map 11.1. At least 10 Israeli aircraft were brought down during the first afternoon: when the IAF planes tried to fly under the range of the Dvinas, they ran into the Neva and Kub fire units; below that, they flew into the waiting SA-7 gunners, Shilkas, and automatic weapons. Egypt had closed the gaps in its air defense coverage. Orders were soon sent out to stay a safe distance away from the barrier. The crossing continued unhindered by Israeli airpower.

In the north it was a slightly different situation. Additional Soviet weapons were shipped to Syria in 1972 and included 50 battalions of Dvinas and Nevas. Ten new batteries of Kubs were sent in along with ZSU-23-4s. Much of this material was deployed around the Golan Heights. Under tight Soviet control, these weapons were kept silent even as air battles raged above them prior to the outbreak of actual hostilities.

The Israelis were unpleasantly surprised therefore to discover a new and fairly effective air defense net operating over the Golan under the command of Colonel Ali Saleh. The IAF lost 30 aircraft to the Syrian Air Defense Barrier in the first afternoon. Clearly, such losses could not be sustained for long.

The Israelis responded with a four-day air defense suppression campaign that began on 6 October. Despite the fact that the Golan Heights was a relatively small area to defend and that the weapons and tactics the Syrians were using were the same being effectively practiced by the Egyptians, the Syrian Air Defense Barrier suffered 50 percent losses.

The attrition suffered by the Syrian forces could be attributed to the ferocity of the Israeli attacks and a few key weaknesses of the Syrian missile defenses. The Soviets apparently provided no long-range surveillance radars for the bar-

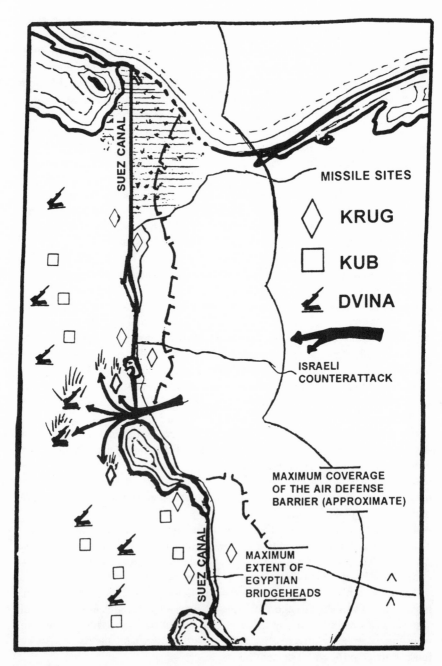

Map 11.1
Egyptian Air Defense Umbrella, 1973

rier, which allowed Israeli planes to get within strike range of the missile battalions with little advance warning. Nor was weapons integration fully satisfactory.

The intensity of the air attacks against the barrier was more than the Syrians were prepared for, and Israeli raids in the interior of the country also alarmed the country's leadership. The surviving missile units were withdrawn to protect Damascus and other strategic targets, leaving the ground forces on their own. By accepting high attrition for a short period of time, the Israelis won a free hand in the skies over the Golan.

In the south, Egyptian troops crossed the Suez Canal under the protection of air defense missiles and guns, while in the north Syrian armored columns made progress virtually immune from enemy air attack. But most of the Arab missile batteries remained in place during the war, and the coverage of the air defense barriers remained fixed. Though a few Kub batteries were carried over the canal, there were apparent problems reintegrating them into the barrier. Plus, the Kub suffered a long site preparation and orientation time (reportedly, six hours). "Down time" would have been a serious consideration for the Egyptians.

After a few days the very progress of the Arab troops began to work against them as they moved out from under the forward edge of the missile defense and became easy prey for the IAF. Until the Israelis could effectively deal with the new problem presented by the next generation of Soviet missiles, they would hit forces not protected by them as hard as they could.

Several Egyptian armored thrusts in the Sinai were repelled with the help of IAF airpower. The Egyptians ordered their forces to pull back under the protection of the barrier on 14 October and in doing so let the initiative pass to the Israelis.

The Israelis followed the enemy columns closely, but out of range of their antitank weapons. They brought up their long-range artillery and began to bring the enemy bridges and SAM batteries under attack. Meanwhile, IAF planes struck at Syrian and Egyptian targets not as heavily defended as the barriers. Local defenses were usually provided by automatic weapons, sometimes fixed in concrete bunker structures.

The Israelis, having forced the Egyptians to depend on their air defense umbrella to protect their troops on the east bank of the Suez Canal, then proceeded to knock that umbrella out. Operation Gazelle was put into operation.

First proposed during the War of Attrition, Operation Gazelle was based on the premise that Israel might not be able to defeat the enemy missile sites from the air. Instead, the Israelis would strike the batteries and battalions where they were most vulnerable, on the ground.

Operation Gazelle began on 15 October, as an Israeli armored column made its thrust to the canal. It carried with it bridging equipment with which to force a crossing to the west bank.

Having secured a foothold on the east bank after some spirited fighting, the

Israelis shuttled individual tanks on pontoons to the far side of the Great Bitter Lake. By dawn on the 16th the Israelis had a small armored force on the far side.

Israeli tanks immediately went to work, hitting individual missile units vital to the maintenance of the barrier. The main guns and machine guns of the tanks made short work of the radars and other support equipment. Faced with Israeli tanks, there was little the missile crews could do; they were simply not equipped with antitank weapons. In desperation, one unit reportedly tried to fire a Dvina missile point-blank at an Israeli tank, unsuccessfully.

As the Dvinas and Kubs were taken out on the ground, gaps began to appear in the barrier. Air defense coverage over the east bank ceased in some sectors, and the IAF took advantage of the gaps, working closely with troops on the ground to isolate and destroy the enemy. The IAF also continued to fly SAM suppression.

Neutralization of the ''Guideline'' threat was routine to the Israelis because of their experience with it during the 1967 War and the War of Attrition, but the concentration and variety of the air defense systems of the barrier as a whole precluded any simple solutions. New ECM pods were used, having arrived too late from the United States for the Battle of the Missile Box. Fitted onto Israeli aircraft, the pods proved only marginally effective in dealing with the Dvinas and Nevas and virtually useless against the Kub. The United States had more advanced models, but did not share them with Israel for fear of their capture.

SAM radars could be jammed and deceived in a number of ways. Broadcasting a strong signal on the same frequency makes it impossible for the radar to ''see'' anything in the area the signal is originating from. One ECCM is frequency agility, switching the radar's frequency so it no longer matches the jammer's transmitting frequency, clearing up the ''noise'' on the radar screen. Other radars are capable of ''burning through'' jamming through brute power or using a video system to track without the use of radar.

Another countermeasure is range deception, broadcasting a false return signal to the radar so that the target is indicated either farther or nearer than its actual position. Different counter-countermeasures can be used to counteract range deception, like the use of range-only radar and special signal discrimination.

Some electronic countermeasures are not electronic but tactical. Doppler radars depend upon the signal of an aircraft either approaching or heading away from the broadcaster. By going into a shallow curve, an aircraft can maintain the same distance from the radar, going into ''zero-doppler.'' Since the aircraft is not approaching or receding, the doppler radar cannot pick it up. Such a tactic cannot be maintained for long even by the best pilots.

IAF planes dropped chaff to confuse the radars associated with the Soviet missile systems and proved effective. The Israelis also reportedly exploited the ''dead zone'' of radar coverage directly above the missile sites, but this may have taken place during the latter stages of the war when command and control links were being broken and as mutual coverage was eliminated through attrition.

Against the Kub Israeli aircraft employed lo-hi-lo tactics, approaching the enemy air defense battery on a very low approach, hugging the ground to lose itself in ground clutter, "popping up" after passing the site, and then dropping conventional bombs, preferably on the fire-control radar. The aircraft would leave the way it came in, dropping close to the horizon while releasing flares to confuse any SA-7 Strelas the air defenders might have available. The lo-hi-lo approach took advantage of the Kub's slow launcher-elevation rates.

As the threat from the Egyptian missiles was lessened, the IAF began going after the canal bridges in earnest. The three Egyptian armies on the eastern side soon found themselves isolated as more and more Israeli troops were shuttled to the western shore. The Egyptians were facing complete annihilation when they agreed upon the 24 October ceasefire.

The IAF had suffered relatively large losses, mostly to the Arab antiaircraft artillery, with few aircraft downed in air-to-air combat. With the new Arab emphasis on a missile-based air defense, it would be logical to conclude that most of these losses were due to SAM engagements. However, most Israeli losses were due to low-altitude automatic weapons like the ZSU-23-4, incurred as IAF aircraft tried to dive below the minimum engagement altitude of the missile systems.

Arab losses amounted to over 450 aircraft. In contrast to the IAF, most of their losses occurred in air-to-air combat rather than to ground-based air defense weapons. This phenomenon would be repeated during the Gulf War.

The Israeli Defense Force/Army was provided tactical air defense through units of its Artillery Corps. Higher-altitude missiles were operated under the control of the IAF and were largely used in air base defense.

Israeli antiaircraft artillery has largely consisted of automatic weapons. Its 20mm, 37mm, and 40mm guns were available in various models, including the excellent Bofors and its upgraded L/70 version. Israel retrofitted U.S. quad M2 12.7mm machine-gun mounts into twin 20mm weapons. Towed and self-propelled Vulcan models were later purchased for use from the United States.

In heavier guns, the 3.7-inch gun inherited from the British provided most of the higher altitude flak, along with captured 57mms. In fact, several Soviet-made weapons would find their way into the Israeli arsenal after the IDF found itself in the possession of the battlefield.

American-built HAWK missiles were owned and operated by the IAF, who put them to good use. More versatile and electronically agile than Soviet SAMs, HAWK earned a creditable combat record in IAF service, beginning with the War of Attrition. On 21 May 1969 an IAF HAWK intercepted and destroyed the formation leader of an Egyptian raid, the first-ever combat use of HAWK. The U.S. missile system would also show its worth during the 1973 War.

The high-medium altitude HAWK was later supplemented by low-altitude weapons like Chaparral and Redeye. Chaparral used large pedestal-mounted heat-seeking missiles, while the Redeye was a first-generation MANPADS, a shoulder-fired antiaircraft missile. With the acquisition of these last two weapons, Israel had a good mix of automatic weapons, radar-guided missiles, and IR-guided missiles.

The IAF air defense commander for each airfield's antiaircraft weapons also held the position of base commander's assistant for air defense, a staff position. But Israel put little reliance on defensive armament, believing that the key to their survival depended upon the aggressive destruction of the enemy before they could scramble. Air defense was only needed in case a few surviving enemy aircraft managed to reach targets within Israel. Air defense of Israel could be characterized as "thin," relying largely on interceptors for protection. This is practical in a country as small as Israel.

In the aftermath of the 1973 War, Egypt made a separate peace with Israel, broke its close ties to the USSR, and instead turned to the West. Accordingly, Egypt slowly began to phase out its Soviet-designed air defense arsenal, purchasing Western aircraft while looking for new sources to provide spare parts and missiles for its SAM systems. Egypt also began producing Soviet-inspired indigenous designs, such as the Sakr Eye handheld missile system.

Syria turned towards even greater ties with the USSR. After the 1973 debacle they requested even more sophisticated weapons. They would eventually receive the S-200, a disquieting turn of events to the Israelis since the "Gammon's" air defense coverage would reach all the way into Israeli airspace, even from as far away as Damascus. S-200s remained under PVO control, however, and the Soviets threatened direct action against Israel should any attempt be made to knock them out.

A sophisticated command-and-control system was installed, and other losses to the Syrian air defense forces were replaced. One estimate claims that 70 percent of Syria's procurement budget went towards air defense costs. Syria's air defenses would continue to improve and be formidable, but Syria would later find that it was not as easy to expand those defenses into Lebanon.

In the meantime, the IAF turned its sights eastward, towards Iraq. Although without a common border with Israel, Iraq considered itself an uncompromising enemy of the "Zionist state." Iraq's Ba'athist dictator Saddam Hussein made not-so-veiled threats against Israel, threatening to use "weapons of mass destruction."

This was not all bluff. Aside from efforts to create chemical and biological weapons, Iraq also possessed a formidable nuclear weapons program. The Osirak reactor complex promised to provide weapons-grade material for a primitive fission device were it allowed to become fully operational. Israel was determined to prevent this.

Destroying Osirak would be a formidable task. Aside from the 960km distance to the target, the Israelis would have to fly over Saudi Arabian and Jordanian territory (a somewhat shorter route over Syria was far more dangerous).

Entering Iraqi airspace held dangers of its own, as Iraq and Iran were in a state of war and naturally would be more alert to intruders.

And finally, there were the air defenses at Osirak itself: 23mm and 57mm guns provided flak coverage of the site, along with Kub batteries. Defenses at Osirak alone may have been at brigade strength and there was a possibility that the air defenses of nearby Baghdad might overlap that of Osirak. The Iraqi defenders of the reactor were alert to the danger of a raid, even though they were expecting it from an Iranian source.

The 7 June 1981 raid of Osirak went perfectly, with no Israeli losses. Surprise was total as Israeli F-16s dropped chaff to confuse the radar-guided guns and Kub missiles. Some missiles lifted off, but didn't lock. As the Israeli force turned toward Jordan and home, the air defense of Baghdad belatedly began throwing up a barrage at imagined enemy aircraft. Osirak's dome had been cracked open and its reactor rendered useless.

Following border attacks from terrorist groups in southern Lebanon, the IDF launched Operation Peace for Galilee. In June 1982 Israeli armor rolled northward. Syria decided to intervene, first sending in its air force; once they started losing planes in air-to-air combat, the Syrians committed a portion of their excellent air defense arsenal into Lebanon.

The Syrians pushed an air defense force of 19 fire units into Lebanon, consisting of Dvinas, Nevas, and Kubs. These units were arrayed in Lebanon's Bekaa Valley to protect Syrian armor columns entering the fray. The air defenses were dense and had the advantage of calling in air support from bases across the border in Syria.

The Israelis defeated the Bekaa Valley defenses in a short, intense campaign. Seventeen of the 19 fire units were destroyed, along with 29 Syrian aircraft in air battles on 9 June, without the loss of a single IAF plane. Israel could thank its intense planning, using RPVs to scout out the location of the missile sites before their attack and then employing ARMs to take out the fire units. Reportedly, a new missile called the Zeev was employed. Ground launched, the Israeli Zeev would home in on and destroy enemy radars.

As the war in Lebanon continued, the Syrians next tried to regain the upper hand by deploying new weapons. Romb units were sent into the battle. Each of the large six-wheeled vehicles was a self-contained fire unit, able to detect and engage two targets simultaneously. Israel managed to knock out at least three of them, despite the fact that they were partially operated by PVO crews. IR-guided Strela 1s also found their way into the fighting: IAF aircraft knocked out several of these, and ground forces also managed to capture a few.

The Arab experience of war during the last 50 years has shown that the use of ground-based air defense weapons can hold back enemy air forces, but only as long as the nature of the weapons involved remains novel. Static defenses can be studied long enough to be overcome. The Arab nations turned to ground-based weapons after a disenchantment with their airpower. Thus, they were largely deprived of the interceptor element of what would have otherwise been formidable air defense networks.

Israel has solved its problem of air defense by aggressively striking at its enemies before its enemies could strike at Israel proper. The IDF fought to seize and maintain the initiative, making its enemies' forces primary concern survival, not attack.

Israel, ever concerned about its security, acquired the Patriot missile system from the United States to supplement and at some later date supersede HAWK. Recognizing the growing threat posed by tactical ballistic missiles, Israel also began a joint program with the United States to produce the Arrow ATBM system. But while being foresighted, Israel would find that it had not planned soon enough: The ATBM threat would become a reality before Israel could field either weapon.

12

Persian Gulf: Aerospace Defense Artillery

Never has a country been so reliant on ground-based air defense at the beginning of a war and never has one been so disappointed by the results as Iraq was during the Gulf War. On the other hand, never was a weapon system so underrated as Patriot was prior to the Gulf War. This chapter looks at two very different stories of air defense.

It was Kuwait that took the initial brunt of Iraqi aggression. Iraq invaded the small country with overwhelming force, employing heliborne commandos to seize key points in the emirate and to increase the shock of invasion while armored units crashed through the country's nearly undefended frontier.

The Kuwaiti Air Force's Air Defense Brigade was equipped with a HAWK II battalion, 35mm guns, and Soviet Romb, Kub, and Strela 2 missile systems. There were some reports of SA-7 Strela kills following the 2 August 1990 invasion, but it was HAWK that made the biggest dent in the Iraqi Air and Air Defense Force (AADF).

Kuwait had four HAWK batteries but insufficient manpower for all of them. One battery was inactive, and another provided training only. But two of the batteries were deployed south of Kuwait City, with one fire platoon operating on Faylakah Island off the Kuwait coast.

The Faylakah site was the first HAWK unit to engage the Iraqis, its first missile taking out an unidentified aircraft early in the morning of 2 August. The

Iraqis gave the island a wide berth at first, then attempted to assault it with two helicopters. One of the low-flying helicopters was destroyed, and the other fled. By the time it was forced to abandon its equipment, the HAWK Assault Fire Platoon had destroyed seven aircraft. The two Kuwait City batteries each took out eight aircraft.

The Kuwait missile sites and airfields were overrun. The small Kuwait Army and Air Force had fought well in some cases, and valiantly in others, but in the end the Kuwaitis were doomed. Some made it to Saudi Arabia while others continued the struggle underground.

Iraq's Army, flushed with success, was then in a position to continue southward, invading Saudi Arabia and possibly other Gulf states. Saudi Arabia and Kuwait's government in exile called for assistance, and the world answered.

The Coalition air defense net initially grew out of Royal Saudi Air Defense Force's 33 batteries under the command of Lieutenant General Prince Khalid Bin Sultan al-Saud (Prince Khalid would later become second-in-command of Coalition forces under U.S. Army General Schwarzkopf). For high- and medium-altitude coverage, the Saudis deployed the U.S.–made HAWK missile system. Lower-altitude coverage was provided by the French-made wheeled Crotale missile system and its tracked variant, the Shahine. The other differences between the systems was the Crotale's 4-missile launcher as opposed to the Shahine's 6-missile launcher, and the Shahine's superior fire control and engagement capabilities. Targeting was done with a radar on board the system launcher. The Crotale/Shahine missile had a range of about 12km.

To supplement the missile systems, some of the batteries were equipped with French AMX-30SA twin 30mm antiaircraft cannon, using a turret-mounted search-and-acquisition radar. The tracked antiaircraft vehicle was basically the same as the Shahine's and the AMX-30 main battle tank employed by the Saudis. Also in use was the self-propelled version of Vulcan, the M163, and a few other older antiaircraft guns with the Royal Saudi Land Forces. The RSLF also possessed the Redeye and Stinger missiles.

A tactical control center existed for Saudi Arabia, but it was not normally manned. A national air defense system would have been impractical for the country, considering how huge it was and how small a population pool the Saudis could draw from. Instead, air defense units were stationed near the few vital population centers, military bases, Gulf and Red Sea ports, and of course oil production installations. The guns and missiles would largely provide point defense.

The Royal Saudi Air Force (RSAF) was to play a key role in air defense, as its excellent planes could be vectored over the vast emptiness of Saudi Arabia to intercept enemy planes. Its well-trained and highly motivated pilots were among the best in the Middle East: Pilot-for-pilot, the RSAF was superior to the AADF.

Some antiaircraft systems were placed in hardened sites, just as the excellent F-15 and Tornado fighters were kept in hardened hangers. All systems were mobile to one degree or another.

The AADF possessed over 600 combat aircraft. Largely Soviet, Iraq also flew French and Chinese models. Of these, less than a hundred could be called first-rate or nearly on par with Western designs, including a few MiG-29 Fulcrums, the very best the Soviets had produced.

Iraq's air force had combat experience, of a kind. The AADF was used during the 1980–1988 Iran-Iraq War primarily in the tactical support role, much as the USSR's air force was employed. Iraq even performed Wild Weasel attacks on the few Iranian HAWK sites that were still operational. But Iraq's air defenses earned a reputation for fratricide: Many Iraqi aircraft wound up being shot down by Iraqi antiaircraft artillery.

Of more immediate concern to Central Command, as the deployment of Allied forces began to enter the country, was the existence of Iraq's tactical ballistic missile (TBM) force. Iraq had several different TBM variants, all based on the Soviet SS-1, NATO code name: Scud.

During the Iran-Iraq War both sides exchanged missiles in combat. In the "War of the Cities" Iraq soon found itself at a disadvantage: The Scud's 180km range gave Iran the ability to hit Baghdad (Iran also purchased Scuds) but made it impossible for the Iraqis to hit Tehran. The solution was to modify the missiles themselves, reducing the size of the warhead to save on weight and extending the size of the body to increase fuel and oxydizer capacity. The Al Hussein missile was a Scud with its 800kg warhead reduced to 250kg and with 15 percent more fuel to make the range 650km. This was used against Tehran. The Al Abbas was modified to reach targets 800km away, but the warhead was only 125kg. Ominously, this one was capable of hitting Israel.

The missiles themselves were virtually inconsequential as a military weapon: The SS-1 entered the Soviet inventory in the 1950s and was never particularly accurate. Iraqi modifications decreased accuracy even further; the missiles were capable of the large target areas they were aimed at, but nothing further could be promised of them.

But some of the technology purchases Iraq made on the open market pointed toward the construction of chemical warheads. Iraq already produced chemical weapons and had used them against Iranians and its own Kurdish population.

To deploy chemical weapons on missiles called for technological sophistication: The chemical agent would have to survive the freezing temperatures of space as it reached the peak of its curve and then the searing heat of reentry. The chemicals had to be dispersed near the ground, but before the missile drove itself deep below the surface and after the point at which the agent would disperse harmlessly over the target.

To protect the airfields and the ports against a chemical missile attack, U.S. Army Patriot missile batteries from the 11th Air Defense Artillery Brigade were deployed to the Middle East and began arriving on C-5 Galaxy transports on 13 August 1990. The first unit, Bravo Battery, 2nd Bn 7th Air Defense Artillery Regiment, was operational by 15 August. The 2-7 ADA had begun training with Patriot's new ATBM capability just the month before.

Patriot represented a whole new generation in air defense weapons. Originally conceived in the 1960s as SAM-D, Patriot was originally seen as a SAM having some capability as a missile interceptor; after all, HAWK and Nike had proved that interception was possible under controlled conditions, and they were originally designed solely to deal with "air breathers." This capability was eliminated during the arms limitations talks of the 1970s and while the system was slowly developing.

SAM-D took the name Patriot in 1976, during the U.S. Bicentennial. Patriot employed up to eight launchers per battery, each equipped with four sealed missile cannisters. Each cannister was a zero-maintenance container that would keep its missile protected until it was fired. Only one Radar Station was needed, providing both acquisition and targeting functions. Unlike conventional radars, the Patriot RS did not provide 360° coverage. Instead, it "looked" in a fan-shaped pattern, its so-called footprint. The missile system was controlled from a van called the Electronic Control Post, where data exchange and decision-making took place. Patriot battalions began to deploy in the early 1980s as the last of the U.S. Nike-Hercules units were being deactivated.

Even as Patriot was taking its place in Europe and the United States, the missile system was being reconsidered for the ATBM role. A Patriot improvement program provided increased radar capability. The PAC-1 phase, tested in the mid-1980s, provided limited ATBM ability with just slight software changes on the existing missile design. PAC-2, tested a few years later, involved hardware changes to produce a PAC-2 missile. The PAC-2 warhead relied on shorter reaction time, greater proximity sensitivity, and improved explosives to destroy the target. PAC-2 missiles were just reaching Army units in small numbers in 1990.

In the ATBM mode, Patriot looks at a narrow corridor (known as a "footprint") for the high-speed objects approaching at a steep angle, which can safely be assumed to be enemy missiles. Typical interception is seen in Figure 12.1. The operator had only a few seconds to decide to fire under computer guidance or to override.

In tests, Patriot had achieved a 100 percent kill rate against TBMs, but under ideal conditions. How effective it could be against Scud variants in combat was still an unknown factor. The simple fact of the matter was that there was no choice: Even though Patriot was given the ATBM role (again) after the fact, it was the only missile interceptor available.

Patriot batteries were deployed at first around the Dharhan-Dammam population center. Dharhan possessed a vital RSAF base where aircraft were arriving every hour with reinforcements for Saudi Arabia's defense, while Dammam was the port where most heavy equipment shipped to the theater would arrive. As more Patriot units were made available, Riyadh, Al Jubayl, Tabuk, and King Khalid Military City were provided ATBM point defense.

Not all Patriot units were committed to the defense of the cities. Other Patriot units were sent to the field to protect the ground forces from the unlikely pos-

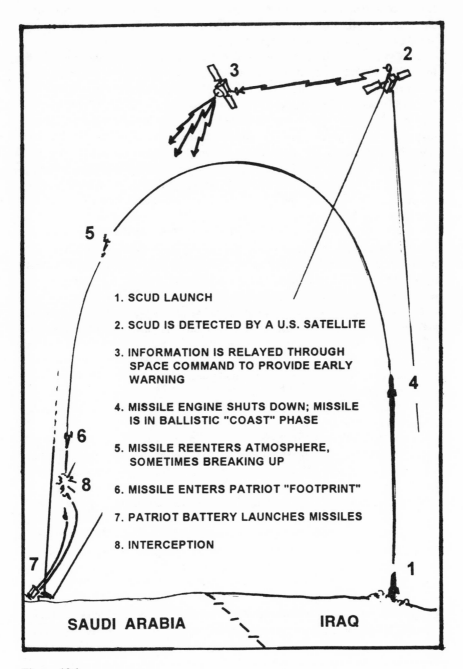

1. SCUD LAUNCH

2. SCUD IS DETECTED BY A U.S. SATELLITE

3. INFORMATION IS RELAYED THROUGH
   SPACE COMMAND TO PROVIDE EARLY
   WARNING

4. MISSILE ENGINE SHUTS DOWN; MISSILE
   IS IN BALLISTIC "COAST" PHASE

5. MISSILE REENTERS ATMOSPHERE,
   SOMETIMES BREAKING UP

6. MISSILE ENTERS PATRIOT "FOOTPRINT"

7. PATRIOT BATTERY LAUNCHES MISSILES

8. INTERCEPTION

SAUDI ARABIA   IRAQ

Figure 12.1
Patriot ATBM Engagement

sibility of a Scud attack on ground troops. U.S. Army HAWK was sent to work with Patriot in the very first air defense task forces, while USMC HAWK provided air defense in Marine Light AntiAircraft Missile batteries.

All available Coalition ground forces were deployed along the Iraqi border following the beginning of the Air War on 17 January 1991. These consisted of XVIII Airborne Corps on the left flank, VII Corps in the center, and the Joint Forces Command along the Gulf Coast facing Kuwait. XVIII ABN Corps was provided Task Force Scorpion for its defense, using 2nd Battalion 1st Air Defense Artillery Regiment (HAWK) for its core unit, augmented by three batteries from 3rd Battalion 43rd Air Defense Artillery Regiment (Patriot). VII Corps' air defense was provided by Task Force 8-43, with 8th Battalion 43rd ADA providing Patriot coverage and 6-52 ADA using HAWK. Joint Forces Command relied on Marine HAWK and lower-altitude AD systems for protection.

Task Force Scorpion was the world's very first electronic task force. Integration between Patriot and HAWK computers was made possible by improvements in both missile systems that took place in the 1980s. Even though it was possible in theory, integration had never been done prior to the war. ADA officers were unable to make the task-force concept work until their experimentation in the port of Dammam successfully resulted in data and command transfer.

In a HAWK-Patriot task force both missile systems were centrally controlled and shared source data not just between each other but also from outside sources such as AWACS. It was therefore unnecessary to have each fire unit continuously active (and thus increasing the possibility of detection); instead, radar coverage duties were rotated among batteries. Intersystem integration was another example of a force multiplier.

Divisional air defense was provided by Vulcans or Chaparral in U.S. divisions. The 3rd Armored Cavalry Regiment was defended by a platoon of Avenger HUMMVs, the first ones available to the Army. Avenger was a pedestal-mounted Stinger vehicle that could provide point defense against air attack with either its eight Stingers, augmented by a Forward Looking Infrared, or with its .50 cal machine gun if the target got too close to engage with missiles.

MANPADS Stingers provided a defensive capability, having superseded Redeye. The Stinger was an all-aspect missile that could engage an enemy aircraft from any direction, with a seeker that was resistant to IRCM. The handheld system also included an IFF transceiver. U.S.–supplied Stingers had proven themselves in Afghanistan; their employment by Mujideen gunners had prevented the Soviets from securing that Central Asian country.

The French Daguet (''Dagger'') Division, deployed with XVIII Airborne Corps, was equipped with Crotale, Matra Mistral, and Stinger missile systems. The single deployed Crotale battery was employed to defend the division's headquarters. Mistral, a short-range man-portable system, was operated from a small tripod that broke down for transport. The missile could engage targets up to 6km. Both Stinger and Mistral provided tactical defense for the troops, along with twin and single 20mm guns.

The 1st (UK) Armored Division was defended by Javelin and Roland missile systems. Roland had proven itself in combat during the Falklands War and had been adopted for service by several Latin and European countries. The Shorts Javelin came into service with the British Army following the Falklands War and had replaced Blowpipe as the standard MANPADS weapon in use with active units. Javelin employed a semiactive TV guidance system that makes IR countermeasures, the means usually employed against MANPADS, totally ineffective.

Syria brought its Rombs, Strela 1s, Strela 2s, and possibly the newer MAN-PADS Strela 3s to provide close-range air defense for its 9th Armored Division, while its divisional Kub missile regiment protected the Syrians from higher altitude aircraft. The Kub presented integration problems for the Coalition, as its Soviet electronics could not be integrated into the air defense net with the rest of the Allied HIMAD missile systems, nor could the Soviet interrogator sets interact with NATO IFF receivers on board Allied aircraft. The solution was to deploy the Syrian regiment in a "gap" between Task Force 8-43's coverage in the west and USMC HAWK coverage in the east. Coalition aircraft were vectored around the Kub's acquisition zone.

Egypt sent its 3rd Mechanized Division and 4th Armored Division to help defend Saudi Arabia. Air defense was provided by Strela 2s or their Egyptian-made equivalent, the Sakr Eye. Converted M113A2s provided mobile antiaircraft capability by mounting a French-made turret armed with a twin ZU-23 gun flanked by two Sakr Eye launch tubes on each side. Known as the Nile 23, it was augmented by a fire-control radar mounted on an M113A2.

Even the most pessimistic Coalition air defense planners knew that eventually the Iraqi air force would be destroyed. The AADF's aircraft were simply outmatched when compared to Coalition planes. But there was the possibility of what was called an "Air Tet," a mission whose objective would be political rather than military: to inflict as many Allied casualties as possible and bolster the voices of appeasement at home.

One possible scenario is illustrated in Map 12.1 and might go like this: Iraq would bring its planes out of their bunkers or from "safe zones" designated by the Allies to be off limits (the AADF parked its planes near mosques, schools, hospitals, and the like, knowing that to attack them would be too politically risky for the Allies). The aircraft would proceed to staging areas where they would be armed with air-to-air and air-to-surface missiles, bombs, and chemical weapons. They would then proceed to attack on a narrow front after knocking out at least one AWACS, which they could accomplish if they were willing to accept high casualties.

Once past the area where fighter patrols were active, the remaining Iraqi planes would be free to attack one or two major targets, causing enormous casualties. Few of Iraq's aircraft would return from such an attack, but they would have the opportunity to cause disaffection in the Coalition rear and possibly create rifts and recrimination among the Allies. After all, the AADF was

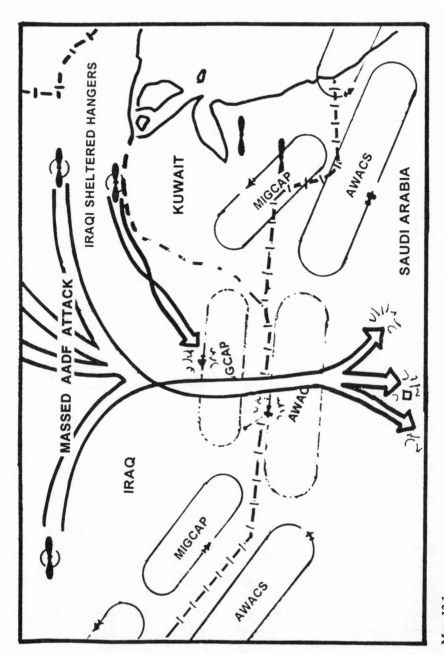

Map 12.1
One Scenario: Air Tet

accomplishing nothing by trying to avoid the bombs except to slow the rate of attrition.

Such a plan made no sense militarily, but was militarily feasible. In fact, such a "Mini Tet" took place when Iraqi armored forces unexpectedly crossed the border from Occupied Kuwait and took the Saudi town of Khafji on 29 January 1991. The Battle of Khafji accomplished nothing, indeed could not accomplish anything. It was merely the sacrifice of at least one mechanized infantry division.

If Saddam was willing to sacrifice a division, he might be willing to throw away his air force. Therefore it was necessary for the task forces not only to protect the corps but also to provide an air defense net that paralleled the Iraqi border and provided a de facto shield that any air attacker would have to pass through to reach targets in Saudi Arabia. Incidentally, the net also screened the redeployed Coalition ground forces from detection by RPVs, which Iraq possessed in numbers. Rear areas not covered by Patriot or Saudi HAWK were defended by a few United Arab Emirates HAWK batteries that were rotated in country. The air defense net was centrally controlled from a forward Tactical Operations Center located in King Khalid Military City (KKMC).

Either Patriot or HAWK covered the common border as far west as Rafha, and most of the frontier was protected by both. Various Allied SHORAD weapons provided low-altitude coverage. Their dissimilarity would have normally been a weakness, but it actually may have been a strength in the case of the Gulf War: Not knowing whether they might face Vulcans, Rapiers, Chaparrals, Crotales, Strela 1s, 20mm guns, Nile 23s, Javelins, or Stingers must have been a nightmare for any Iraqi officer planning a mission against Coalition forces.

To form the air defense net, air defense units with VII Corps and XVIII Corps were redeployed from a defense in depth of the Coalition divisions in their holding areas in the Eastern Province to the Saudi border with Iraq (Joint Forces Command was already positioned for its role in the war). The "Hail Mary" Move took place immediately after the Air War began on 17 January 1991.

Instead of using their air force, the Iraqis responded with their Scud missiles the following day. Scuds were aimed at Israel and Saudi Arabia. As air raid sirens wailed, "A" Battery, 2-7 ADA succeeded in the first combat missile-on-missile interception, destroying a Scud missile over Dhahran. It would not be the last, as further Scud attacks would be aimed at Damman, Riyadh, KKMC, and the tiny Gulf emirate of Bahrain. The sound of air-raid sirens or field alarms would become familiar to virtually any soldier or civilian in Saudi Arabia.

Air-raid sirens would also sound in Israel as Iraq began targeting it with its arsenal of missiles. Israel had been working with the United States to build its own Arrow ATBM system and in the meantime was acquiring Patriot but had no operational units available when the Gulf War broke out. In a diplomatic move vital to preserving the Coalition, the United States deployed Task Force Patriot-Defender from 32nd Army Air Defense Command in Germany. The task force was Patriot-pure, composed of fire units from 4-43 ADA and 1-7 ADA and later supplemented by two Israeli units that were rushed into operation.

The Defense of Israel was vital to the Coalition in order to keep Iraq from drawing it into the Gulf conflict. Protecting the Israeli people from the Scud missiles was of course the foremost concern of the Israeli government, especially since Saddam Hussein had promised that in a war the country would be ''consumed in fire.'' This was generally perceived to mean chemical weapons would be used against Israel.

If Iraq were willing to strike at Israel, it might also attack Turkey, which was not actively participating in the war but was providing air bases from which Coalition attacks could take place. Task Force Proven Force, a USAF organization, incorporated 4-7 ADA (Patriot) units deployed from Germany to protect the airfields from missile or air attacks. As part of its commitment to defending a NATO ally, the Netherlands also sent Patriot units. Short-range air defense was provided by Turkish forces. Iraq never launched Scuds at Turkey, perhaps for fear of involving even more countries in the conflict.

The campaign against the Scud missiles was actually twofold. Enormous effort was put into locating and destroying the mobile launchers and the permanent launch sites, which drew sorties that might otherwise have been used against other vital military targets. Iraq turned out to have more missiles than U.S. intelligence had believed at the beginning of the war, and despite the Allies' best efforts Scuds remained difficult to find and destroy. Iraq continued to launch Scuds right up to the very end of the war, and once launched the missiles could only be intercepted by Patriot.

Almost every night of the war was punctuated by the wail of air-raid sirens, then the sudden launch of a Patriot missile streaking upward, to explode just a few hundred meters above the ground. The scenes of the Patriot intercepting Scud missiles were beamed around the world as Allied airmen and soldiers risked staying above ground to view the ''fireworks.''

Patriot, after being armed with PAC-2 missiles, achieved a 70 percent interception rate in Saudi Arabia and a 40 percent rate in Israel, an interception being defined as a warhead kill or a mission kill. A warhead kill resulted in the total destruction of the warhead, nullifying its capacity to destroy. A mission kill resulted when a Patriot exploded close enough to the missile to divert it from its target or reduce its destructive capacity.

Unlike the prewar targets, Scuds tended to break up in flight, due to the shoddy workmanship of the Iraqis during their modification. This degraded their accuracy even further, but the erratic, unpredictable behavior of the Scuds made it difficult for the Patriot computer to deal with the intercept problem. The Scuds aimed at Israel were more extensively modified and would break up sooner in their flight, showing a greater tendency towards erratic behavior and resulting in fewer intercepts.

Iraq's only hope to cause significance damage in either Israel or Saudi Arabia was to saturate a single target with as many missiles as could be fired simultaneously. With a finite number of Patriot missiles available per fire unit, this was militarily feasible. But this option proved unworkable for the shattered Iraqi command and control network. One attempt at saturation was apparently caught prior to launch, and the missile force was destroyed before the Iraqis could fire their missiles at Israel.

In the end, between the inaccuracy of the weapons and Patriot intercepts, only 14 of the 91 Scuds launched actually struck the targets they were aimed at. None of them were armed with chemicals, although U.N. weapon inspectors discovered such warheads following the war.

Another Iraqi weapon that Coalition air defense would have been called upon to deal with was the so-called Supergun. It was a long-range weapon designed by a renegade Canadian scientist for Saddam Hussein, in theory capable of reaching Israel with its huge shells. Fortunately for the Coalition, the gun was not complete; in any case Patriot probably would have been able to destroy the incoming projectiles much as it destroyed Scud missiles.

AADF aircraft were largely destroyed by interceptors before they could ever reach the air defense net. Saddam Hussein authorized suicide raids for any pilot that wished to conduct one, but it seemed that no one volunteered. Most of Iraq's other planes were destroyed as their bunkers were destroyed with ''smart'' weapons, but the Coalition never succeeded in destroying all of Iraq's planes. The possibility of Air Tet, though lessened every day, was never completely eliminated.

Soon after the beginning of the Air War, AADF aircraft began to flee to Iran. The exact status of the Iraqi warplanes is still unclear; were the pilots defectors or were they under orders to deliver their warplanes to Iran to prevent their destruction? During the war, it appeared that the two countries might have struck a deal, a deal that could have included allowing Iraqi planes to operate from ''safe havens'' in Iran.

Afterward, none of the 150 AADF planes that fled to Iran were returned to the Iraqi government. Soon, they were appearing with Iranian insignia. If there was a deal struck between the two countries, it was not honored by the Iranians.

It should have come as no surprise that the very first Iraqi target struck was an air defense facility. U.S. Army helicopters crossed the border and struck a surveillance radar site south of the town of As Salman. Once knocked out, the Iraqi radar net had a gap along its border through which F-15 fighter-bombers entered to destroy the nearest air defense command post. It would be the first of many to be destroyed.

General Schwarzkopf was determined to ''attrit'' the Iraqi divisions facing the Coalition by cutting off their supply routes, destroying their supporting infrastructure, and bombing them directly prior to invading Iraq and liberating Kuwait. This was a tall order, as much of the road networks, telephone lines, power grids, and water supplies normally used by the civilian populace were drafted to support the Iraqi armed forces, or could do so in an emergency. An additional objective for the Coalition was the destruction of Hussein's nuclear, biological, and chemical weapon programs.

This could be accomplished only if the Allies possessed absolute control of the air. To gain such control, they would have to defeat the Iraqi Air Defense Force.

The Integrated Air Defense System (IADS) used by Iraq was centrally controlled from Baghdad, coordinating all elements of the Air Defense Force (IADF), a branch subordinate to the AADF and under command of Lieutenant General Hamid Sha'aben al Khazraji. IADS controlled IADF fighters, surface-to-air missiles, and antiaircraft guns through radio and possibly fiber optics, a relatively new communications technology.

The IADF was divided into air defense sectors, each with its own assigned acquisition radars, interceptors, guns, and missiles. Sector command posts were placed in above-ground, reinforced concrete bunkers from which they could receive information from subordinate units, send out orders, and maintain contact with the central command post. IADS computers were housed in the bunkers. Such an integrated air defense system can be seen in Figure 12.2.

IADF interceptors were controlled by GCI, much as their Soviet counterparts were; these quickly ceased to be a factor in the war, as the ground-based radars they depended on were knocked out. Iraqi air defense pilots probably had as little initiative as their Soviet counterparts. They rarely tried to intercept Coalition aircraft and after the first few days rarely flew at all except to flee to Iran. What success Iraq would enjoy would be due entirely to its antiaircraft artillery.

Iraq's antiaircraft artillery consisted mainly of Soviet systems; ZU2, ZU4, ZU-23-4, ZU-57-2, KS-12, KS-19, KS-30, and S60 guns, Strela 2, Strela 3, and Igla MANPADS, and Dvina, Neva, Kub, Romb, Strela 1, and Strela 10 mobile SAMs. These were augmented by some Roland and Mistral missile systems purchased from France, as well as some Swiss-made Skyguard radar-controlled guns presumably captured from Iran. Kuwait's HAWK batteries had been captured during Iraq's invasion, and it was assumed that the system might be used by the Iraqis. In all, Iraq had some 7,000 antiaircraft guns and perhaps 16,000 individual surface-to-air missiles.

Theoretically, such a variety of weapons, if deployed in large enough numbers and effectively controlled, should have formed a formidable air defense barrier, one nearly impossible to breach. However, the very centralized nature of the system turned out to be its primary weakness.

Few Iraqi radars were operating at the time of the first attacks. Realizing that the Coalition possessed excellent electronic intelligence-gathering aircraft, the IADF limited their emissions. As a result, few of the first attacking aircraft were detected as they approached their primary target: the air defense net itself.

Sea-launched cruise missiles were part of the first wave, hitting targets all across the country, including Baghdad. Fired from the Red Sea and the Persian Gulf, the missiles were small and hugged the ground as they followed their

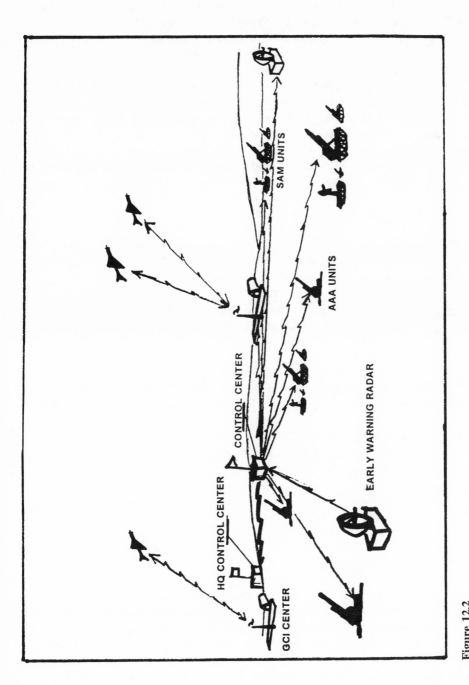

Figure 12.2
A Typical Integrated Air Defense System

preprogrammed routes. They were nearly impossible to detect, much less hit, although the Iraqis did succeed in shooting down a few of them.

Stealth planes were the only manned aircraft used to strike at Baghdad, Iraq's capital and an area which contained many military targets because of the nature of the country's centralized totalitarian regime. It was correctly assumed that the city would be heavily defended. F-117A Nighthawk fighter-bombers were not totally invisible to radar but presented a far smaller radar signature, lessening the amount of time radar-guided missiles and guns would have to react and engage. Stealth pilots considered themselves the masters of the night as they dropped their bombs with pinpoint accuracy.

Stealth fighters, cruise missiles, and conventional aircraft all struck at targets simultaneously or nearly simultaneously all over Iraq, concentrating on command-and-control nodes like the air defense sector command posts, as well as vital radars. The Iraqi air defense net began to unravel as first the national command post was knocked out and the sector command posts were isolated. The isolated posts were blinded if not knocked out, and poorly operated. IADS never recovered from the shock of the first few days of the Gulf War, showing that while the Iraqis might be able to buy such a sophisticated system they did not have the means to fix it. Soon, the system was reduced to isolated missile and antiaircraft gun units, each fighting its own little war for survival. *

Isolated air defense units were dealt with by Suppression of Enemy Air Defense (SEAD) tactics. With no mutual support by other units, they were comparatively easy to eliminate.

Iraq was operating pretty much the same radar-guided missiles used during the Vietnam War and the October 1973 War, so ECM pods were already available for dealing with IADF weapons. Wild Weasel aircraft took a heavy toll of SAM sites: USAF F-4Gs, USN F/A-18s, and RAF Tornados sought out and destroyed missile sites with ARMs, the HARM in the case of U.S. forces and the ALARM when launched from British aircraft.

Electronic warfare aircraft escorting attack aircraft could render the fire control radars of SAMs and antiaircraft artillery useless, blinding them or causing them to get misleading information. Strike aircraft could use the emissions from fire control radars to locate and destroy the weapons, but radar-guided guns rarely employed their fire-control equipment for fear of detection and instead would usually just fire at sound, an extremely ineffective technique against jet aircraft.

Iraqi gunners often sprayed the skies with blind bursts of flak when their receivers picked up escort jamming. After Allied pilots realized this, they would often jam targets they had no intention of bombing, causing the Iraqis to waste their ammunition.

The night skies over major Iraqi cities were often lit up with tracers arching upward and tracer streams searching the skies. One of the few Iraqis to earn the respect of Coalition pilots was an antiaircraft gunner they nicknamed the Red Rope Ranger. The Red Rope Ranger got his name from the tracer stream fired almost straight upward every night of the Air War, flying into the sky from Bubiyan Island. The red tracer stream could be seen by Coalition pilots as they flew towards targets in Kuwait, the single gunner prominent against the huge volume of flak being fired over Kuwait City just over the horizon.

The single gunner on Bubiyan became a target for Coalition pilots returning to their bases. If they had unexpended ammunition they would make a point of dropping it on the Red Rope Ranger, even though he was accomplishing nothing with his antics and so far as Central Command knew he was not defending anything of military significance. Thus, tons of munitions were dropped on a target that otherwise warranted none at all.

Despite the tons of bombs being dropped on him, the Red Rope Ranger continued firing his lone gun until the last day of the war. As it turned out, the Iraqi gunner was busy attracting attention to an infantry brigade that Coalition intelligence didn't even know was on Bubiyan Island.

Some SAM units launched their missiles "blind," without radar. These unguided missiles would claim no downed aircraft, requiring blind luck to hit their targets.

The United States and its Allies used other technological advantages to overwhelm the Iraqis. Cruise missiles were very effective because of their accuracy, the virtual lack of countermeasures available against them, their ability to evade detection, and the fact that there was no pilot to be concerned about. Air-breathing cruise missiles were not fast, but they were small. They fly close to the ground, checking preprogrammed maps against the terrain they were following. Often, cruise missiles followed roads, and one was observed in Baghdad flying down a street and making a right-hand turn to hit its target.

Cruise missile accuracy seemed to go down after the initial phase of the war. As many of the landmarks used by the cruise missiles were in fact targets for other missiles or aircraft, as the Iraqi landscape became devastated by Coalition airpower it became unrecognizable to the cruise missiles' computer memory.

Stealth technology was never defeated by the Iraqis. None of the 42 aircraft lost because of combat actions were F-117s, even though every target hit in Baghdad was struck by Nighthawks if not taken out by cruise missiles.

The physical design of the F-117A helped it avoid detection, utilizing flat surfaces to deflect radar waves instead of reflecting them back to their source and buffers to suppress and redirect the IR signature. The plane itself was made of special radar-absorbing materials.

Stealth technology is not cheap. If the composite material were replaced by gold of the same weight, it would be only slightly more expensive. The justification of the cost of the planes is that Stealth planes can attack targets with absolute impunity. Yet with the defeat and total collapse of the Iraqi air defense net, all aircraft were de facto stealth aircraft. Yet there were still Coalition air losses right up to the end of the war; stealth did not mean invulnerability to air defense.

But Coalition losses were light, far lighter than most analysts thought they would be. After the IADF was defeated during the Air War, it set the stage for the Ground War. The emphasis of Coalition airpower switched from the strategic to the tactical, with attack aircraft conducting interdiction strikes to isolate the battlefield. The battlefield meant southern Iraq and Kuwait itself.

Such attacks were fought with small arms, MANPAD missiles, and automatic antiaircraft weapons. Visually aimed or passively guided, these weapons could not be easily countered, yet they did little to stem the Allied tide. Coalition aircraft would go out of their way to destroy any location from which antiaircraft fire originated as they flew in support of the ground troops, and most Iraqi units were so demoralized by the time the Ground War came that they felt little incentive to risk their lives in such a pointless engagement.

Some tactical air defense weapons were withdrawn from the troops to defend the Scud launch sites, just as some tactical aircraft from the Coalition forces were diverted from attack missions on behalf of the Ground Forces to "Scud-hunting" duty. The USAF could do little about the missiles once they had been launched, but they could try to destroy them before they lifted off.

The defense of the launch sites was as unsuccessful as that of the rest of the country. Coalition aircraft never managed to find and destroy all the Scud Trans-port-Erector-Launchers, but they made the crews live in fear of their lives every time they fired and defeated several missile attacks before they ever took place. Scud hunting was much like the Allied air missions against V-2 sites at the end of World War II.

The failure of the IADF was hardly total, but it was enough for Saddam Hussein. Lieutenant General Khazraji was reported executed shortly after the beginning of the Air War. He was not present to see the contrast of end results for both the Coalition and Iraq.

On one hand, the Coalition achieved all post-invasion air kills in air-to-air combat (or by small-arms fire as Iraqi air bases were overrun). The only excep-tion was the ATBM intercepts made by Patriot; no other ground-based air de-fense system had the opportunity to destroy the enemy.

Iraq achieved all its aerial kills with ground-based antiaircraft weapons. Its combat aircraft never shot down a single Coalition plane, but its gun batteries and missile battalions succeeded in bringing down 39 aircraft of all types, only slightly twice as many as were lost for noncombat reasons.

The Gulf War was a vindication for antiaircraft artillery. Even without a sophisticated air defense network coordinating its missiles, guns, and intercep-tors, indeed, without the interceptors at all, Iraq still managed to shoot down some of the most sophisticated aircraft ever built. However sophisticated, air-planes were still vulnerable to ground fire.

For the Coalition and the war against the Scuds, Patriot not only proved to be militarily effective but also important for morale. Just as the sound and sight of British antiaircraft artillery firing at German bombers during the Blitz reas-sured the residents of London, the sight of a Patriot missile streaking upward to destroy Scuds made soldiers and civilians alike feel as if they had rendered

Hussein's most fearsome weapon (such as it was) useless. Patriot became a symbol of American technological supremacy and promised even greater things to come.

The Gulf War vindicated those theorists who believed the ballistic missile was not invulnerable, that a "bullet could hit another bullet." Imperfectly done, but then again the first attempts to shoot down airplanes was done imperfectly in the beginning. ATBM technology could be improved upon.

Coalition air defense could rightly claim 100 percent success against Iraq's AADF. This success was due more to the Iraqis' reluctance to challenge the array of air defense weapons and fighters that were deployed in Northern Saudi Arabia than to any combat attrition due to combat. But Iraq's reluctance to challenge the air defenses may arguably be credited to the very capabilities of those weapons. The Gulf War can be viewed as virtual attrition at its most extreme.

The ceasefire ended the war, but it did not entirely end the conflict. As part of the United Nations efforts to keep the renegade Iraqi state under control, "No-Fly Zones" were established, one in the north, where Kurdish rebels were trying to win their independence, and one in the south, where Shi'ites were in insurrection.

No Iraqi aircraft from the devastated IADF were permitted to fly in these zones, and they were patrolled by Allied aircraft. Some of the remaining Iraqi missile batteries were moved into this zone to challenge Coalition airpower, with predictable results: Iraq ended up with fewer radars, and the Allies retained absolute air supremacy in both zones.

The Coalition also proved it could strike at Iraq any time it wished. U.S. cruise missiles were sent in twice to destroy strategic targets in Iraq, with the IADF apparently just as incapable of dealing with them as they were in the first hours of the Gulf War, despite Iraq's unique and unwanted experience in such warfare.

13

The Future of Air Defense

What of the future? Airpower has proved that it is here to stay. Air defense has likewise proved throughout its short but intense history that it will also continue to have a role to play.

Following the advent of jet aircraft and nuclear weapons it was assumed that short-range automatic weapons would no longer have a role to play against aircraft. But radar and electrical firing systems helped to prove the worth of such weapons in the Middle East and Vietnam, bringing down even the fast-flying jets as they attempted to complete their missions. Even older automatic guns devoid of radar guidance such as those used in the 1983 invasion of Grenada can still bring down enemy aircraft and provide a deterrence effect.

Newer light weapons, such as the Stinger and Strelas, may someday replace automatic antiaircraft guns for low-level point air defense on the battlefield, but not in the foreseeable future. The soldier in the field must have a visible means of defense when all other air defenses have been defeated or evaded.

Heavy antiaircraft guns have likewise continued in service, although they are clearly inferior to missile systems in every way except cost. Even with radar guidance, computer prediction, and proximity fuzes the best that can be hoped for with antiaircraft artillery is a deterrence effect. All major military powers have rid themselves of conventional heavy guns or are in the process of doing so; antiaircraft artillery use in the Gulf War may have been its "last gasp."

But we may yet see the weaponry of air defense come full circle, back to the heavy antiaircraft gun. In the early 1990s the FMC Corporation was working on sophisticated gun designs, one employing electrothermal (ET) technology and the other an electrothermal-chemical (ETC) propulsion system. Such research might result in hypervelocity guns capable of enormous speed and kinetic killing power. If successful, we may yet see a gun capable of taking on a missile in flight.

Smart munitions are also becoming a possible factor in air defense. "Smart rounds" have already been developed for use with field artillery pieces. Electronic packages small enough and strong enough to survive the stresses of ballistic firing are being developed to provide guidance after the round leaves the barrel of the gun, using gas thrusters or vanes to change course in flight.

Such rounds could be given course corrections by radio after firing, defeating any maneuvers an aircraft might make. Detonation patterns could also be introduced for maximum effectiveness, or the rounds could be programmed to approach the target from above, where it might be more vulnerable.

But the future clearly belongs to the surface-to-air missile. In today's world there is a missile system in service for every type of air threat, except possibly Stealth. Missiles have been designed with optical, IR, laser, and radar tracking. They vary from the lightweight, shoulder-fired Redeye to the large S-300. The very versatility of missile design makes the ADA concept of "mix," combining SAMs with different capabilities and engagement systems, practical and effective. When confronted with several different missile systems, a pilot's chances of returning from a mission are considerably lessened.

The role of SAMs was expanded during the Gulf War. Regardless of how effective Patriot was during the conflict, it seems that defense from ATBMs will become a future requirement for armies in the field just as defense from more conventional aircraft is currently a part of strategic planning. This job is the sole domain of missiles; interceptors currently cannot perform the ATBM role.

The Gulf War, combined with the realities of the post–Cold War era, has resurrected the idea of a national air defense system, not against bombers but against limited nuclear strikes. With the breakup of the Soviet Union and the spread of missile and nuclear weapon technologies, the threat of a single nuclear attack of just a few missiles from some small country has become a possibility. An Anti-Ballistic Missile defense capable of defeating the entire Soviet Strategic Rocket Forces' arsenal would have been a massive undertaking for the United States, but a defense against a limited strike from North Korea or Iran is within reach of present American technologies.

Such technology is available in part because of the Strategic Defense Initiative of the 1980s. Whereas the Sentinel ABM would have been based on just two missile interceptors, SDI planned to employ an entire series of weapons to prevent a successful missile attack. The liftoff of enemy missiles would be detected by the network of surveillance satellites already in orbit for that purpose, then a few would be destroyed during ascent stage, a few more after engine burnout, another percentage at reentry, and the last of them at terminal approach.

To accomplish this, a truly varied and exotic series of weapons even the maddest mad scientist couldn't have dreamed of were explored: particle beam weapons capable of frying the electronics of an inbound missile, pop-up-X-ray lasers literally requiring the power of an exploding atom bomb to power them, electromagnetic rail guns whose rounds would destroy targets through sheer kinetic killing power, chemical lasers that would cut through the skin of a missile like a knife through butter, kinetic kill vehicles launched from satellites and smart enough to "hunt" their prey, and free-electron lasers whose ground stations would hit the incoming targets via orbiting mirror satellites, to name but a few.

These weapons all had one thing in common: none of them was ready to be deployed. In fact, most of the technologies involved were barely proven under laboratory conditions. This was far from the technological expertise needed to deploy them as field weapons.

Remarkably, the largest hurdle to the deployment of SDI was not technological, but political. Opponents to the development of such a strategic defense were concerned that if SDI were to succeed it would be "destabilizing," that such a system would be perceived as a threat to the USSR. The Soviets never seemed to have such qualms, continuously working on ABM systems and beam weapons. Opponents rather disingenuously argued simultaneously that the system could not possibly work and that when it did it would change the balance of power.

One serious argument against the SDI program was the idea that America would develop a "Maginot Line Syndrome," in which the American people would incorrectly believe they were safe from a nuclear attack when in fact there would always be a window of vulnerability. But the casual attitude many American politicians exhibited towards the Soviet strategic buildup caused a Maginot Line Syndrome to develop—without a Maginot Line.

In fact, the wrong lesson is drawn from the Maginot Line. The Maginot Line did not fail because it was poorly conceived and built; in fact, the Maginot Line withstood every German attempt to take it. The Maginot Line failed because it was not adequately funded and because the politics of its construction took precedence over the tactics of its use.

The Maginot Line as originally envisioned by the French in the 1930s would have created a deep defensive zone all along the French frontier. But because of politics, the Maginot Line stopped at the Belgium frontier; it did not extend all the way to the Channel coast, and the French politicians turned a blind eye to the fact that the Germans could outflank the line.

The Germans had to outflank the line. Despite problems, the Maginot Line functioned as designed. The Wehrmacht failed to take it by force, even from behind. Similarly, a dynamic defense network, using many different technologies, would be virtually impossible for an enemy to get through, even through the expedient of increasing the size of the missile force.

Many of the opponents of SDI hailed the collapse of the USSR as the end of missile defense. But the success of Patriot and the missile threat posed by an increasing number of third-world countries ensured the survival of at least a small program. In May 1993 the Strategic Defense Initiative Organization became the Ballistic Missile Defense Organization, or BMDO.

BMDO's emphasis would be aimed at a limited missile defense against shorter-range missiles. Space-based weapons were dropped from the research program, reducing the organization's main weapons to ground-based missile systems, with beam weapons possible later on. Airborne weapon systems might also find their way into BMDO. BMDO's efforts can be generalized into two different fields known by their official acronyms as TMD and NMD.

Tactical Missile Defense, or TMD, presently relies on future upgrades to Patriot and the U.S. Navy's Aegis program to defend U.S. and Allied forces in combat. Patriot is scheduled to be augmented by THAAD, the Theater High-Altitude Air Defense system by the mid-1990s. Corps SAM and Erint missile systems are also presently under development or study: Corps SAM to provide air defense above Patriot and below THAAD, while Erint would be a short-range interceptor based on the Patriot system. Each Patriot-type cannister would contain four Erint missiles, giving each launcher 16 missiles. Being small and relying on an impact kill, Erint will have limited range and lethality.

American HIMAD missile systems under development and future such systems will no doubt be designed for interoperability with each other and with current missile systems. U.S. success with electronic task forces during the Gulf War point to continued developments to maximize the effectiveness of available air defense resources, no matter how slim these might be. Interoperability might even be extended to future SHORAD systems and to Allied systems in development.

National Missile Defense (NMD) is the planned defense of the United States against a limited missile strike. TMD systems and many technologies originally developed for SDI might find their way into NMD, including kinetic kill vehicles. In 1991 such a weapon called ERIS was proven to be feasible, intercepting a simulated ICBM high above the Pacific Ocean.

Assuming that at least some of the projected missile systems reach operational status, the United States Army Air Defense Artillery could possibly set up an improvised ABM defense during a crisis using ADA batteries assigned to the field corps. In a more optimistic scenario, future air defense units might be deployed in strength enough to provide all-around coverage against a sudden missile attack. National Guard units could be used to man a permanent shield against missile attack, just as they helped protect America against nuclear bombers during the 1950s and 1960s.

Russia has inherited the bulk of the USSR's strategic defense arsenal, including its original ABM system fielded during the 1960s and follow-on research into exotic weapons technology. The Russian missile defense system is not very extensive, confined as it is to the Moscow District, nor does it appear to be very sophisticated. But against a limited strike the Russian system would probably be capable of defending the Russian capital, and new PVO missile systems like the S-300 and S-300V could deploy to defend likely targets in Russia or other CIS states.

Missile defense is not just a concern of the United States and Russia: NATO's AGARD Committee met in January 1993 to study the future of a European missile defense, and in April the Western European Union met to determine what steps, if any, should be taken to establish a common ABM defense. The original SDI program was based on a Free World versus Communist World ideology and as such probably would have eventually defended Europe as well as North America.

With widespread reduction in military spending and greater emphasis on welfare spending in the United States, Europe is clearly on its own for a truly strategic regional defense network; the best it can hope for is to buy into American THAAD and Corps SAM should they survive and to use Patriot to provide a minimal interim defense until a European system can be developed, such as SAM-T. With Russian interest in exporting the S-300, Europe might even operate a mixed system of American, European, and Russian systems, assuming that military budgets do not become the overriding consideration on the Continent as well.

The electronic infrastructure of air defense continues to improve. In June 1993 the IUKADGE, Improved United Kingdom Air Defence Ground Environment, came on-line. IUKADGE tracks all aircraft within the UK and can control interceptor and SAM units in its defense. Using a variety of sources and datalinks, the Air Defence Operations Center (ADOC) can be assured of an accurate air picture at all times, and the system has been designed to "degrade gracefully" in the event of system failure or combat attrition. Eurofighter 2000 and MSAMS are scheduled to see service in IUKADGE.

The Medium-range Surface-to-Air Missile System (MSAMS) was meant to replace the Bloodhound missile system, which was withdrawn from service in 1991 and not replaced. However, with budget constraints and the disappearance of the Soviet bomber threat, politics may result in the death of MSAMS.

Future integrated air defense systems might some day incorporate artificial intelligence to aid human operators to identify, track, and formulate strategies for dealing with enemy aircraft. Clearly, however, human operators must retain the power of decision-making. Whenever human lives are involved, humans must still make the decisions.

Tactically, automated air defense weapons of a different kind might be developed for use on the battlefield: antiaircraft mines. The Soviets developed a weapon called "Strela-Blok" which was a Strela-2 missile armed with an acoustic sensor. It was designed to be placed by Spetsnaz teams near NATO airfields, where they would automatically fire at enemy aircraft as they took off. ADA also studied the idea of antiaircraft mines in the 1980s, but to date no such weapon is commonly in service. However, the technology is already available for such weapons, and antiaircraft mines might be useful for denying air routes to low-flying aircraft or could be used to force enemy planes to a higher altitude before reaching a target.

Though exotic beam technologies have mainly been developed for ASAT or ABM purposes, there is potential for such weapons on a tactical level. Germany has looked into the possibility of building a self-propelled High Energy Laser system, which can cause critical damage to enemy aircraft. HEL technology is still some years off, it it is practical at all.

Fighter aircraft of course remain a key element in air defense and will remain so in the foreseeable future. A growing emphasis is on agility and maneuverability, as opposed to sheer speed. Improved controls have cut fractions of a second off of engagement, the only difference between life and death in air-to-air combat. Someday, thought controls which respond directly to brain impulses might be incorporated into avionics systems to maximize flight response beyond that of the best human reflex.

While air-to-air missile technology continues to grow in sophistication, aircraft guns have returned to aerial combat. Faster-firing, and using more sophisticated engagement technology than their predecessors, these aircraft cannons are nonetheless descendants of machine guns carried on board the early biplanes.

Combat aviation technology continues to grow in expense as well. Versatility is the growing order of the day, as opposed to the specialization shown in having fighters, fighter-bombers, bombers, electronic warfare aircraft, and recon aircraft. To reduce costs, future airframes should be capable of flying several different types of missions.

To counteract SAM and antiaircraft radars, ECM pods are being replaced by on-board electronic modules. Such black boxes can be swapped out as more advanced models become available or as the threat changes. But an aircraft will always be hampered by its finite limitations of physical size and power; even mobile ground-based systems can in theory draw on far more power than a fighter-bomber's on-board generators can produce and can operate large radars that can blanket out enemy transmissions.

Radar stealth technology made its first combat appearance during Operation Just Cause over Panama, and succeeded in inflicting heavy damage on the Iraqis during the Gulf War. However, despite misconceptions to the contrary, stealth aircraft are not "invisible" to radar, they merely have a much smaller radar cross-section, which makes detection difficult—but not impossible.

Stealth aircraft will usually become visible to radar, but at much closer range where radar transmissions are strongest. Fire-control radars employing intense continuous-wave beams might be able to detect stealth aircraft at greater ranges through a programmed search pattern. Stealth-specific detection technology is already being researched: The simplest might be a bistatic radar that employs a transmitter located some distance from a passive receiver; computer analysis would provide data on stealth target location. Another method is magnetic anomaly detection (MAD), a technology used successfully during World War II to detect and destroy mines and currently used against submarines. MAD technology depends upon the effect large amounts of metal have on the Earth's magnetic field.

Passive sensor technology could conceivably be developed from the revolutionary new astronomical techniques available today, utilizing thermal imaging, gas spectrometry, and millimeter-wave radiometry to detect enemy stealth aircraft. Even sound detection might be revived for use against Stealth; it was one of the few means the Iraqi antiaircraft gunners had to engage the F-117A.

This is bad news to USAF and USN planners who wish to incorporate Stealth characteristics into the next generation of combat aircraft. If Stealth is going to be of little use against such new technologies, can the enormous cost of incorporating it into already expensive planes be justified?

Further steps could be taken to minimize aircraft detection due to these technologies as well, but there is only so much that can be done to an aircraft to make it "invisible" and still make it a usable combat plane. Stealth technology, already being explored by Russian scientists, may prove to be a technological dead end.

Not only is air defense firmly established in modern warfare, it is still growing in capability and responsibility. Whether an army or air force's air defense arm is protecting a rifle squad or an entire country from a missile attack, the function of air defense has been successfully demonstrated around the world, in many battles and campaigns. The future belongs to Aerospace Defense Artillery.

Glossary

AA (Anti-Aircraft): A term used to describe weapons or tactical measures specifically designed for use against aircraft, such as "AA gun" or "AA missile."

AAA (Anti-Aircraft Artillery): A term that describes gun-based antiaircraft weapons. Sometimes refers to AAA as an air defense component, similar to the use of the terms SAM or GCI.

AA Service (Antiaircraft Service): The air defense force of the AEF during World War I. The first formal U.S. Army antiaircraft organization.

AADCOM (Army Air Defense Command) (U.S.): The largest unit of the Air Defense Artillery after the deactivation of ARAADCOM. An AADCOM controls two or more ADA brigades.

AADF (Air and Air Defense Forces): The branch of the Iraqi armed forces charged with controlling both offensive and defensive air weapons.

ABM (Anti-Ballistic Missile): A missile capable of intercepting and destroying ICBMs. Usually part of a large and complex missile system.

Ack-Ack (British): Slang term for antiaircraft fire, taken from the initials "AA." Commonly used by the British to describe their own air defenses.

Ack Girls (British): Slang term for female antiaircraft auxiliaries.

ADA (Air Defense Artillery) (U.S.): The combat branch of the U.S. Army that provides ground-based air defense.

ADC (Aerospace Defense Command) (U.S): A change in the name of the USAF's ADC made when greater emphasis was placed on detecting and intercepting enemy aircraft in the upper atmosphere.

ADC (Air Defense Command) (Egyptian): The branch of the Egyptian armed forces charged with defending Egypt and its ground forces against air attacks during the 1973 War. Manned and operated the Air Defense Barrier.

ADC (Air Defense Command) (U.S.): Component of the USAF responsible for interception of enemy aircraft approaching the United States.

ADF (Air Defense Force): The North Vietnamese military component charged with defending DRV airspace against enemy air attack.

ADGB (Air Defence Great Britain): An interservice command charged during World War II with defending British airspace against air attack.

ADIZ (Air Defense Identification Zone) (U.S.): A volume of airspace surrounding the United States; aircraft entering an ADIZ must provide identification with local airspace control or be intercepted.

ADMF (Air Defense Missile Force): The North Vietnamese military component given control of the SAM air defense component during the Vietnam War.

AEF (American Expeditionary Force): The U.S. Army in Europe during World War I.

AFP (Assault Fire Platoon): The basic fire unit in HAWK.

ALARM: A type of British ARM with a "loitering" capability. ALARM is fired at SAM sites, which then will sometimes shut down their radars; the missile then releases a parachute and waits for the radar to be switched back on; it then reactivates to home in on and destroy the enemy radar. First used during the Gulf War.

ARAACOM (Army Antiaircraft Command) (U.S.): The post–World War II Army component charged with ground-based air defense of the United States.

ARADCOM (Army Air Defense Command) (U.S.): The missile-based successor to ARAACOM.

Archie (British): Antiaircraft artillery. A slang term originated by World War I pilots to describe enemy antiaircraft fire, but often used to describe Allied AA fire.

Area Defense: A defense intended to protect a large area with several potential targets. An area defense is the opposite of a point defense.

ARM (Anti-Radiation Missile): An air-launched missile designed to home in on and destroy enemy radars, usually those associated with SAMs.

ARP (Air Raid Precautions) (British): Civil defense organization created during World War II.

ARVN (Army of Vietnam): South Vietnam's (RVN) army.

ASAT (Antisatellite): Missile and beam systems designed to destroy enemy satellites in orbit.

ATBM (Anti-Tactical Ballistic Missile): A battlefield missile system designed to destroy enemy short-range missiles.

ATS (Auxiliary Territorial Service) (British): Female service organization that performed military duties during World War II. Some ATS members served with air defense units.

AW (Automatic Weapons) (U.S.): Term for light Rapid-firing antiaircraft weapons such as Bofors and AA machine guns.

AWACS (Airborne Warning and Control System): A Boeing E-3A aircraft equipped with radar and other electronics capable of tracking and controlling air battles in its sector.

Barrage: A large volume of antiaircraft fire created by preset guns to deny airspace to the enemy. Barrages can be employed in several ways, but they require large numbers of guns to be effective. Barrages originated in World War I.

Barrage Balloon: A tethered balloon used to deny the enemy airspace by use of steel cables.

BEF (British Expeditionary Force): The British Army force on the Continent during World War I.

Blitzmadchen (German): Lightning Girl. German nickname for female AA gunners during World War II.

BMDO (Ballistic Missile Defense Organization): The post–Cold War successor to the SDIO.

Bofors (Swedish): A Swedish armanents company most famous for its 40mm automatic antiaircraft gun, designed shortly before World War II. This weapon was commonly called "Bofors" and was in service with both Allied and Axis countries.

Bollongeschutz (German): Balloon shooter. A gun designed for shooting down balloons during the Prussian siege of Paris in 1870. The first weapon designed solely to shoot down enemy aircraft.

BOMARC: A USAF unmanned air defense interceptor deployed in the 1960s.

CAC (Coast Artillery Corps) (U.S.): The branch of the U.S. Army originally given the responsibility of antiaircraft defense during World War I.

CDF (Canadian Defense Forces): The Canadian component of NORAD.

CH (Chain Home) (British): The radar system used by the British to detect approaching enemy aircraft during World War II.

CHL (Chain Home Low) (British): A radar system set up to detect aircraft flying below the coverage of Chain Home.

Command Guidance: A system for guiding surface-to-air missiles. Radio directions are constantly broadcast to an airborne missile to ensure the interception of enemy aircraft. Command guidance is typically susceptible to jamming.

ConAC (Continental Air Command) (U.S.): The post–World War II USAF organization responsible for Air Force units within the continental United States, including ADC.

CONAD (Continental Air Defense Command) (U.S.): A joint command controlling both ARAACOM and USAF interceptor forces. Formed in the 1950s.

Cwt: Hundredweight. Term used as a designation for individual British antiaircraft artillery guns, such as the 3 in. 20 cwt.

DAT (Defense Aerienne du Territoire) (French): Territorial Air Defense. The strategic, or national, air defense forces of France. Originated during World War I.

DCA (Defense Contre Aeronifs) (French): Antiaircraft Defense. Used to refer to French tactical air defense, as opposed to strategic air defense. Term originally used during World War I. DCA has also come to refer to tactical air defense weapons.

Dead Zone: An area not covered by antiaircraft radar or missiles.

DEW (Distant Early Warning) Line: A NORAD radar net designed to pick up Soviet aircraft approaching North America from over the Arctic.

Director: see Predictor.

DMZ (Demilitarized Zone): An area from which two opposing military powers agree to withhold their forces. DMZs were established between North and South Vietnam and between North and South Korea.

Dodge City: USAF pilot's nickname for Hanoi during the Vietnam War, because of the need to "dodge" AA fire.

Down Time: The term for the period of time during which a fire unit is not available to engage the enemy. Includes time for moving and emplacing the system, maintenance, and system failures. Also see Red Time.

Drahtfunk (German): A World War II air-raid warning device. A drahtfunk receiver monitored a continuous transmission that would warn German civilians if an attack was possible or imminent.

DRV (Democratic Republic of Vietnam): The official name for North Vietnam.

Dvina: A Soviet SAM system also known as the V-75 or by its NATO code name SA-2 Guideline. The basic fire unit of the Dvina is the missile battalion. The missile was a two-stage liquid-fuel missile employing command guidance. Named after a Russian river.

ECCM (Electronic Counter-Countermeasures): Measures taken by ground-based radars to defeat ECM. Frequency-hopping is an example of ECCM.

ECM (Electronic Countermeasures): Measures taken by aircraft to deceive or confuse enemy radars. Jamming is one kind of ECM.

ECM Pod: A device designed to defeat enemy radars. Carried externally by aircraft.

Engagement: The sequence of events involved in destroying an enemy aircraft.

ERIS (Exoatmospheric Reentry-vehicle Interceptor Subsystem): A weapon system designed to destroy ballistic missiles with a kinetic kill vehicle.

ET (Electrothermal): A technology being explored to produce hypervelocity AA guns. Utilizes plasma propulsion to create enormous chamber pressure and achieve high ballistic speeds.

ETC (Electrothermal-Chemical): A variation of ET, utilizing plasma injection into chemical propellents. Weapons operating on an ETC principle could conceivably control ballistic characteristics by changing electrical impulses.

EW (Electronic Warfare): Military action involving the use of electromagnetic energy to determine, exploit, reduce, or prevent hostile use of the electromagnetic spectrum and to retain friendly use of the electromagnetic spectrum. Includes ECM and ECCM, as well as standard uses of radar.

Festung Europa (German): Fortress Europe. The German name for the defenses of Nazi-occupied Europe; included strategic air defenses.

Festung Ploesti (German): Fortress Ploesti. World War II nickname for the German air defenses of the Romanian city of Ploesti. Ploesti was a strategic oil center.

FEZ (Fighter Engagement Zone): A volume of airspace in which interceptor aircraft have engagement priority.

Fire Unit: The smallest missile unit capable of engaging and destroying an enemy aircraft with the system it is equipped with. For the Stinger, a fire unit is the individual gunner; for HAWK it is the Assault Fire Platoon; for Patriot it is the battery.

Flak (Flugzug Abwehr Kanonen) (German): Antiaircraft guns. First so termed during World War I. Originally used when referring to German air defense weapons, but also used to describe almost any kind of antiaircraft fire.

Flak Kampfhelferinnen (German): Antiaircraft female volunteers. Women auxiliaries who mostly served in noncombat roles in Germany's air defense forces during World War II.

Flakscheinwerfer (German): Searchlight.

Flak Suppression: Tactics to reduce the effectiveness of enemy antiaircraft fire, usually at a particular target. Flak suppression could be as simple as the use of designated fighters to strafe enemy antiaircraft guns during a mission.

Flaktower: Special structure built to give antiaircraft guns unrestricted fields of fire and protection against bomb damage. Used in Festung Europa during World War II.

Flak Trap: The deliberate luring of an enemy aircraft to a position where it can be engaged by antiaircraft weapons. Usually, enemy aerial reconnaissance is tricked into believing that a military target exists, when actually large numbers of AA guns were massed to destroy the planes as they approach the fake target.

Flak Wehrmaenner (German): Antiaircraft fighting men. A type of German AA reserve that employed industrial workers to defend their factories against air attack during World War II.

Flintenweiber (German): Gun woman. Nickname of female auxiliaries manning antiaircraft weapons during World War II.

Flying Telephone Pole: USAF pilots' nickname for the Dvina during the Vietnam War.

Footprint: The term for a fixed radar coverage. Commonly used when referring to Patriot.

Force Multiplier: Weapons and weapon systems that make maximum use of other friendly assets.

Freikorps (German): Free Corps. Collective term for paramilitary units that formed in post–World War I Germany. Some of these were formerly German Army units, including some antiaircraft batteries. These units served different political interests.

Frequency Hopping: An ECCM tactic used by radars to defeat fixed-frequency jamming.

GCI (Ground Control Interception): Interception of enemy aircraft by use of ground radar surveillance, central controllers, and radio links to friendly fighters.

GDA (Gun Defended Area) (U.S.): A volume of airspace in which antiaircraft artillery is given engagement priority.

GLO (Gun Liaison Officer) (British): An officer assigned to coordinate AAA fire with interceptors. Part of the ADGB system during World War II.

GOC (Ground Observer Corps) (U.S.): A volunteer organization that provided the "eyes" of the U.S. national air defenses during World War II and the early Cold War period.

GU-PVO (Russian): Main Administration of the PVO. Soviet air defense organization responsible for training and administration of the PVO, but not command functions.

Happy Valley: British nickname given to the Ruhr industrial area in Germany because of its air defenses during World War II.

HARM (High-speed Anti-Radiation Missile): A second-generation ARM, also known as the AGM-88. Designed to attack enemy radars at twice the speed of sound and with an improved radar-killing warhead.

HAWK (Homing All the Way Killer): A U.S. SAM originally deployed in the 1950s. Currently, HAWK III is still in service, providing HIMAD coverage in conjunction with Patriot. The AFP is the basic fire unit of HAWK.

HEL (High Energy Laser): A new type of antiaircraft technology under development.

HIMAD (High-to-Medium Air Defense): The upper zone of air defense.

Himmelbett (German): Heaven bed. Codename for German radar defenses. Himmelbett refers to a four-poster bed, which the defense resembled.

Hypervelocity Guns: Antiaircraft guns capable of firing projectiles at speeds many times that of conventional antiaircraft guns.

IADF (Iraqi Air Defense Force): The branch of the Air and Air Defense Force charged with controlling AAA, SAMs, and interceptors.

IADS (Integrated Air Defense System): The electronic network used by the Iraqis to control their air defenses during the Gulf War.

IAF (Independent Air Force) (British): An inter-Allied bombing force created in 1918 to attack strategic targets in Germany and Occupied France.

IAF (Israeli Air Force): The component of the Israeli armed forces responsible for offensive and defensive air weapons.

IAZ (Inner Artillery Zone) (U.S.): A volume of airspace reserved solely for antiaircraft engagements. Friendly aircraft are prohibited from entering an IAZ.

IFF (Identification Friend or Foe) (U.S.): An electronic system for identifying friendly aircraft. An IFF interrogator transmits a coded signal to an unknown aircraft; if the aircraft is friendly, it will have a transponder that will transmit the correct response code. Though IFF usually refers to the system in use with NATO, the USSR also developed IFF systems.

Igla (Russian): Needle. The third-generation Soviet MANPADS. Utilizes improved IRCM capabilities.

Interceptor: An aircraft whose function is to find and destroy hostile aircraft.

IR (Infra-Red): A portion of the invisible spectrum militarily useful for detecting enemy aircraft. IR guidance is used for some types of SAMs, such as the Stinger and the Strela series.

IRCM (IR Counter-Measures): Technology and tactics used to defeat IR-seeking missiles. Dropping flares is one form of IRCM.

Jinking: The flying tactic of making sharp, sudden moves to the left and right to avoid flak.

Kammhuber Line: The code name for German's frontier air defenses. Named after Major General Joseph Kammhuber. Incorporated Himmelbett cells.

Kommandogerat (German): Command device. A later model predictor.

Kommandohilfsgerat (German): Command aid device. A World War II German antiaircraft predictor.

Koshaho (Japanese): Antiaircraft gun.

Koshaho Chutai (Japanese): Antiaircraft battery.

Kosha Kikanho (Japanese): Antiaircraft machine cannon.

Kosha Kikanju (Japanese): Antiaircraft machine gun.

Krug (Russian): Circle. A Soviet tactical surface-to-air missile system also known as the SA-4 Ganef. The missile utilizes external solid rocket boosters and a ramjet sustainer motor. A Krug battery is the basic fire unit.

Kub (Russian): Cube. Also known as Kvadrat in export version. Identified by the NATO designation SA-6 Gainful. Kub missiles utilize a rocket/ramjet motor. The basic fire unit of the Kub is the missile battery.

LAAM (Light AntiAircraft Missile): USMC designation for air defense units employing missiles.

LADA (London Air Defence Area) (British): The primary air defense zone created by the British during World War I.

Lashup (U.S.): The first post–World War II radar network employed around the continental United States.

Leaker (U.S.): Term for a hostile aircraft that penetrates forward air defenses to attack rear areas.

Leuchtspucker (German): Lightspitter. The nickname for female auxiliaries manning tracking boards.

LSW (Luftschutz Warndienst) (German): Air Raid Warning Service. The World War II German civil defense organization.

Luftsperre (German): Air Barrier. A tactic employed by World War I fighters to prevent enemy aircraft from reaching rear areas. Relied on a heavy concentration of friendly fighters along a single sector of the front.

Luftstreitkrafte (German): Combatant Air Forces. World War I German air arm, also responsible for antiaircraft artillery.

Luftwaffe (German): Air Force. Responsible for offensive and defensive air weapons, except for flak units attached to the German Army.

Luftwaffehelfern (German): Air Force Volunteers. A World War II auxiliary that employed youths not yet of draft age to help man antiaircraft guns.

MAD (Magnetic Anomaly Detection): A technology being explored for stealth detection. Employs the measurable effect large amounts of metal have on the Earth's magnetic field.

MANPADS (Man-Portable Air Defense System): Shoulder-fired missile systems, such as the Redeye or Blowpipe.

MEZ (Missile Engagement Zone): A volume of airspace in which surface-to-air missile systems are given engagement priority.

Mid-Canada Line: A microwave "fence" deployed in the 1950s to provide early warning for NORAD.

MiG Alley (U.S.): An area along the Sino-Korean border that was a haven for MiG-15 jet fighters during the Korean War.

MIGCAP (MiG Combat Air Patrol) (U.S.): USAF and USN fighters that patrol to prevent MiG aircraft from reaching other air formations.

NATO (North Atlantic Treaty Organization): The defensive alliance formed between the United States and Western European nations in the face of Communist aggression.

Neva: A Soviet SAM system also known as the S-125, or by its NATO designation SA-3 Goa. The Neva missile is a two-stage solid-fuel missile system. The export version of Neva is known as Pechora. The basic fire unit of the Neva system is the missile battalion.

Nike-Ajax: The first SAM developed for use by the U.S. Army. Provided HIMAD coverage.

Nike-Hercules: An improved missile similar to Nike-Ajax. Most Nike equipment was compatible with both systems.

NMD (National Missile Defense) (U.S.): The use of various technologies to protect the United States from a missile attack.

NORAD (North American Air Defense Command): The interservice Canadian-American organization charged with air defense of the North American continent.

NVA (North Vietnam Army): A common term used to describe the army of the DRV. The official designation was the People's Army of Vietnam (PAVN).

Patriot: An improved high-to-medium altitude SAM system designed to replace Nike, Hercules, and Hawk. Capable of providing limited defense against tactical ballistic missiles.

PAVN (People's Army of Vietnam): The official designation of North Vietnam's army.

Pdr: Pounder. Term used as a designation for individual British antiaircraft artillery guns, such as the 3 in. 20 cwt.

Phased Array Radar: A system that transmits radar beams in different directions while the antenna remains fixed. Patriot and S-300 missile systems employ phased array radars.

Pinetree Line: A network of radars along the U.S.–Canadian border to provide final warning for U.S. air defenses of enemy bombers approaching over the Arctic.

PKO (Protivo-Kosmicheskaya Oborona) (Russian): Antispace Defense. Soviet ASAT missile and beam technologies designed to deny the use of space to the enemy. Part of PVO.

Point Defense: A defense intended to protect a single target. The opposite of an area defense.

Pom-Pom (British): The nickname for fast-firing antiaircraft guns. Earned during World War I by the sound the guns made when firing.

Predictor: Mechanical and electric devices used prior to the invention of computers to determine the probable future position of an aircraft based on available tracking information. Also called a director.

PRO (Protivo-Raketnaya Oborona) (Russian): Antirocket Defense. Strategic ABM defenses within the PVO.

Proximity Fuse: An antiaircraft shell fuze designed to detonate when an aircraft is in the vicinity.

PVO (Protiovozdushnoi Oborony) (Russian): Air Defense Force. The branch of the Soviet armed forces charged with air defense. Used as generic term for Soviet air defenses.

PVO Strany (Russian): National Air Defense Force. Those air defense weapons deployed for the defense of the USSR, as opposed to the tactical air defense weapons defending the Soviet Army.

PVO SV (PVO Sukoputnikh Voisk) (Russian): Ground Forces Air Defense Force. The element of the Soviet Army charged with tactical air defense.

R-113: An early Soviet SAM designated SA-1 Guild. Liquid-fuel and based around Moscow.

RA (Royal Artillery) (British): The branch of the British Army that was initially put in charge of antiaircraft weapons.

RAA (Regiment d-Artillerie Antiaerienne) (French): Antiaircraft artillery regiment.

RAD (Reichsarbeitdienst) (German): Reich Labor Organization. Some RAD members were drafted into auxiliary antiaircraft units.

RADCA (Regiment d'Artillerie de DCA) (French): DCA artillery regiments formed during the interwar period.

RAF (Royal Air Force) (British): The branch of the British armed forces responsible for military aviation.

Ramjet: A type of aircraft engine that has no moving parts; it relies on the aircraft's tremendous speed to provide enough air compression for the jet engine to function. Several missile designs have utilized ramjets, including BOMARC and Krug.

RCAF (Royal Canadian Air Force) (Canadian): The branch of the Canadian armed forces responsible for military aviation.

RE (Royal Engineers) (British): The branch of the British Army originally responsible for operating searchlights.

Redeye: The first U.S. MANPADS. It employed an IR seeker and a throw-away launcher.

Red Time: The period of time during which a missile system is not functioning because of technical failure.

Reichswehr (German): The national armed force established by treaty for Germany following World War I.

RFC (Royal Flying Corps) (British): The branch of the British Army originally responsible for military aviation. Was merged with the RNAS to form the RAF.

RHA (Royal Horse Artillery) (British): The branch of the British Army first put in charge of tactical air defense for the BEF.

RLB (Reichsluftschutzbund) (German): Reich Air Protection League. A German World War II organization responsible for early warning and tracking, similar in function to the GOC or the ROC.

RNAS (Royal Naval Air Service) (British): The air arm of the Royal Navy during World War I. Merged with the RFC to form the RAF.

ROC (Royal Observer Corps) (British): A volunteer organization originally formed to detect and track aircraft over England.

Romb (Russian): Diamond. A Soviet tactical air defense system designated SA-8 Gecko by NATO. The six-wheeled Romb vehicle serves as the system fire unit: detection, tracking, fire-control, and launch functions are all performed on board.

RPV (Remotely Piloted Vehicle): An unmanned aircraft controlled by radio link. Used mainly for reconnaissance.

RSAF (Royal Saudi Air Force): The branch of the Saudi Arabian armed forces responsible for military aviation.

RSLF (Royal Saudi Land Forces): The branch of the Saudi Arabian armed forces responsible for ground combat.

RTV (Radiotekhnicheskiye Voiska) (Russian): Radio-Technical Troops. Branch of the PVO responsible for early warning and national tracking radars.

RVN (Republic of Vietnam): The official name of South Vietnam.

S-200: A strategic Soviet SAM developed in the 1960s. Also known as the SA-5 Gammon.

S-300: A Soviet SAM system developed for tactical or strategic use, depending upon its configuration. Designated SA-10 or SA-12, the S-300 is highly mobile.

SA-1: See R-113.

SA-2: See Dvina.

SA-3: See Neva.

SA-4: See Krug.

SA-5: See S-200.

SA-6: See Kub.

SA-7: See Strela-2.

SA-8: See Romb.

SA-9: See Strela-1.

SA-10: See S-300.

SA-11: NATO code name: Gadfly. A Soviet tactical air defense system, mounted on self-propelled tracked vehicles. Apparently a replacement for the Kub system.

SA-12: See S-300.

SA-13: See Strela-10.

SA-14: See Strela-3.

SA-15: A Soviet tactical air defense missile system that was still in testing and deployment stage when the USSR collapsed.

SA-16: See Igla.

SAGE (Semi-Automatic Ground Environment): A U.S. electronic system for controlling interceptors and AA weapons. Developed during the 1950s.

SAM (Surface-to-Air Missile): A generic term for ground-based antiaircraft missiles. Commonly used to describe missiles as a component of an air defense.

SAM-D: See Patriot.

SDI (Strategic Defense Initiative): Research begun in the 1980s to develop a serious antimissile defense system for the United States. Sometimes called Star Wars.

SDIO (Strategic Defense Initiative Organization): The Department of Defense branch responsible for SDI research. Renamed BMDO.

SEAD (Suppression of Enemy Air Defenses) (U.S.): Formal name for wild weasel and flak-suppression tactics; used in the process of gaining air supremacy.

Searchlight: A device for creating an intense beam of light, usually by concentrating an arc light with mirrors. Used to detect and engage aircraft flying at night.

Shilka: Russian name for the ZSU-23-4 self-propelled antiaircraft gun.

SHORAD (Short Range Air Defense): The lower zone of air defense.

Smart Munitions: Shells capable of guiding themselves to a target after firing.

Sonderkommandos (German): Special Detachments. World War II Luftwaffe units formed at the end of the end of the war for the purpose of ramming enemy bombers.

Sortie: A single flight by a single aircraft. Twenty sorties could be two missions of 10 planes each, four missions of five planes each, or 20 missions by a single plane.

Sound Detector: A device for detecting and tracking aircraft by the sound of their engines.

Spoofing: Fooling electronic devices by means of false signals.

Star Wars: See SDI.

Stealth: Aviation technology designed to minimize the detection of an aircraft by means of radar or infrared.

Stinger: The second-generation U.S. MANPADS. Designed with IRCM and an IFF system.

Strela-1: A Soviet pedestal-launched IR-seeking missile mounted on an armored car. Tactically, it operates in an air defense battery with ZSU-23-4 Shilkas. Known in the West as the SA-9 Gaskin.

Strela-2: The first Soviet MANPADS weapon to be developed. Known as the SA-7 Grail.

Strela-3: The second-generation MANPADS weapon, which includes some IRCM capabilities. Code-named SA-14 Gremlin.

Strela-10: A second-generation pedestal-launched IR-seeking missile mounted on a tracked vehicle. Tactically, it appears to be intended to operate in air defense batteries with the Tunguska gun/missile system. Code-named SA-13 Gopher.

TA (Territorial Army) (British): A reserve component of the British Army. In the 1930s much of the antiaircraft strength of the British Army was relegated to the Territorial Army.

THAAD (Theater High Altitude Area Defense) (U.S.): A missile system under development to provide a first line of defense against tactical ballistic missiles, relegating Patriot to a point defense TBM system.

TMD (Tactical Missile Defense) (U.S.): The use of various missile systems to protect an army in the field.

Transloader: A vehicle designed to carry and reload missiles.

Tunguska: Russian name for the gun/missile system meant for use with the Strela-10 SAM.

USAAF (United States Army Air Forces): The component of the U.S. Army responsible for military aviation during World War II.

USAF (United States Air Force): The branch of the U.S. military responsible for most military aviation. Responsible for manned and unmanned interceptors.

USN (United States Navy): Naval branch of the U.S. military. Responsible for carrier and other types of naval aviation.

Virtual Attrition: The degrading of an enemy's offensive airpower caused by measures needed to counteract friendly air defenses. Reducing bombload in order to carry an ECM pod is one example of virtual attrition; relegating some fighter-bombers in a strike mission to the role of wild weasels instead of bomb carriers is another example.

VNAF (Vietnamese Air Force): The air force of South Vietnam.

VNOS (Vozdushnoye Nablyudenie Opoveshchenie Svyaz) (Russian): Aerial Observation, Warning and Communications Service. An auxiliary service meant to provide detection and tracking of aircraft. Served the same function as the U.S. GOC.

Wilde Sau (German): Wild Boar. Term used to describe independent Luftwaffe fighter tactics free of ground control.

Wild Weasel: U.S. Anti-SAM aircraft and tactics. Generically used to described the anti-SAM tactics of other countries.

Zahme Sau (German): Tame Boar. Term used to describe fighters under ground control.

ZAV (Zenitniye Artilelriskiye Voiska) (Russian): Zenith Artillery Troops. The branch of the PVO responsible for surface-to-air missiles.

Zero-doppler: The point at which a doppler radar loses a track when it enters a shallow turn.

Selected Bibliography

AAA Research Board. *Survey of the Japanese Antiaircraft Artillery.* GHQ USAFPAC: (Army publication), 1946.

Addington, Larry. *The Patterns of War since the Eighteenth Century.* Bloomington: Indiana University Press, 1984.

AF Pamphlet 200-21, Soviet Aerospace Handbook. Washington, D.C.: U.S. Government Printing Office, 1978.

Aker, Frank. *October 1973.* Hamden, Conn.: Archon Books, 1985.

Antiaircraft Defense. Harrisburg, Pa.: Military Service Publishing Company, 1940.

Ashmore, Major-General Edward B. *Air Defence.* London: Longmans, Green and Co., 1929.

Barnard, Lieutenant-Commander Roy S. *The History of ARADCOM.* Vol. 1: *The Gun Era, 1950–1955.* Headquarters ARADCOM: Historical Project ARAD 5M-I.

Beckett, Ian, ed. *Communist Military Machine.* London: Hamlyn Publishing, 1985.

Berger, Major Maurice. "Employment of Hertzian Waves for Stopping Aeroplanes in Flight." *The Coast Artillery Corps Journal* 60 (May 1924): 434–35.

Bidwell, Shelford, ed. *Brassey's Artillery of the World.* New York: Brassey's Publishers, 1981.

Bishop, Chris, and David Donald, eds. *The Encyclopedia of World Military Power.* New York: Military Press, 1988.

Blau, Tim. "TMD in the Clinton Era." *Military Technology* 17 (1993): 16–18, 20, 21.

Brits, Lieutenant-Commander Vladimir. "Repelling Air Attacks." *Soviet Military Review* (January 1988): 20–21.

Broughton, Jack. *Going Downtown: The War against Hanoi and Washington.* New York: Orion Books, 1988.

Bruce-Briggs, B. *The Shield of Faith.* New York: Simon and Schuster, 1988.

Bullock, David L. *Allenby's War: The Palestine-Arabian Campaigns, 1916–1918.* London: Blandford Press, 1988.

Campbell, D'Ann. "Women, Combat, and the Gender Line." *Military History Quarterly* 6 (Autumn 1993): 88–97.

Carter, Ashton B., and David N. Schwartz, eds. *Ballistic Missile Defenses.* Washington, D.C.: Brookings Institution, 1984.

Cave, Dorothy. *Beyond Courage: One Regiment against Japan, 1941–1945.* Las Cruces, New Mexico: Yucca Tree Press, 1992.

Chant, Christopher. *Air Defence Systems and Weapons: World AAA and SAM Systems in the 1990s.* London: Brassey's Defence Publishers, 1989.

Cohen, Stan. *V for Victory: America's Home Front during World War II.* Missoula, Mont.: Pictorial Histories Publishing Company, 1991.

Cole, Christopher, and E. F. Cheesman. *The Air Defence of Britain, 1914–1918.* London: Putnam, 1984.

Conn, Stetson, Rose C. Engelman, and Byron Fairchild. *The Western Hemisphere: Guarding the United States and Its Outposts.* The United States Army in World War II Series. Washington, D.C.: Office of the Chief of Military History, Department of the Army, 1964.

Cooksley, Peter C. *Flying Bomb: The Story of Hitler's V-Weapons in World War II.* New York: Charles Scribners' Sons, 1979.

Cordesman, Anthony H., and Abraham R. Wagner. *The Lessons of Modern War.* Vol. 2; *The Iran-Iraq War.* San Francisco: Westview Press, 1990.

Cullen, Tony, and Christopher F. Foss, eds. *Jane's Battlefield Air Defence, 1988–89.* Coulson, Surrey, UK: Jane's Information Book, 1988.

Cuneo, John R. *The Air Weapon: 1914–1916.* Harrisburg, Pa.: Military Service Publishing Company, 1947.

Darwish, Adel, and Gregory Alexander. *Unholy Babylon: The Secret History of Saddam's War.* New York: St. Martin's Press, 1991.

Davis, Burke. *The Civil War: Strange and Fascinating Facts.* New York: Fairfax Press, 1982.

"Doctrine of Anti-Aircraft Defense in France." *The Coast Artillery Corps Journal* 58 (February 1923): 54–59.

Dokuchayev, LTC Anatoly. " 'We, Too, Defended Vietnam.' " *Soviet Military Review* (September 1989); 34–35.

Dommett, William E. *Airplanes and Airships.* London: Whittaker and Co., 1915.

Dudgeon, Air Vice-Marshal A. G. *The War That Never Was.* Shrewsbury, UK: Airlife Publishing, 1991.

Dugan, James, and Carroll Stewart. *Ploesti: The Great Ground-Air Battle of 1 August 1943.* New York: Random House, 1962.

Dunnigan, James. *How to Make War.* New York: William Morrow and Company, 1982.

Dzhugashvili, Colonel Yevgeny. "Air Defence in Local Wars." *Soviet Military Review* (April 1987): 18–19.

Eglin, James Meikle. *Air Defense in the Nuclear Age.* New York: Garland Publishing, 1988.

Ely, Lieutenant Hiram B. "Sound Locators: Their Functions and Limitations." *The Coast Artillery Corps Journal* 65 (August 1926): 123–31.

Emry, CW4 Jack K. *Blazing Skies.* Bend, Oregon: Maverick Publications, 1990.

Everett-Heath, John. *Design, Development and Tactics: Soviet Helicopters.* London: Jane's Publishing Company, 1983.

FM 44-1: U.S. Army Air Defense Artillery Employment. Washington, D.C.: Headquarters, U.S. Army, 1983.

FM 44-8: Small Unit Self-Defense against Air Attack. Washington, D.C.: Headquarters, U.S. Army, 1981.

Fontaine, G. "Barrage Balloons." *The Coast Artillery Journal* 58 (February 1923): 141–43.

Ford, Brian. *German Secret Weapons: Blueprint for Mars.* New York: Ballantine Books, 1977.

Foss, Christopher F. *Artillery of the World.* New York: Charles Scribner's Sons, 1974.

Fredette, Raymond H. *The Sky on Fire: The First Battle of Britain 1917–1918.* Washington, D.C.: Smithsonian Institution Press, 1991.

French, Mary. "Women in ADA." *Air Defense Artillery* (September-October 1988): 28–39.

Friedman, Norman. *Desert Victory: The War for Kuwait.* Annapolis, Md.: Naval Institute Press, 1991.

Futernick, LTC Allan J. "The Air Defense of Colorado." *Air Defense Artillery* (Spring 1983): 5–9.

Gander, Terry J. *The 40mm Bofors Gun.* Wellingborough, UK: Patrick Stephens, 1990.

Gervasi, Tom. *Arsenal of Democracy II.* New York: Grove Press, 1981.

Greenwald, Captain Bryan E. "The Legitimacy Struggle." *Air Defense Artillery* (September-October 1992): 6–15.

Gunston, Bill. *Air Superiority.* London: Ian Allen, 1985.

———. *An Illustrated Guide to the Modern Soviet Air Force.* New York: Arco Publishing, 1982.

Gunston, Bill, and Mike Spick. *Modern Air Combat.* New York: Crescent Books, 1983.

Hahn, Fritz. *Deutsche Geheimwaffen 1939–1945* [German Secret Weapons 1939–1945]. Heidenheim: Erich Hoffman Verlag, 1963.

Hallion, Richard P. *Storm over Iraq: Air Power and the Gulf War.* Washington, D.C.: Smithsonian Institution Press, 1992.

Harmon, Captain Benjamin F. "The Archies and the Anti-Aircraft Service." *Journal of the United States Artillery* 56 (June 1922): 528–51.

———. "The Past and Future of Defense against Aircraft." *The Coast Artillery Corps Journal* 63 (December 1925): 555–56.

Harries, Meirion, and Susie Harries. *Soldiers of the Sun: The Rise and Fall of the Imperial Japanese Army.* New York: Random House, 1991.

Hartcup, Guy. *The War of Invention: Scientific Developments 1914–18.* New York: Brassey's Defence Publishers, 1988.

Haythornthwaite, Philip J. *The World War One Source Book*. London: Arms and Armour Press, 1992.

Henry, Lisa B., ed. *Arabian Knights*. Fort Bliss, Tex.: Air Defense Artillery Magazine, 1991.

Herzog, Chaim. *The Arab-Israeli Wars*. New York: Vintage Books, 1984.

Hinman, Captain Dale D., and Captain Maurice Morgan. "Contangent Method of Anti-Aircraft Searchlight Control." *The Coast Artillery Journal* 57 (November 1922): 435–48.

Hogg, Ian V. *Anti-Aircraft: A History of Air Defence*. London: MacDonald and Jane's, 1978.

————. *The Guns: 1939–45*. New York: Ballantine Books, 1970.

————. *The History of Fortification*. New York: St. Martin's Press, 1981.

Insight Team of the London Sunday Times. *The Yom Kippur War*. New York: Doubleday and Company, 1974.

Irving, David. *The Mare's Nest: The German Secret Weapons Campaign and Allied Countermeasures*. Boston: Little, Brown and Company, 1965.

Isby, David C. *War in a Distant Country—Afghanistan: Invasion and Resistance*. New York: Sterling Publishing, 1989.

Johnson, Curt. *Artillery*. London: Octopus Books, 1976.

Kennedy, William V. *Intelligence Warfare*. New York: Crescent Books, 1987.

Kennett, Lee. *The First Air War, 1914–1918*. New York: Free Press, 1991.

————. *A History of Strategic Bombing*. New York: Charles Scribner's Sons, 1982.

Kerr, E. Bartlett. *Flames over Tokyo: The U.S. Army Air Forces' Incendiary Campaign against Japan 1944–1945*. New York: Donald I. Fine, 1991.

Kilner, Captain H. R. "Notes on Colonel Steger's Proposed Method of Anti-Aircraft Fire." *Journal of the United States Artillery* 56 (May 1922): 437–38.

Kirkpatrick, Major Charles E. *Archie in the AEF*, Fort Bliss, Tex.: U.S. Army Air Defense School, 1984.

Kirsanov, Colonel Anatoly. "More Concern for People." *Soviet Military Review* (April 1989): 14–15.

Knyazkov, Colonel Viktor. "Self-Propelled AD System ZSU-23-4." *Soviet Military Review* (March 1987): 47–49.

[Koker, Hubert]. "Clark Field: Air Defense Debacle in the Philippines." *Air Defense Artillery* (January-February 1992): 24–30.

Korionov, Vitaly. "Why Destroy Missiles." *Soviet Military Review* (April 1989): 56.

Kreis, John F. *Air Warfare and Air Base Air Defense*. Washington, D.C.: Office of Air Force History, 1988.

Lanning, Michael Lee, and Dan Cragg. *Inside the VC and the NVA: The Real Story of North Vietnam's Armed Forces*. New York: Ballantine Books, 1992.

Lowther, William. *Arms and the Man: Dr. Gerald Bull, Iraq and the Supergun*. Novato, Calif.: Presidio Press, 1991.

Macksey, Kenneth. *Technology in War*. New York: Prentice-Hall Press, 1986.

Magini, Publio. "Secret Mission to Tokyo." *Military History Quarterly* 5 (Summer 1993): 98–103.

Mason, Air Vice Marshal R. A., and John W. R. Taylor. *Aircraft, Strategy and Operations of the Soviet Air Force*. London: Jane's Publishing Company, 1986.

Maurer, Maurer, ed. *The U.S. Air Service in World War I.* Washington, D.C.: Office of Air Force History, 1979.

McCoy, James W. *Secrets of the Viet Cong.* New York: Hippocrene Books, 1992.

McKenney, Janice E. *Air Defense Artillery.* Washington, D.C.: United States Army Center of Military History, 1985.

McWilliams, Barry. *This Ain't Hell . . . But You Can See It from Here.* Novato, Calif.: Presidio Press, 1992.

McWilliams, James P. *ARMSCOR: South Africa's Arms Merchant.* London: Brassey's (UK), 1989.

Mettler, Major C. G. ''Anti-Aircraft.'' *The Coast Artillery Corps Journal* 63 (December 1925): 543–54.

Mikesh, Robert C. *Japan's World War II Balloon Bomb Attacks on North America.* Washington, D.C.: Smithsonian Institution Press, 1973.

Morse, Stan, ed. *Gulf Air War Debrief.* Westport, Conn.: Airtime Publishing, 1991.

Naisawald, L. Van Loan. *Grape and Cannister: the Story of the Field Artillery of the Army of the Potomac, 1861–1865.* New York: Oxford University Press, 1960.

Nash, Trevor. ''The Changing Face of AD in the UK.'' *Military Technology* 17 (1993): 24, 26.

National Research Council. *Star 21: Strategic Technologies for the Army of the Twenty-First Century.* Washington, D.C.: National Academy Press, 1992.

Nicholson, General Sir Cameron, Editor-in-Chief. *The History of the Royal Artillery: 1919–1939.* United Kingdom: Royal Artillery Institution, 1978.

Nikanorov, LTC Vladimir. ''SDI Version for Europe.'' *Soviet Military Review* (August 1988): 55–56.

Nissen, Jack, with A. W. Cockerill. *Winning the Radar War.* New York: St. Martin's Press, 1987.

O'Ballance, Edgar. *The Electronic War in the Middle East, 1968–70.* Hamden, Conn.: Archon Books, 1974.

———. *No Victor, No Vanquished: The Yom Kippur War.* Novato, Calif.: Presidio Press, 1991.

Orlov, Colonel Aleksandr. ''Chasing After a 'Miracle Weapon.' '' *Soviet Military Review* (April 1987): 45–46.

''Patriot: A Reason to Be Proud.'' *Air Defense Artillery* (January-February 1993): 24–27.

Piekalkiewicz, Janusz. *The German 88 Gun in Combat: The Scourge of Allied Armor.* West Chester, Pa.: Schiffer Military History, 1992.

Pike, Douglas. *PAVN: People's Army of Vietnam.* Novato, Calif.: Presidio Press, 1986.

Pile, General Sir Frederick. *Ack-Ack: Britain's Defence against Air Attack during the Second World War.* London: George G. Harrap and Co., 1949.

Pocock, Rowland F. *German Guided Missiles.* New York: Arco Publishing Company, 1967.

Poolman, Kenneth. *Zeppelins against London.* New York: John Day Company, 1961.

Price, Alfred. *Luftwaffe Handbook 1939–1945.* New York: Charles Scribners Sons, 1977.

Roof over Britain: The Official Story of the A.A. Defences, 1939–1942. London: His Majesty's Stationary Service, 1943.

Rottman, Gordon, and Ron Volstad. *Armies of the Gulf War*. London: Osprey Publishing, 1993.

Ryabokon, Colonel Georgy. "The Successors of the Putilov Regiment." *Soviet Military Review* (April 1987): 23–26.

Schaffel, Kenneth. *The Emerging Shield: The Air Force and the Evolution of Continental Air Defense 1945–1960*. Washington, D.C.: Office of Air Force History, 1991.

Schofield, Carey. *Inside the Soviet Military*. New York: Abbeville Press, 1991.

Schwarzkopf, General H. Norman. *It Doesn't Take a Hero*. New York: Linda Gray Bantam Books, 1992.

Scott, Harriet Fast, and William F. Scott. *The Armed Forces of the USSR*. Boulder, Colo.: Westview Press, 1979.

"SDI: Who Stands to Gain?" *Soviet Military Review* (September 1988): 50–51.

Sechkin, Lieutenant-General Nikolai. "Guarding Soviet Airspace." *Soviet Military Review* (April 1987): 5–8.

Semmens, Colonel E. Paul. *The Hammer of Hell*. Fort Bliss, Tex.: Air Defense Artillery School, 1989.

Shcherbakov, Colonel Sergei. "Speciality Initiation Ceremonies." *Soviet Military Review* (March 1988): 14, 15.

Shores, Christopher. *History of the Royal Canadian Air Force*. London: Bison Books, 1984.

Stevens, Major Phillip H. *Artillery through the Ages*. New York: Franklin Watts, 1965.

Stone, Secretary of the Army Michael P. W. "Closing the Patriot Controversy." *Air Defense Artillery* (January-February 1993): 27–28.

Streetly, Martin. *Airborne Electronic Warfare: History, Techniques and Tactics*. London: Jane's Publishing Company, 1988.

Strelnikov, Colonel-General Vladimir. "Fighting an Air Enemy." *Soviet Military Review* (October 1988): 49–51.

Sumin, A. "Russian Air Defence Forces." *Military Technology* 17 (1993): 27, 28.

Taylor, Michael, and David Mondey. *Guinness Book of Aircraft Facts and Feats*. Enfield, UK: Guinness Superlatives, 1984.

TM-E 30-451: Handbook on German Military Forces. Washington, D.C.: United States Government Printing Office, 1945.

TM-E 30-480: Handbook on Japanese Military Forces. Washington, D.C.: United States Government Printing Office, 1944.

Trotter, William R. *A Frozen Hell: The Russo-Finnish War of 1939–1940*. Chapel Hill, N.C.: Algonquin Books, 1991.

"2S6M Tunguska: The World's First Gun/Missile SP AA System." *Military Technology* 17 (1993): 38–42.

Van Dyke, Jon M. *North Vietnam's Strategy for Survival*. Palo Alto, Calif.: Pacific Books, 1972.

Venkus, Colonel Robert E. *Raid on Qaddafi*. New York: St. Martin's Press, 1992.

Volkogonov, Dmitry, ed. *The Soviet Army*. Moscow: Planata Publishers, 1988.

Waddell, Colonel Dewey, and Major Norm Wood, eds. *Air War—Vietnam*. New York: Arno Press, 1978.

Wagner, Ray, and Heinz Nowarra. *German Combat Planes.* New York: Doubleday and Company, 1971.

Watson, Bruce W., ed. *Military Lessons of the Gulf War.* Novato, Calif.: Presidio Press, 1991.

Watt, Richard M. *The Kings Depart.* New York: Simon and Schuster, 1968.

Werrell, Kenneth P. *Archie, Flak, AAA, and SAM: A Short Operational History of Ground-Based Air Defense.* Maxwell AFB, Ala.: Air University Press, 1988.

Westwood, J. N. *The History of the Middle East Wars.* New York: Exeter Books, 1984.

Wood, Derek. *Attack Warning Red: The Royal Observer Corps and the Defence of Britain 1925–1975.* London: MacDonald and Jane's, 1976.

Wood, Tony, and Gill Gunston. *Hitler's Luftwaffe.* New York: Crescent Books, 1978.

Yevtushenko, Valery. " 'Afghanistan, Part of my Life.' " *Soviet Military Review* (September 1988): 49.

Zologa, Steven J. *Soviet Air Defense Missiles: Design, Development and Tactics.* Surrey, UK: Jane's Information Group, 1989.

———. *Target America: The Soviet Union and the Strategic Arms Race, 1945–1964.* Novato, Calif.: Presidio Press, 1993.

Zuyev, Alexander. *Fulcrum: A Top Gun Pilot's Escape from the Soviet Empire.* New York: Warner Books, 1992.

Index

About the Author

JAMES D. CRABTREE's experience in air defense began in 1982 when he enlisted as a private in the U.S. Army Air Defense Artillery. He was trained in Hawk II, Patriot and Stinger Missile systems and was then sent back to the United States from West Germany with an active duty ROTC scholarship. Returned to active duty as a 2nd Lieutenant, Crabtree served as a Hawk III Tactical Control Officer during Desert Storm and led a survey team into southern Iraq. Before leaving the service, he was assigned to a General Staff position.

ISBN 0-275-94792-0

HARDCOVER BAR CODE